STUDIES IN GERMAN LITERATURE,
LINGUISTICS, AND CULTURE
Vol. 27

STUDIES IN GERMAN LITERATURE, LINGUISTICS, AND CULTURE

Editorial Board

CAMDEN HOUSE
Columbia, South Carolina

Music and Mozart in the Life of Goethe

Die

Zauberflöte.

Eine

Oper in drei Aufzügen,

neubearbeitet

von

C. A. Vulpius.

Die Musik ist von Mozart.

Aufgeführt auf dem Herzoglichen Hoftheater zu
Weimar zum erstenmal am
16. Januar 1794.

Leipzig, 1794.
bei Johann Samuel Heinsius.

Die Zauberflöte 1794: title page of the Vulpius version

Robert Spaethling

Music and Mozart in the
Life of Goethe

CAMDEN HOUSE

Set in Palatino type and printed on acid-free Glatfelder paper.
Copyright 1987 by
CAMDEN HOUSE, INC.
Drawer 2025
Columbia, SC 29202 USA

Library of Congress Catalog Card Number:86-72131
All Rights Reserved
Printed in the United States of America
First Edition

ISBN:0-938100-47-5

To Ellen
and our many years together

List of Illustrations

Abbreviations of Works Frequently Cited

Eckermann
"Eckermann Gespräche."
Eckermann, Johann Peter. *Gespräche mit Goethe in den letzten Jahren seines Lebens*. Munich: Deutscher Taschenbuch Verlag, 1976. Reprint. *Goethe Gedenkausgabe*, vol. 24.

Faust
Faust. A Tragedy by Johann Wolfgang Goethe. Edited by Cyrus Hamlin. Translated by Walter Arndt. New York: W. W. Norton, 1976.

GA
"Gedenkausgabe."
Gedenkausgabe der Werke, Briefe und Gespräche Johann Wolfgang Goethes. 24 vols. Edited by Ernst Beutler. Zurich: Artemis Verlag, 1948-54.

GZB
"Goethe-Zelter Briefwechsel."
Der Briefwechsel zwischen Goethe und Zelter. 3 vols. Edited by Max Hecker. Leipzig: Insel Verlag, 1913-18.

HA
"Hamburger Ausgabe."
Goethes Werke. 14 vols. Edited by Erich Trunz. Hamburg: Christian Wegner Verlag, 1948-60.

IJ
"Italian Journey."
J. W. Goethe, *Italian Journey 1786-1788*. Translated by W. H. Auden and Elizabeth Mayer. New York: Pantheon Books, 1962. Reprint. San Francisco: North Point Press, 1982.

WA
"Weimarer Ausgabe."
Goethes Werke. 143 vols. Edited by Gustav von Loeper, Erich Schmidt, Hermann Grimm *et al.* Weimar: Hermann Böhlau, 1887-1912.

K
"Köchelverzeichnis."
Ludwig Ritter von Köchel, *Chronologisch-thematisches Verzeichnis sämtlicher Tonwerke Wolfgang Amadé Mozarts*.

6th ed. Edited by Franz Giegling, Alexander Weinmann, and Gerd Sievers. Wiesbaden: Breitkopf and Härtel, 1964.

LM   "Letters of Mozart."
The Letters of Mozart and His Family. 3rd ed. Edited by Emily Anderson. New York: W. W. Norton, 1985.

Contents

Acknowledgments

Segments of "Goethe and Music" are reprinted from "Music in Goethe's Thought and Writing" by permission of the editors of *The Romantic Tradition: German Literature and Music in the Nineteenth Century*. Edited by G. Chapple, F. Hall, and H. Schulte. Lanham, London, New York: University Press of America, 1987.

The chapter "*The Abduction* in Weimar" is reprinted by permission of the President and Fellows of Harvard College from *Essays in Honor of James Edward Walsh on his Sixty-Fifth Birthday*. Edited by Hugh Amory and Rodney G. Dennis. Cambridge: The Goethe Institute of Boston and the Houghton Library, 1983.

Goethe's *Magic Flute, Part II*, translated by Eric Blom, is reprinted by permission of the editors of *Music and Letters*. Oxford: Oxford University Press.

"Szenenentwurf zur Zauberflöte," a sketch in pen and ink of the Queen of the Night by Goethe, and "Kostümierung zur Zauberflöte," a watercolor by G. M. Kraus, are reproduced by permission of the *Nationale Forschungs- und Gedenkstätten der klassischen deutschen Literatur in Weimar*.

The frontispiece, a facsimile reproduction of the title page of *Die Zauberflöte* as arranged by C. A. Vulpius for the Weimar Court Theater, is reprinted by permission of Freies Deutsches Hochstift, Frankfurt a. M.

A phenomenon like Mozart will always remain a miracle that cannot be explained. But how else can the divinity create miracles if not at times through extraordinary individuals whom we behold in awe and wonder but cannot grasp whence they come.

Goethe to Eckermann,
February 14, 1831

Preface

JOHANN WOLFGANG GOETHE, THE GREATEST POET in the German language, and Wolfgang Amadeus Mozart, possibly the most gifted composer of all time, were close contemporaries. Goethe was born on August 28, 1749 in the Imperial City of Frankfurt. Mozart, more precisely, Johannes Chrysostomus Wolfgangus Theophilus Mozart, came into this world less than seven years later, on January 27, 1756, in the ancient town of Salzburg. In spite of their closeness in age and geography, the two artists never met, never established a personal relationship, and never even corresponded. Once, in 1763, the fourteen-year old Johann Wolfgang Goethe saw the wunderkind from Salzburg give a performance in Frankfurt, but the two youngsters did not come face to face, not then and not later in their lives.

Yet it is possible to view and discuss Goethe in relation to Mozart. We can base such an association on the more than two hundred references to the composer and his music which we find in Goethe's diaries, letters, and documented conversations. These observations not only testify to Goethe's steadily growing admiration for the composer, but contain occasional reflections by the poet linking his own artistry with that of Mozart's. Goethe's remark to Johann Peter Eckermann, for instance, that "Mozart ought to have composed the music for Faust,"[1] tells us two

---

[1] Johann Peter Eckermann, *Gespräche mit Goethe in den letzten Jahren seines Lebens* (Munich: Deutscher Taschenbuch Verlag, 1976), p. 313. As there is no complete modern English translation of the "Conversations," I will use this German edition as a reference (a dtv reprint of vol. XXIV of the *Goethe Gedenkausgabe*, ed. Ernst Beutler, Zurich: Artemis Verlag). The translations are my own unless otherwise noted. The "Conversations" with Eckermann will hereafter be cited in

things: how highly Goethe valued Mozart as a composer and, secondly, how appropriate he felt Mozart's music would have been for his play. The latter implicaton fascinates in particular because it betrays Goethe's strong desire for proportionate and balanced form, even in his most metaphysical drama. That he himself pointed to Mozart's *Don Giovanni* as a model in this context is therefore not surprising. Even in his last days, when the aged poet described his *Faust* drama, the work of a lifetime, as one of these "very serious jests" — "diese sehr ernsten Scherze"[2] — we can hear the echo of Mozart. For to the degree that Goethe's sagaciously ironic formula fits his own masterpiece, it also fits *Don Giovanni, Cosi fan tutte, Die Zauberflöte.* It may indeed be the most succinct characterization of Mozart's music, its mysterious blend of graceful form and emotional appeal, its playfulness and poignancy.

Goethe's knowledge of Mozart's music grew in the course of fifty years from superficial acquaintance to an intelligent, even profound understanding of his art. When the poet remarked, late in his life, that the works of Mozart belonged to those creations in the world which are of "consequence" and "permanence," that Mozart's music possessed "procreative power" — "eine zeugende Kraft" — that will carry it "from generation to generation" (Eckermann March 11, 1828), he made an observation that was not only perceptive but rather uncommon for his time. Mozart was often thought to be either too difficult or too light; some critics considered his music to be demonic and mystical, others judged it unproblematical, sunny, and "Olympian." Even his G Minor Symphony, K. 550, today referred to as a work of "passion" (Leonard Bernstein),[3] or as an "expression of suffering" (Charles Rosen),[4] was then regarded as a work of charm, serenity, and grace.[5] Rarely was Mozart's music described as vital and energetic, as art filled with "procreative power."

---

the text as "Eckermann" followed by the date of conversation. This remark dates from February 12, 1829.

[2] "Diese sehr ernsten Scherze." Letter to Wilhelm von Humboldt, March 17, 1832. This was Goethe's last letter. Cf. *Johann Wolfgang Goethe, Gedenkausgabe der Werke, Briefe und Gespräche,* ed. Ernst Beutler, vol. XXI, *Briefe der Jahre 1814-1832* (Zurich: Artemis, 1951), p. 1043, cited hereafter in the text as GA followed by volume and page numbers.

[3] Leonard Bernstein, *The Unanswered Question. Six Talks at Harvard* (Cambridge: Harvard University Press, 1976), p. 39.

[4] Charles Rosen, *The Classical Style. Haydn, Mozart, Beethoven* (New York: W.W. Norton, 1972), pp. 324-325. Rosen makes his remarks not only about the G Minor Symphony, but also about *Don Giovanni,* and the G Minor Quintet.

[5] Robert Schumann, for instance, referred to the symphony as "diese griechisch-schwebende Grazie..." Cf. Schumann, *Gesammelte Schriften über Musik und Musiker* (Leipzig: Breitkopf und Härtel, 1914) I, 105.

Goethe knew, especially toward the end of his life, that Mozart's music was more than elegant artistry, that it was like his own poetic creations: the fullness of life rendered into art.

Goethe's artistic and intellectual relationship to Mozart was completely one-sided. While we have ample evidence of what Goethe thought of Mozart, we have no direct knowledge of what Mozart thought or knew about Goethe. Wolfgang Hildesheimer informs us that Mozart read Goethe's best-selling novel *The Sufferings of Young Werther*,[6] and there is reason to believe that Mozart was familiar with Goethe's play *Clavigo*,[7] but in neither case do we have proof. Not even Goethe's poem "Das Veilchen" ("The Little Violet," 1785, K. 476), the only text by Goethe which Mozart set to music, gives clear indication that Mozart knew the author of the poem. Mozart's autograph is inscribed "Das Veilchen vom Göthe" at the top of the first page, presumably in the composer's own hand.[8] It is generally believed, however, that Mozart did not take the text directly from a Goethe edition (the poem appeared first as a song in the bucolic *Singspiel Erwin und Elmire*, 1775; it was reprinted as a single poem in subsequent Goethe editions and in numerous anthologies). Most musicologists agree that Mozart took the poem from a collection of songs, *Sammlung Deutscher Lieder für das Klavier*, published in Vienna between 1778 and 1782 by the "k.k. Hofklaviermeister" Joseph Anton Steffan.[9] The popular "Veilchen" was printed twice in that edition, in volumes I and III, both times with musical notes but in neither case with Goethe's

[6] Wolfgang Hildesheimer, *Mozart*, trsl. Marion Faber (New York: Farrar Straus Giroux, 1982), p. 197.

[7] Mozart's brother-in-law Joseph Lange (who also painted Mozart's most famous portrait) played the title role in Goethe's sentimental tragedy *Clavigo*, which was performed at the Burgtheater in Vienna in 1786. It is unlikely that Mozart was totally unaware of this. Cf. *Mozart. Briefe und Aufzeichnungen, Gesamtausgabe*, ed. Wilhelm A. Bauer and Otto Erich Deutsch (Kassel: Bärenreiter Verlag, 1971). Kommentarband, ed. Heinz Eibl, vol. VI, 314: "Am 7.1 1786 wurde es [*Clavigo*] am Burgtheater in Wien erstaufgeführt; die Hauptrollen spielten Freunde und Bekannte Mozarts: Joseph Lange (Clavigo), Gottlieb Stefan d.J. (Carlos)..." Also: Leopold Mozart mentioned the play when it was first performed in Salzburg. He writes to his daughter Maria Anna on October 20, 1786: "Heute wird Clavigo...aufgeführt." *Mozart. Briefe und Aufzeichnungen, Gesamtausgabe*, III, 597.

[8] The musicologist Paul Nettl suggests that Mozart added Goethe's name later. Cf. Paul Nettl, *Goethe und Mozart* (Esslingen: Bechtle Verlag, 1949), p. 8.

[9] *Sammlung Deutscher Lieder für das Klavier* (Wien, bey Joseph Edlen von Kurzböck, 1778-1782). The collection contains musical settings by Steffan, Friebert, and Hoffman. Carl Friebert probably edited volume III.

name.[10] If Mozart indeed used Steffan's anthology as a source for his text
— and Otto Erich Deutsch confirms that Volume III of the anthology was
found among Mozart's possessions[11] — he could not have known that
Goethe had written the poem.

This study, then, is about Goethe and the role of music, particularly
Mozart's music, in Goethe's life and art. The book does not endeavor to
explain Mozart or his music; rather it seeks to describe Goethe's
awareness of Mozart and draw parallels between the two artists
wherever possible.

Part One of the study, "Goethe and Music," examines the full range of
the poet's personal and artistic attitudes to music, his scientific interest in
music as an acoustical phenomenon, and his thematic and metaphoric
usage of music in his writing. Music was a supreme art form for Goethe;
he regretted his lack of musical literacy. Yet his perception of this art form
was often uneven and idiosyncratic. He shunned the Romantics and their
"new" music, and measured musical accomplishments with yardsticks of
the past rather than the future. Because of this limitation he had
difficulties understanding some of his own great contemporaries:
Beethoven, Schubert, Berlioz. But the music of Mozart, once he had
opened himself up to it, fully satisfied his personal as well as his aesthetic
and philosophical needs.

The existing scholarship on the subject of "Goethe and Music" is rich
and varied, ranging from venerable nineteenth-century musicologists and
Goethe scholars, such as Max Friedlaender, to the comprehensive studies
of Hermann Abert and Wilhelm Bode early in our own century. Of the
numerous books and articles that have appeared since, I will mention
only Friedrich Blume's *Goethe und die Musik,* Willy Tappolet's
Begegnungen mit der Musik in Goethes Leben und Werk, and the illuminating
essays by Edgar Istel, "Goethe and Music," W.C.R. Hicks, "Was Goethe

[10] In volume I (1778) the poem is attributed to the German poet Johann Wilhelm
Ludwig Gleim. The title reads "Das Veilchen auf der Wiese von Gleim." This
volume contains another poem by Gleim, entitled "Das Veilchen im Hornung"
which may have led to the error. In volume III (1780) the poem appears without
any name. The version of Goethe's poem printed in volume I shows many
differences from both Goethe's and Mozart's versions. The text in volume III
differs from Mozart's in only one word: "Und sank...!"; Mozart: "es sank..." It
seems likely, therefore, that Mozart used the text of volume III.

[11] Otto Erich Deutsch, *Mozart. Die Dokumente seines Lebens* (Kassel: Bärenreiter
Verlag, 1961), p. 317.

Musical?," and John Neubauer, "Absolute and Affective Music: Rameau, Diderot, and Goethe."[12]

The second major segment of the study concentrates on Goethe's experience and understanding of the music of Mozart. Here I describe Goethe's association with the composer from various perspectives: the popular perception of the two artists as the two "Olympians" of German-Austrian culture; Goethe's personal and intellectual encounters with the works of Mozart, specifically *Die Entführung aus dem Serail, Don Giovanni, Die Zauberflöte*; and, most important, Goethe's attempt to write a sequel to the latter: *Der Zauberflöte zweiter Teil*. In the chapter "Parallels of Styles and Artistic Attitudes," I present some stylistic comparisons between Goethe's and Mozart's artistic languages, describing parallels in their period styles (Rococo, Storm and Stress, etc.) as well as similarities in their individual artistic idioms.

Bibliographical sources for this section of the study are decidedly less numerous, especially in English, than for the first part. Yet here too some ground has been broken. Paul Nettl's concentrated monograph *Goethe und Mozart*, Emil Staiger's inspiring essay "Goethe und Mozart" in *Musik und Dichtung*, and Ernst Beutler's Goethe essay "Begegnung mit Mozart," are basic introductions to this subject which I seek to widen and complement.

To round off my presentation I included Goethe's fragment *Der Zauberflöte zweiter Teil* in the appendix. This aborted sequel to the Mozart-Schikaneder libretto is printed here in German and English, the latter in the rhymed verse translation by Eric Blom, one of the great Mozart scholars. The fragment, admittedly not one of the great works of Goethe, nonetheless deserves to be better known in English as well as in German.

This study follows, in the main, the traditional path of humanistic scholarship which requires no special methodological introduction. However, the chapter on "Parallels of Styles and Artistic Attitudes," an attempt to compare poetry and instrumental music, leads us into an interdisciplinary approach that calls for a brief explanation.

I believe strongly that different art forms, even those of different disciplines, can be fruitfully compared, that they can be compared in their structure-content relationships and in the meanings they evoke. Music, at least instrumental music, is a non-verbal medium, it does not express emotion or denote meaning. Music produces sound, not meaning. Yet,

---

[12] The complete bibliographical references of these books and articles are listed under the authors' names in the bibliography section of the book. One recent publication, *Goethes Gedanken über Musik*, ed. Hedwig Walwei-Wiegelmann (Frankfurt: Insel Taschenbuch, 1985), appeared too late to be considered here.

the organization of that sound and the mode of its delivery make it meaningful to us, the listeners. A dissonance placed within a diatonic structure, a simple withholding of an expected resolution will generate certain reactions within us to which we assign, wittingly or unwittingly, some form of meaning. Music, therefore, can be understood as a means of communication with its own inherent forms that function like a language. Charles Rosen expressed this thought with refreshing simplicity: "The limits set by the composer belong to a system which is in many respects like a language: it has an order, a syntax, and a meaning."[13] Languages, be they musical, poetic, or philosophical, are indeed comparable; they are often, as Marshall Brown explains, only different expressions of the same cultural "infrastructure."[14] Scholarship in this area is not new. Beginning with the music theorists of eighteenth-century France (Rameau, Rousseau, Momigny), musicologists as well as literary historians have long sought to find precise formulations in describing the relationship between words and music.Steven Paul Scher's critical and bibliographical accounting of these complex issues, their definitions and history, merits our thanks.[15]

The general aim of this study is straightforward: I wish to present a significant aspect of Goethe's personal and creative life, namely his relationship to music and to Mozart. In so doing, I hope to contribute to our understanding of these two exceptional artists, especially of Goethe who, some one hundred and fifty years after his death, is still less well known in the English-speaking world than he deserves to be. Secondly, I wish to illuminate through these associations the unique gift that Goethe and Mozart bestowed on their culture and the world. For they have created in their art a form of universe based on harmony, reconciliation, and the golden mean. They resisted the lures of inwardness and death, of nihilism and nationalism, so ever-present in their cultures, particularly Germany, and instead produced in their art an uncommon state of clarity, balance, and universal appeal. Goethe and Mozart belong, in that sense,

---

[13] Charles Rosen, *The Classical Style*, p. 196.

[14] Marshall Brown, "Mozart and After: The Revolution in Musical Consciousness," *Critical Inquiry*, 7 (1981), 689-706.

[15] Steven Paul Scher, "Literature and Music," in *Interrelations of Literature*, eds. Jean-Pierre Barricelli and Joseph Gibaldi (New York: MLA, 1982), pp. 225-250. "Literatur und Musik — Eine Bibliographie," in *Ein Handbuch zur Theorie und Praxis eines komparatistischen Grenzgebietes* (Berlin: Erich Schmidt Verlag, 1984), pp. 404-420. "Theory in Literature, Analysis in Music: What's Next?", *Yearbook of Comparative and General Literature*, 32 (1983), 50-60.

to those ultimate harmonizers and supreme creators of whom Coleridge has said that they are "Gods of Love who tame the chaos."[16]

For me to write about these two artists was a personal need as much as a scholarly challenge. I could not have undertaken this task without the practical and moral support of friends who helped in so many ways to bring this study to a conclusion: Professors Henry Hatfield of Harvard University; Alfred Hoelzel, University of Massachusetts, Boston; Eugene Weber, Swarthmore College. And, last but not least, Professor Takenori Inoki, Osaka University, with whom I had so many inspiring conversations about Mozart. In addition, I wish to acknowledge the patient help I received from Marie Steffen and Tom Ingemanson in preparing the manuscript. To all these friends as well as the National Endowment for the Humanities I am deeply indebted for help, encouragement, and guidance.

R.S.
Cambridge, Mass.

[16] Quoted by Emerson R. Marks in *Coleridge on the Language of Verse* (Princeton: Princeton University Press, 1981), pp. 103-104. The complete reference is as follows: "Poets are Bridlers by Delight, the Purifiers, they that combine [fancy, imagination, superstition, etc.] with reason & order, the true Protoplasts, Gods of Love who tame the chaos."

Part One:

Goethe and Music

GOETHE'S MUSICAL INTELLIGENCE, HIS KNOWLEDGE OF music and his interest in the art, have elicited over the years many differing and even contradictory opinions. Egon Friedell, a cultural historian, concluded that music had little attraction for Goethe. "He looked on it as a subsidiary art; the world of 'absolute music' was closed to him."[1] Calvin S. Brown, a knowledgeable scholar of literature and music, speaks of Goethe's "rather severe musical limitations,"[2] but the most unexamined judgment comes from William H. Hadow who states with blissful superficiality: "We are told that he [Goethe] was once moved by *Die Zauberflöte* and conceived for a moment the idea of supplying it with a sequel; but the interest, to whatever cause attributable, was no more than a wave on the surface."[3]

Many Germanists and musicologists take a different view. Friedrich Blume speaks for most when he asks with impatience: "How can anyone doubt the deep and intrinsic relationship Goethe had to music?" And to support his contention he quotes from a letter Goethe wrote to the composer Johann Friedrich Reichardt, in which the poet requests of his musical friend some new compositions, something uplifting after a severe illness which had almost taken his life in January 1801. "The first nobler impulse I felt after my illness," Goethe wrote in that letter, "was to hear music."[4]

---

[1] Egon Friedell, *Cultural History of the Modern Age* (New York: A. Knopf, 1931) II, 412.

[2] Calvin S. Brown, "The Relation Between Music and Literature As a Field of Study," *Comparative Literature*, 22 (1970), 105. Cf. also Wilhelm Bode, *Die Tonkunst in Goethes Leben* (Berlin: E.S. Mittler und Sohn, 1912) I, vi and vii, and W.C.R. Hicks, "Was Goethe Musical?" in *Publications of the English Goethe Society*, N.S., 27 (1958), 73-139.

[3] William H. Hadow, "A Comparison of Poetry and Music," in *Collected Essays* (London: Oxford University Press, 1928), p. 222.

[4] Friedrich Blume, *Goethe und die Musik* (Kassel: Bärenreiter Verlag, 1948), p. 19. Goethe's letter is dated February 5, 1801; cf. GA XIX, 406.

It may well be that Goethe himself furnished the basis for these different assessments of his musical competence. For on the one hand he thought of himself as a "Ton- und Gehörloser," someone without a good ear for music.[5] On the other hand he had sufficient knowledge to read musical scores — and was proud of it. For example he read the scores of compositions by Zelter (motets and songs) and Handel's *Messiah*;[6] the latter, incidentally, in the arrangement by Mozart. We know that his deepest attachment belonged to the sciences, the visual arts, perhaps to his beloved Homer, even to his rock collection. Yet it is also evident that music represented a genuine need in his life. Quite often he complained about being "too cut off from music," from all "Sang und Klang" and "musical imagination" (GZB I, 67, 79, 168, 327, etc.).

Goethe's relationship to music is highly differentiated and complex. It is at times uncertain and even biased, but on the whole consistent with his general mode of thinking and creativity. It is a relationship formed over many years and influenced by his own diverse scientific and poetic interests as well as by his many musical friends and advisers. In Italy he learned about music from the young German composer Philipp Christoph Kayser; later, in Weimar, he profited from Johann Friedrich Reichardt's compositions and Karl Eberwein's direction, and he began a highly fruitful correspondence with Karl Friedrich Zelter, director of the famed "Singakademie" in Berlin. Goethe was an incessant learner. He studied minerals and human anatomy, Persian and Chinese poetry, the Old Testament and modern physics, he was interested in architecture and knowledgeable about theater. In Bohemia he conducted geological experiments and in Rome he delved into the visual arts. Music was no exception. He learned about music all his life and as he learned he explored, as was his wont, the laws and principles of sound as a natural phenomenon. He approached music as a scientist, as a theater director, as a poet, and as a simple listener. He enjoyed Handel, Italian church music, the *Lieder* of Reichardt and Zelter, some of the keyboard music of Johann Sebastian Bach. The latter shows a considerable independence of judgment, for the old master was anything but popular in Goethe's time. But the musical experience most in accord with Goethe's own aesthetic sensibilities and needs was the music of Wolfgang Amadeus Mozart. It was with this composer that the poet formed an intellectual and artistic

---

[5] The complete passage of the letter reads as follows: "Und so verwandle ich Ton- und Gehörloser, obgleich Guthörender, jenen großen Genuß in Begriff und Wort. Ich weiß recht gut, daß mir deshalb ein Drittel des Lebens fehlt; aber man muß sich einzurichten wissen." *Der Briefwechsel zwischen Goethe und Zelter*, ed. Max Hecker (Leipzig: Insel Verlag, 1913-18) II, 57; May 2, 1820. Hereafter cited in the text as GZB followed by volume and page number.

[6] For the *Messiah* reference see GZB II, 268; for Zelter see GZB I, 605. Goethe writes that he listened to Zelter's motets with his "eyes."

relationship that endured from 1785 to his death — a period of nearly fifty years.

There are, of course, the celebrated blind spots in Goethe's musical life, his notorious "misjudgments," such as his preference for compositions by Kayser, Reichardt, Zelter, and a host of other minor musicians over compositions by Schubert, Berlioz, and Beethoven. These preferences have long been considered a sign of musical ignorance, embarrassing lapses in artistic taste — and from a certain post-Romantic point of view that may well be true. But it is also true that not all the relevant facts underlying Goethe's judgments in music have been duly examined. It is with this in mind that I will discuss in this part of the book three aspects of Goethe's musical involvement: music and music-making in Goethe's life, Goethe's theoretical approaches to music, and Goethe's use of music in his poetic writings.

1

Music and Music-Making in Goethe's Life

BY ALL ACCOUNTS GOETHE CAME from a music-loving family. His mother played the harpsichord and sang, his father played both the flute and the lute — although, as Goethe recalled in his autobiography, *Dichtung und Wahrheit*, his father "tuned his lute longer than he actually played it."[1] At age thirteen young Wolfgang took piano lessons together with his younger sister Cornelia. Their initial enthusiasm was, however, quickly snuffed out by the pedantry of the teacher. Not even the wunderkind from Salzburg, who was just then dazzling the burghers of Frankfurt with his musical skills, could inspire young Goethe to higher flights. The dullness of the teacher won out and Johann Wolfgang quit the piano.

Next came the flute. We do not know exactly how long or how well young Goethe played this instrument, but it must have been a fleeting affair, for he soon left the flute in favor of the cello, where he progressed far enough to venture into performances of "sonatas for two basses" with his teacher, "Violincellmeister Busch," in Strasbourg.[2] This seems to have

---

[1] *Goethes Werke*, ed. Erich Trunz (Hamburg: Wegner Verlag, 1955) IX, 338. Hereafter cited in the text as HA (Hamburger Ausgabe) followed by volume and page numbers.

[2] This somewhat unusual piece of cello literature is mentioned by Goethe in a letter to Johann Daniel Salzmann, February 3, 1772: "Wollten Sie bey Gelegenheit meinen Violincellmeister Buschen fragen, ob er die Sonaten für zwey Bässe noch hat, die ich mit ihm spielte, sie ihm abhandeln und baldmöglichst mir

been the highest level of Goethe's instrumental accomplishment. There are indications that he played the piano now and then, and on one occasion he even tried his hand at composing. In a letter to Zelter the poet confessed that, in a moment of solitude in Bohemia, he attempted a choral composition, "In te Domine Speravi," for four voices (GZB I, 374-375). But this is an isolated reference and for all practical purposes Goethe was neither a composer nor a polished instrumentalist.

What appealed to Goethe more than composing or music-making — this remained true throughout his life — were the pleasures of listening to music. While still a youngster, Goethe made frequent visits to the French opera in Frankfurt, where he saw Jean Jacques Rousseau's *Devin du Village*, Pierre Alexandre Monsigny's and André Grétry's *Rose et Colas*, and Charles Simon Favart's *Annette et Lubin*. And only a few years later, as a student in Leipzig (Goethe had just turned sixteen when he arrived at the university there), he was drawn to the German *Singspiel* and became acquainted with one of the genre's leading exponents, Johann Adam Hiller, who was just beginning to organize a series of concerts that has continued as the famous *Gewandhauskonzerte* to the present day.

Of no small importance for Goethe's expanding musical interests was his friendship with the Breitkopf family in Leipzig, the sons (Goethe's fellow students at the university) and daughters of Bernhard Christoph Breitkopf, head of the famous publishing house. Goethe was not only exposed to music and musical discussions in this lively, intellectual family, but the youngest son of the family set Goethe's first collection of (anacreontic) poems to music: *Neue Lieder in Melodien gesetzt von Bernhard Theodor Breitkopf*, Leipzig, bei Bernhard Christoph Breitkopf und Sohn, 1770.[3] Goethe was now nineteen years old and on his way to Strasbourg where he studied law, read Homer and Shakespeare, and wrote the "Sesenheimer Lieder," poems that swept across the German lands like a storm in spring time, filled with music and the exuberance of young love.

The following two decades were of utmost importance for Goethe's musical development. In 1775 he moved to Weimar as the friend and companion of the youthful Carl August, Duke of Sachsen-Weimar-Eisenach; in 1785 he saw a performance of Mozart's *Die Entführung aus dem Serail*, and in 1786 he departed on a journey to Italy that would keep him there for nearly two years.

Weimar was not one of Europe's cultural capitals. Yet the mid-sized town of about 6,000 could boast of a good theatrical tradition, a decent university in nearby Jena, and, after 1772, the presence of Christoph

zuschicken. Ich treibe die Kunst etwas stärker als sonst." Max Morris, *Der junge Goethe* (Leipzig: Insel Verlag, 1910) II, 121.

[3] I am following here the accounts of Wilhelm Bode, *Die Tonkunst in Goethes Leben*, I, 19-41; and Albert Bielschowsky, *Goethe. Sein Leben und seine Werke* (Munich: C.H. Beck'sche Verlagsbuchhandlung, 1911) I, 69 f.

Martin Wieland, one of Germany's foremost writers, who had accepted an appointment in the ducal household as a tutor to the princes. More important perhaps: Weimar possessed a source of artistic energy and resourcefulness lacking in many a larger city — Anna Amalia, the dowager duchess, a woman of charm, erudition, and inspiration. She was the major force in overcoming the cultural stagnation that had beset Weimar ever since a fire on May 6, 1774 had destroyed most of the palace and with it the court theater. Herself a pianist and skilled lutist — and one of a number of composers to set Goethe's *Singspiel Erwin und Elmire* to music — she had assembled a group of good amateur musicians that gathered regularly at the *Fürstenhaus* to play ensemble music. So intense and stimulating were the performances that Wieland, half amused, half enthusiastic, wrote to Johann Heinrich Merck in August 1779: "There was such a plucking and a fiddling, a blowing and a piping that the angels in heaven looked on with joy" — "Es wurde geklimpert, gegeigt, geblasen und gepfiffen, daß die Engel im Himmel ihre Freude daran hatten."[4] As far as we know, Goethe did not actively participate in these high-spirited musicales, but he came to listen, and we may assume that his admiration for the Duchess as well as the congenial atmosphere did much to shape and sharpen his musical taste. Besides, many of his friends in Weimar were excellent amateur musicians, Charlotte von Stein among them, and Goethe was treated quite often to some very good *Hausmusik*.

On September 3, 1786, Goethe embarked quietly and secretly on a journey that would become one of the most decisive learning experiences in his life.

> I have slipped out of Carlsbad at three in the morning; otherwise, I would not have been allowed to leave. Perhaps my friends, who had so kindly celebrated my birthday on August 28 [Goethe's thirty-seventh], had thereby acquired the right to detain me, but I could wait no longer... The morning was misty, calm and beautiful, and this seemed a good omen.[5]

With these words Goethe describes the beginning of his Italian journey, which took him in the course of twenty months to Venice, Rome, Naples, Sicily, Rome, and back to Weimar. The trip began as an escape from life at court and personal involvements, and it became a time of complete personal and artistic renewal, a kind of elementary rebirth, as Goethe himself soon recognized and noted in his travel log: "The rebirth which is transforming me from within continues. Though I expected really to learn something here, I never thought I should have to start at

---

[4] Quoted by Bode, *Die Tonkunst in Goethes Leben*, I, 58-59.

[5] J.W. Goethe, *Italian Journey*, trsl. W.H. Auden and Elizabeth Mayer (San Francisco: North Point Press, 1982), p. 5, hereafter cited as IJ followed by page numbers.

the bottom of the school and have to unlearn or completely relearn so much" (IJ 138-39).[6]

There was much to be seen and learned in Italy. Goethe studied art history, Renaissance architecture and ancient sculpture, drawing, geology, the formation of minerals and plants. And, of course, music. When Goethe's young composer friend from Frankfurt, Philipp Christoph Kayser, announced his visit, the poet was jubilant: "I shall probably have the pleasure of seeing Kayser in Rome. So music will join the other arts and close the circle they have formed around me, as if they wished to make a wall between me and my friends" (IJ 387). Later, in Rome, Goethe felt inspired to rework several of his Singspiele. He and Kayser even collaborated on a new one, Scherz, List und Rache, which Kayser ultimately left unfinished.[7] But most important for the moment: Kayser, who had come to Italy to study old music, taught Goethe how to listen, he taught him the beauty of a capella singing and seventeenth-century choral music: "My friend Kayser," Goethe wrote in his "Retrospect," "stimulated and broadened my love for music, which had hitherto been limited to opera. He followed with interest all the church festivals and induced me to listen with him to the solemn Masses which are sung on those days" (IJ 418). Shortly before returning to Germany, Goethe recorded one of his most memorable music experiences of the entire journey, a ceremony combining sacred music and church ritual at Easter time:

> The music in the Sistine Chapel is unimaginably beautiful, especially the Miserere [by Vittorio Allegri] and the so-called Improperi [by Palestrina], that is, the Crucified's reproaches to His people, which are sung on Good Friday. The moment when the Pope is stripped of his pontifical pomp and steps down from his throne to adore the cross, while all the others stay where they are in silence, until the choir begins — Populus Meus, quid feci tibi? — is one of the most beautiful of all these remarkable rites. You shall hear more about it all in detail when I get back, and such of the music as is transportable Kayser is going to bring with him (IJ 482-483).

Goethe returned to Weimar in June of 1788 and immediately fell into a busy schedule of writing, botanical and optical studies, and matters of state. The French revolution sent its first tremors through the world, including the small Duchy of Sachsen-Weimar-Eisenach. Political and military events would sweep across Europe in the next ten to fifteen

---

[6] Melitta Gerhard has pointed out how much Goethe had to learn and relearn in Italy; even his visual sense had to be developed. Cf. "Rom in seiner Bedeutung für Goethe — Eine 'Neue Welt.'" Jahrbuch des Freien Deutschen Hochstifts 1977, pp. 85-91.

[7] Goethe reworked most of his Singspiele in Italy: Erwin und Elmire, Claudia von Villa Bella, Lila, Jery und Bäteley — all were "so revised," he wrote on February 1, 1787, "that nobody will recognize them" (IJ 470).

years, absorbing much of Goethe's attention. Yet, in spite of the turbulent times, court life at Weimar continued apace and with it the life and musical development of its most prominent citizen.

In the spring of 1791 Goethe was appointed Director of the Weimar Court Theater. Surprisingly enough, he held this time-consuming post for twenty-five years. Goethe's directing career was often filled with frustrations, with moments of failure, but certainly one of his most propitious experiences was his coming into contact with the operas of Mozart. Under his aegis Mozart's stage works became the most frequently performed operas in Weimar. *Die Zauberflöte* ranked first in frequency of performance with eighty-two, *Don Giovanni* second with sixty-eight, *Die Entführung aus dem Serail* was staged forty-nine times, *Cosi fan tutte* thirty-three, *La Clemenza di Tito* twenty-eight, and *Le Nozze di Figaro* twenty times.

All in all, 280 performances of Mozart operas took place during Goethe's tenure at the Court Theater, twice as many as those of the second most popular composer, Karl Ditters von Dittersdorf.[8] We know from the "Chronicles of the Weimar Court Theater" with what energy and personal commitment Goethe involved himself in the production of the operas, particularly *Don Giovanni* and *Die Zauberflöte*, paying attention to the smallest details of staging, lighting, and acting.[9] It is from this basis, from the working knowledge of a stage director, that much of Goethe's admiration for Mozart's musical and dramatic genius evolved.

Goethe's natural inclination towards the music of Mozart was strengthened by many of his friends in Weimar and Berlin. Johann Gottfried Herder, for instance, was a great admirer of Mozart and so was Johann Nepomuk Hummel, a student of Mozart's, who came to Weimar in 1819 as a pianist and *Kapellmeister*. But most of all it was Karl Friedrich Zelter who influenced Goethe's taste for Mozart. The correspondence between the two men, which began in 1801 and continued until 1832, when they both died within months of each other, eloquently testifies to Goethe's musical interests and musical intelligence. We find exchanges on specific works, such as Handel's *Messiah*, Haydn's *Creation*, Mozart's *Requiem*, J.S. Bach's *St. Matthew Passion*, and we find Zelter's famous diatribe against Berlioz's Opus I, *Huit Scènes de Faust*. Most important: we find lengthy discussions on the nature of the art song revealing Goethe's conservative, classical bent in matters of musical accompaniment.

Zelter, half out of courtesy, half out of conviction, flattered Goethe by saying that he was the only one whose judgment in music mattered to

[8] Alfred Orel, *Goethe als Operndirektor* (Bregenz: Eugen Russ Verlag, 1949), p. 190.

[9] Orel, *Goethe als Operndirektor*, p. 67 f. See also: *Gesang und Rede, sinniges Bewegen. Goethe als Theaterleiter*, ed. Jörn Göres (Düsseldorf: Goethe-Museum, 1973), pp. 127-128.

him — "weil Du der einzige Mensch bist, auf dessen Urteil in der Musik ich etwas halte" — (GZB I, 479). The poet returned the compliment by thanking Zelter for helping him understand this elusive art — "If it is possible to teach music through concepts" — "Durch den Begriff die Musik zu erfassen" — then you have accomplished that for me"(GZB II, 308). In the course of this thirty-year correspondence Goethe entrusted Zelter with some of his most private, often rather pessimistic utterences about life and art, and in return Zelter gave Goethe his unwavering loyalty and devotion — and he furthered Goethe's understanding of Mozart whom Zelter perceived as the greatest composer of all time. "I put Mozart above Haydn from whom he descended," Zelter remarked to Kanzler von Müller during a visit in Weimar, "Beethoven stands by himself, but he is not as great as Mozart. Cosi fan tutte and Figaro are Mozart's best operas."[10]

In the winter of 1801-1802 Goethe founded a singing group, perhaps better described as a congenial social club, which he called "Liebeshof" or "cour d'amour." Invited were seven selected couples, among them Friedrich and Charlotte von Schiller, Count and Countess von Egloffstein, and Fräulein von Göchhausen, who would gather at the poet's house every Wednesday night during the winter months, "abends nach dem Theater," for a pot-luck supper. The ladies would bring the food, the men were responsible for the wines. According to the rules and by-laws, drafted by Goethe himself, each member could bring a guest, but only if the others agreed, and there were to be no disturbing topics of discussion — "nothing...that would touch on political or other current problems."[11] The object of the weekly get-togethers was simply to enjoy good food in pleasant company and to engage in some light-hearted singing. Apparently the group succeeded on both counts. One event practiced with particular élan was the presentation of musical parodies. The idea was to write a humorous text which was then sung *prima vista* to a familiar melody. Goethe, so it seems, was one of the prime contributors to this inspirational art form; his " Stiftungslied," of which I will quote the first two stanzas, gives an indication as to the nature of this amusing poetic genre.

> Was gehst du, schöne Nachbarin,
> Im Garten so allein?
> Und wenn du Haus und Felder pflegst,
> Will ich dein Diener sein.

[10] Kanzler von Müller, *Unterhaltungen mit Goethe* (Munich: Verlag C.H. Beck, 1982), p. 107. Zelter's visit took place in November 1823.

[11] Cf. Carl von Beaulieu-Marconnay, "Goethes cour d'amour," *Goethe-Jahrbuch*, 6 (1885), 68.

Mein Bruder schlich zur Kellnerin
Und ließ ihr keine Ruh'.
Sie gab ihm einen frischen Trunk
Und einen Kuß dazu.[12]

(Why are you, beautiful neighbor, / strolling alone in the garden? / When you tend house and field, / won't you let me be your servant. / / My brother sneaked off to the waitress / and would not give her peace. / So she gave him a fresh drink and a kiss to boot. /)[13]

The text was sung to Mozart's popular Papageno tune "Ein Mädchen oder Weibchen wünscht Papageno sich" — a tune that has also become familiar as the accompaniment of Ludwig Hölty's "Üb' immer Treu und Redlichkeit." Goethe's choice of this melody attests both to the general popularity of the Papageno songs ("Der Vogelfänger bin ich ja" and "Ein Mädchen oder Weibchen" were veritable "hit songs" in Austria and Germany at that time) as well as his own fondness of the melody that had everything he cherished in a song: a regular strophic structure and a singable, cheerful melody.[14]

Not all the singing in Goethe's house was tongue-in-cheek. In 1807 the poet assembled another group that he called his "Hauskapelle" or "meine kleine Sang-und Klanggesellschaft." The group, consisting of members from court and theater, met on Thursdays for rehearsals under the direction of Franz Karl Eberwein. In the repertoire were German and Italian choral pieces — e.g. Mozart's offertory "Misericordias Domini," K. 222, Nicolò Jommelli's "Confirma hoc Deus," Kayser's "Weihnachts-kantate," and some works by Zelter, who also sent along some "pieces for four voices by Haydn." Sunday mornings the "Hauskapelle" would present the fruit of their dedicated labor in Goethe's "Haus am Frauenplan." Audiences of up to fifty would come from court and town and listen to the musical offerings. The poet himself not only hosted these festive occasions, but participated with vigor in the bass section of the chorus.

Such were Goethe's direct involvements with music. Singing remained his favored musical expression. At one point (ca. 1820) he acquired a "Streicher" grand piano, reputedly the best of its kind at that

---

[12] *Goethes Werke* (Weimar: Hermann Böhlau, 1893), section 1: vol. I, 109. Future references to this edition will appear in the text as WA (Weimarer Ausgabe) plus number of section, volume, and pages.

[13] Prose renditions of poems are my own unless otherwise indicated.

[14] Cf. Frederick W. Sternfeld, *Goethe and Music. A List of Parodies and Goethe's Relationship to Music* (New York: The New York Public Library, 1954), pp. 13-19.

time.[15] But he himself played little if at all; he was content to sit in a corner of his music room and listen to more qualified performers: Johann Nepomuk Hummel, Maria Szymanowska, Felix Mendelssohn. Felix, who was introduced to Goethe by his teacher Zelter as a twelve-year-old prodigy, completely charmed the old man during his stay in Weimar. "Every afternoon," the young pianist reported to his parents in Berlin, "Goethe opens his piano (aStreicher) with the words 'I have not yet heard you play today — now make a little noise for me.' And then he generally sits down beside me, and when I have finished (I usually extemporize) I ask for a kiss or take one."[16] Years later, when Mendelssohn was already an accomplished pianist and composer, he wrote, after another visit in Weimar:

> I have often played to Goethe in the morning hours. He wanted to get an idea of how music has developed and wished to hear the music of different composers in chronological order. He seemed rather wary of Beethoven, but I could not spare him this acquaintance because he had to hear 'where sounds had turned to,' and so I played for him the first movement of the C Minor Symphony which he liked very much.[17]

Hermann Abert wrote in this connection that "young Felix was the last great musical impression of [Goethe's] life," and he quotes from a letter to Zelter (June 3, 1830) in which Goethe praised Felix Mendelssohn for having given him a sense of history about music, of having presented to him Bach, Haydn, Gluck, Mozart, as well as all the "great new technicians" in a form and order that made them all understandable to him.[18]

"Was Goethe Musical?" — this is a question posed as the title of a stimulating essay by W.C.R. Hicks.[19] Hicks answers in the affirmative, and if interest in music qualifies as musicality then Hicks is unquestionably right. Goethe had well-developed musical sensibilities, he enjoyed music as a listener, he admired music as an art form. But Goethe's true musicality becomes manifest not in his musical endeavors

---

[15] Ferdinand Hiller, *Goethes musikalisches Leben* (Cologne: Du Mont-Schauberg, 1883), pp. 81-82. Hiller says that Goethe bought the "Streicher'sche Flügel" around 1820. "Streicher" pianos were made in Vienna by a daughter of the famous Augsburg piano maker Andreas Stein.

[16] *Felix Mendelssohn: Letters*, ed. G. Selden-Goth (New York: Random House, 1972, rept. Vienna House, 1973), p. 22.

[17] *Mendelssohn: Letters*, p. 81.

[18] Hermann Abert, *Goethe und die Musik* (Stuttgart: J. Engelhorns Nachf., 1922), p. 45.

[19] *Publications of the English Goethe Society*, N.S., 27, (1958), 73 ff.

but in his poetry. Goethe's instrument was the German language and his most euphonious compositions were done in German verse.

2

Goethe's Theories Of Music: Schubert, Beethoven, Berlioz

IN THE SUMMER OF 1810, WHILE vacationing in Bohemia, Goethe sketched out some preliminary ideas concerning a theory of acoustics, a study of the origin and physical laws of sound. This *Tonlehre*, as he entitled the inquiry, was inspired by his *Theory of Colors*, which he had just completed; but, in contrast to the latter, his treatise on sound was never finished. It remained a "naked but well-proportioned skeleton," as he himself referred to it, not without humor, some years later (GZB III, 154).[1] Despite their differences in size — the *Farbenlehre* is comprised of two stately volumes, the *Tonlehre* is drawn up on a single chart — the two inquiries share a number of basic assumptions. One of them, perhaps Goethe's most cherished scientific belief, is the idea that natural phenomena, such as light and sound, stimulate organic sensory

---

[1] Goethe's *Tonlehre* remained a fragment, a "Tabelle" as he called it, and was not printed in his life time. Goethe's ideas of the interrelatedness of physical, physiological, and atmospheric conditions as they are found in both his *Tonlehre* and *Farbenlehre* caused a lot of scientific head-shaking. He shared his *Tonlehre* with his friend Zelter after he rediscovered the fragment in 1826 — "Die Tabelle der Tonlehre ist nach vieljährigen Studien, wenn Du Dich erinnerst, nach Unterhaltungen mit Dir etwa im Jahre 1810 geschrieben" (Letter from September 26, 1826; GZB II, 456). The *Tonlehre* is printed in WA 2: XI, 287-294; it was reprinted in GA XVI and the Deutsche Taschenbuch Verlag, XXXIX. There is also an edition included in Ernst-Jürgen Dreyer's *Versuch, eine Morphologie der Musik zu begründen. Mit einer Einleitung über Goethes Tonlehre* (Bonn: Bouvier Verlag, 1976), pp. 7-40; 219-240.

perceptions and form a symbiosis with the eyes and ears of their receivers. Goethe formulated this concept more than once, even poetically, but nowhere as clearly as in his Introduction to the *Theory of Colors*:

> The eye may be said to owe its existence to light, which calls forth, as it were, a sense that is akin to itself. The eye, in short, is formed with reference to light, to be fit for the action of light; the light it contains corresponding with the light without.[2]

A similar form of interaction between nature and human perception exists, according to Goethe, in the world of sound and the human ear. In his *Tonlehre* he subdivided the production of sound into three basic categories of origin: "The Organic (subjective)" category, musical sound created by the human voice and perceived by the ear for the pleasure and elevation of the listener; the "Mechanical (mixed)" category, i.e. sound generated by certain materials and spatial arrangements (e.g. intervals); finally, the "Mathematical (objective)" sound category, music defined and determined by physical laws and measurements, such as the width of amplitudes and the frequency of vibrations.

Characteristically, Goethe ranked the organic creation of music above any mechanically produced sounds. The singing of songs, Goethe contended, is an autonomous human act in which the sound issues from the voice and returns to the originator through the ears, challenging and heightening in this process man's creative impulses ("Indem sich aus und an dem Menschen die Tonwelt offenbart, 1. hervortritt in der Stimme, 2. zurückkehrt durch's Ohr, 3. aufregend zur Begleitung den ganzen Körper und seine sinnlich-sittliche Begeisterung und eine Ausbildung des innern und äußern Sinnes bestimmend"). Singing, Goethe continued, is an entirely self-sufficient musical act ("Der Gesang ist völlig produktiv an sich," WA 2: XI, 291). And what could be more Goethean and, for that matter, humanistic than the notion that the human being is nature's most perfect instrument and the creation of music by the human voice a process both aesthetic and moral. Singing is perceived here as the highest form of music and the human voice — Goethe expressed this thought so many times — "the highest and most beautiful organic expression which God and nature were capable of rendering."[3] Historically, Goethe followed Rousseau and Diderot in this preference, as John Neubauer has shown in a recent essay on "Absolute and Affective Music." Even though

---

[2] Johann Wolfgang Goethe, *Theory of Colours*, trsl. Charles Lock Eastlake (London: J. Murray, 1840, rpt. Cambridge, Massachusetts: MIT Press, 1970), liii.

[3] Letter from February 1, 1831; GZB III, 378. It is fascinating that Goethe relates the power and ability of the human voice to a certain "high" on the barometer scale, connecting, as he often did, atmospheric conditions with human accomplishments.

the concept of "autonomous" music — "selbständige Kunst" — (e.g. the contrapuntal music of Bach and Handel or virtuoso instrumental music) was not unfamiliar or unpleasant to him, Goethe remained close to "representational" music, music that appeals to "intellect, sensibilities, and passion."[4]

Each natural phenomenon, according to Goethe's understanding, derives wholly from its origin, equipped with a generic blueprint and a potential for all forms indigenous to the species. This thesis is central to his treatise on the *Metamorphosis of the Plants*, it is part of the *Theory of Colors*, and it is contained, if sketchily, in his *Theory of Sound*. Christian Heinrich Schlosser, Goethe's young nephew, had advanced the theory that the major and minor tonalities derived from one indivisible unit of sound, which he called (taking a clue from Leibniz) "*Tonmonade.*" Goethe needed no persuasion. Schlosser's idea suited his own concept of wholeness perfectly:

> Here we are fully in accord when you say that the basis of the so-called Minor lies within the tone-monade. You echo my very thought. The nearest way to a further development of this primal antagonism may be found in the following: When the tone-monade expands, it produces the Major, when it contracts, the Minor (WA 4: XXV, 305).[5]

All sounds, Goethe explained, are monogenetic, natural, and original ("ursprünglich"). For that reason he vehemently opposed the prevalent assumption (shared by Schlosser and Zelter) that the minor third, for instance, was not a natural sound, but a man-made derivative. The minor third was for Goethe as much a "gift of nature" as all the sounds of the diatonic scale. In 1808 Zelter had written to Goethe: "In other words, the minor third is not an immediate *donum* of nature, but rather a product of modern artistry" (GZB I, 198). Goethe lost no time replying: "I object to the notion that only the diatonic scale is natural," and twenty years later he was still adamant. Almost angrily he lashed out at his friend: "Man is worth more [than all your theories], for nature has endowed him with his own minor third to make it possible for him to express his undefinable longings" (GZB III, 401; March 31, 1831).[6]

---

[4] John Neubauer, "Absolute and Affective Music: Rameau, Diderot, and Goethe," in *Johann Wolfgang von Goethe: One Hundred and Fifty Years of Continuing Vitality*, eds. Ulrich Goebel and W. T. Zyla (Lubbock, Texas: Texas Tech Press, 1984), pp. 116, 120, 129.

[5] I am quoting this letter in the translation of Theodore Baker from Edgar Istel's article: "Goethe and Music," *The Musical Quarterly*, 14 (1928), 245. Goethe's letter is dated May 5, 1815 and is marked "Concept," WA 4: XXV, 299-313.

[6] The idea that minor tones evoke melancholic moods as well as the general idea that certain sounds have particular effects upon the human psyche is part of the "Affektenlehre" which was dominant in eighteenth-century Germany. But it also

What emerges from Goethe's theoretical discussions in the realm of music are fundamental assumptions and preferences that are quite consistent with his thinking in other areas of the arts and sciences: it is a tendency to look for indivisible organic entities, for wholeness in every detail, and to shun excessive subjectivism. This was a basic part of his scientific and creative stance — "Goethe's way of seeing and thinking is in terms of totality,"[7] — and it most definitely influenced his judgment of music as an art form.

Both as a listener and as a poet Goethe liked simple music. In song compositions the poet preferred "strophic" settings to "through-composed" accompaniments. (The *Harvard Dictionary of Music* defines "strophic" as a "designation for a song in which all stanzas of the text are sung to the same music;" and "through-composed" as a method "preferred for dramatic or narrative texts in which the situation changes with every stanza, e.g. Schubert's 'Der Erlkönig.'").[8] In a letter to Wilhelm von Humboldt, Goethe explained why he thought so highly of the *Lied* compositions of his friend Zelter. The composer's strophic technique, Goethe wrote, allowed the poem's basic idea to be repeated in each strophe so that it could be heard throughout the text, whereas the technique of through-composition — Goethe actually uses the word "Durchkomponieren" — destroys any such poetic unity (GA XIX, 434; March 14, 1803).

In general, Goethe found that particularly Reichardt's and Zelter's song compositions were very compatible with his own poetic and musical intentions. Reichardt maintained that the art song should be close to the folksong, it ought to have simple melodic lines, the accompaniment should not violate the verbal and structural integrity of the text.[9] Goethe could not have agreed more. He was similarly in agreement with Zelter

finds a close and interesting parallel in Goethe's own theory of colors, particularly as delineated in Chapter VI where Goethe discusses the effects of colors on the human mind. Cf. *Farbenlehre* in HA XIII, 494-503. There is also a good discussion of Goethe's *Tonlehre* in relation to his *Farbenlehre* in W.C.R. Hicks, "Was Goethe Musical?" *PEGS*, 27, 115 ff.

[7] Cf. Carl Friedrich von Weizsäcker, "Nachwort," Goethe's *Farbenlehre*, HA XIII, 537.

[8] *Harvard Dictionary of Music*, ed. Willi Apel (Cambridge: Harvard University Press, 1972), 2nd edition, pp. 811, 850-851.

[9] Walter Salmen, *Johann Friedrich Reichardt* (Freiburg and Zurich: Atlantis Verlag, 1963), p. 298.

whose melodies, he found, supported his verses like "gas inflating a balloon and carrying it aloft."(GZB II, 59). In an earlier letter, Goethe had compared the task of a *Lied* composer to that of a craftsman: "I consider it important for the poet to create his designs on materials that are loosely enough structured so that the composer can have a choice whether to add his embroidery — "Stickerei" — with fine or heavy thread, just as the situation requires" (GZB I, 324f.). This letter, one of several on the subject of *Lied* compositions, is of considerable importance. It reflects Goethe's view that in a collaboration between poet and composer, the writer's work must take precedence, the composer must follow, support, and adorn the poet's design. But this applies only to the composition of *Lieder*. In music theater Goethe granted the final touch to the composer. "The author of a musical piece," he wrote to Philipp Christoph Kayser in May of 1786, "must look upon his text, after he gives it to the composer, like a son or pupil he puts into the service of a new master" (GA XVIII, 925).

In the evolution of the German *Lied* from the eighteenth century to the early nineteenth, we can observe two significant developments. One is the growing availability of poetic texts in collected editions and anthologies. Numerous poems by Goethe, for instance, which had first appeared in plays and novels — Goethe's *Singspiele, Egmont, Faust, Wilhelm Meister* — were beginning to be printed as individual songs and ballads. Poems, such as "Erlkönig" and "Das Veilchen," became accessible to readers and composers who were no longer concerned or even knowledgeable about the original contexts of the poems and focused their interpretations on the text itself, its inherent poetic and musical qualities.

The second development, which goes hand in hand with the first, is an increasing assertion of the composer vis-à-vis the poetic text. Music in general and the art song in particular became individualized and technically diversified. Goethe, Reichardt, Zelter had understood the art song as a medium in which the voice of the poet dominates. Now the voice of the poet was only one of several in the song. Schubert's composition of Goethe's poem "Erlkönig" has become the *locus classicus* for manifesting these changes.

Franz Peter Schubert composed his first Goethe poem, "Gretchen am Spinnrade," in 1814 when he was seventeen. In the course of his short life he set more than sixty texts by Goethe to music. But when in 1816 his friend Joseph von Spaun sent eight of Schubert's early compositions of Goethe poems to Weimar (among them: "Erlkönig," "Gretchen am Spinnrade," "Heidenröslein"), he never received as much as an acknowledgement. Almost ten years later, in 1825, Schubert himself sent his "Opus XIX" to Goethe, which contains his compositions of "An Mignon," "An Schwager Kronos," and "Ganymed" — with these humble words: "Should I succeed by the dedication of these compositions of your poetry in proving my unbound reverence for your Excellency, or in gaining some notice of my unimportance, I should regard this desirable success as the most beautiful event of my life."[10] Again there was no reply. If it were not for a matter-of-fact entry in Goethe's diary on June 16, 1825 — "Mail from Schubert from Vienna, compositions of songs of mine" (WA 3: X, 68-69) — we would not even know that the poet had received the precious gift.

Why was Goethe silent? There are many reasons. Goethe was gravely ill at the time, much of his mail remained unanswered. And Schubert was, after all, an unknown composer — even the music publishers Breitkopf and Härtel had rejected his "Erlkönig" and returned the manuscript by mistake to a Franz Schubert residing in Dresden.[11] But there are other, more compelling reasons. Goethe probably had difficulties in reading and understanding Schubert's music. True, some of the earlier songs, such as "Heidenröslein," are relatively simple and strophic, but "Erlkönig" is quite another matter. Even Schubert's third version — von Spaun had sent this easier version with eighth notes instead of triplets in the right hand — is difficult to perform. But more important: this music went against Goethe's aesthetic grain. Goethe favored folklike, dispassionate music, Schubert's rendering is intense and personal; Goethe liked strophic settings, Schubert's composition is through-composed and highly dramatic, building towards an inevitable climax; Goethe wanted simple accompaniments, Schubert's is complex and difficult to play.

"Erlkönig" was originally written for a *Singspiel, Die Fischerin,* where the female protagonist, Dortchen, opens the play by singing the ballad to herself as one sings a folksong — much like Gretchen sings "Der König in Thule" in *Faust.* In a letter to Philipp Christoph Kayser Goethe described this type of song within a dramatic setting as a "melody of which one assumes that the singer had learned it by heart and is now recalling it in a certain situation. Such songs can and ought to have their own definite and complete melodies which are distinct and memorable" (WA 4: IV, 155f.).

The composer, who seemed to have understood Goethe's dramatic and musical intentions rather well, was the first composer to set this ballad to music: Corona Schröter, actress and singer at the Weimar "Liebhabertheater." She played the title role in Goethe's *Die Fischerin* (first performance in Tierfurt, 1782) and she composed the music for the play, i.e. she wrote melodies for the intermittant songs.

---

[10] Quoted by Newman Flower, *Franz Schubert. The Man and His Circle* (New York: Frederick A. Stokes, 1928), p. 184.

[11] Harold C. Schonberg, *The Lives of the Great Composers* (New York: W.W. Norton, 1970), p. 109.

Schröter's composition consists of eight measures, has a folktune-like simplicity, a dance-like rhythm, and is entirely strophic. But nowhere is the content of the poem, the hectic ride through the night, the child's nightmarish fantasies, reflected in the music. It is an attractive, even memorable tune, providing a simple musical frame for the text with no ambition for interpretation.

Schubert, by contrast, did not provide Goethe's poem with a supportive melody, rather he "appropriated" the text: he first interpreted the poem, then wrote music to suit his interpretation. As Edward T. Cone says: "The composer is not primarily engaged in 'setting' a poem.... to say he 'sets'... is less accurate than to say he appropriates it: he makes it his own by turning it into music."[12] Schubert's compositional technique is decidedly more complex than Schröter's. The singing part alone consists of four different voices: the narrator, who opens and closes the song, the father, the child, and the Erlkönig. They all have, consonant with their rhythmical patterns in the poem, distinct melodic lines. How important the effect of, for instance, Erlkönig's voice was for Schubert is indicated by the fact that he changed the original *fortissimo* in the line "Ich liebe dich, mich reizt deine schöne Gestalt..." to a *pianissimo* in his manuscript, realizing that a whispering Erlkönig is much more alluring and frightening than a shout in the night.[13]

The different voice characterizations are complimented and augmented by an equally diverse and sophisticated accompaniment. The famous *ostinato* that runs through most of the accompaniment creates both a unifying effect of the song and a sense of impending doom. The effect is anything but folksong-like or tonal "embroidery" of the text. It is tense and urgent drama, spooky and threatening, a new expressionism in music.

To the poet at Weimar, who in his later years shunned intense personal expressions, Schubert's rendering must have appeared as an unleashing of all the sinister elements he had taken pains to balance and constrain. Goethe was certainly aware of these elements, for they appear frequently in his writings, but he objected to a compositional technique that would emphasize their presence. Alfred Einstein, the great humanist among musicologists, tells us why:

> When Goethe refused Schubert's songs set to his poems, it was presumably not only for the reason that the amplitude of the music appeared to interfere with the poetic word, but because he felt the 'demon' in them, for he himself had too much of this demoniacal, this abysmal,

---

[12] See Edward T. Cone's excellent book, *The Composer's Voice* (Berkeley: University of California Press, 1974), p. 19.

[13] Max Friedlaender, *Gedichte von Goethe in Compositionen seiner Zeitgenossen* (Weimar: Verlag der Goethe-Gesellschaft, 1896) I, 142.

element to have it stir him in music. It is to be supposed that for him there was also too much of this in Beethoven — but then he knew Beethoven's music only very inadequately.[14]

We know from Goethe's relationship to Heinrich von Kleist that Einstein may well be correct in his observation. Kleist and Schubert touch in their art on problematical aspects in human nature, without erecting sufficient counterweights in theme or structure. Goethe undoubtedly sensed in Schubert's music, as he did in Kleist's dramas, the lure of darkness, and he did what he always did when coming face to face with such problems: he kept his distance.

Yet the poet was not as implacable as it might seem. In April 1830 he received the visit of a brilliant young singer, Wilhelmine Schröder-Devrient (Richard Wagner's first Senta in *The Flying Dutchman* and his first Venus in *Tannhäuser*), who sang Schubert's "Erlkönig" in a recital at the home of the eighty-year-old poet. Goethe apparently enjoyed both the singer and the song. "I have heard this composition before," he is reported to have remarked to Miss Schröder-Devrient, "years ago, when it did not appeal to me at all — but in your presentation everything becomes one visual image" — "...aber so vorgetragen, gestaltet sich das Ganze zu einem sichtbaren Bild."[15]

The musical style that seemed best to satisfy Goethe's requirements of simplicity and melodiousness was the *style galant* that was dominant in the second half of the eighteenth century. It was the musical language of the sons of Johann Sebastian Bach, the early Haydn, and young Mozart. And it was the style practiced by so many of Goethe's musical friends: Reichardt, Seckendorff, the Duchess Anna Amalia, Zelter, Kayser, Corona Schröter. This pleasing, melodic style was not Goethe's final or ultimate choice of musical expression — Italian church music, Handel, the Classical Mozart rated higher — but the requirement that music be simple, harmonic, and ordered ("gesetzlich"), that it be limited in orchestration and dynamic range, remained his strong preference throughout his life.

The latter element especially, the scope of orchestra and sound, seems to have been one reason why Goethe also shied away from the musical titan of his time, Ludwig van Beethoven. Even Mozart's music caused Goethe some consternation when sound and range of orchestration went beyond the familiar as, for instance, in *Die Entführung aus dem Serail*. No wonder that Beethoven's music affected him even more adversely. We

---

[14] Alfred Einstein, *Greatness in Music* (New York: Oxford University Press, 1941), p. 171f.

[15] From Eduard Genast, *Aus dem Tagebuch eines alten Schauspielers*, quoted by Wilhelm Bode, *Die Tonkunst in Goethes Leben*, II, 264-65, and Max Friedlaender I, 142.

know that Felix Mendelssohn, who insisted on introducing the poet to Beethoven's music, had a difficult time in persuading the reluctant listener to sit still:

> He wanted to have nothing to do with Beethoven, but ... I could not let him escape, and played the first part of the symphony in C minor [the Fifth Symphony]. It had a singular effect on him; at first he said, 'This arouses no emotion; nothing but astonishment; it is grandiose.' He continued grumbling in this way, and after a long pause he began again, 'It is very great; quite wild; it makes one fear that the house might fall down; what must it be like when all those men play together!'[16]

Musical dynamics and grandiose designs were but two of the elements that caused Goethe's uneasiness in his relationship with the "unruly" Beethoven. Another decisive factor was undoubtedly the man himself. The two artists met in Teplitz, a Bohemian spa, in 1812. They visited each other, walked together, and the musician entertained the poet with improvisations on the piano. But the meeting produced little more than a host of anecdotes. Edgar Istel is right in observing that this meeting "bequeathed to literature a cloud of legends that more recent investigations have had difficulties in dissipating."[17] The fact remains that the meeting did not result in a meeting of minds, it neither led to a fruitful collaboration, nor did it much to increase Goethe's appreciation of Beethoven. Not that Goethe was insensitive to the genius of the composer. After hearing him play the poet entered into his diary: "[Beethoven] played exquisitely" — "Er spielte köstlich" — and to Zelter he reported a little later: "His talent really surprised me" (GZB I, 328). Goethe, we might speculate, even admired Beethoven in some ways. But the composer's untamed personality as well as the seemingly uncontrolled expressivity of his music filled Goethe's admiration with awe and uneasiness, a reaction for which Zelter found the perfect formulation: "What you are saying of Beethoven is quite natural," he wrote to the friend in Weimar, "I, too, admire him with fear in my heart" — "Auch ich bewundere ihn mit Schrecken" (GZB I, 331).

Beethoven for his part had no such difficulties in relating. He admired Goethe the poet (but not Goethe the courtier) without inhibitions. He was inspired by Goethe's lyrics, and he repeatedly read *Egmont, Faust, Wilhelm Meister*. His *Egmont* music even found the approbation of the poet. And on and off for twenty years he wanted to write music for Goethe's *Faust, Part One*, but the composition never came

---

[16] *Felix Mendelssohn: Letters*, ed. G. Selden-Goth, p. 71.

[17] Edgar Istel, "Goethe and Music," p. 233.

to be.[18] And Goethe, when he spoke of music for *Faust*, mentioned Mozart, Giacomo Meyerbeer, even Zelter and Eberwein — but never Beethoven. Of course, back in the "Storm and Stress" days of his youth, Goethe might have found it possible to collaborate with Beethoven on a Faustian project. Psychologically and aesthetically the poet was then much closer to the tense and energetic music of the composer. But in later years Goethe's aesthetic thinking became more and more dominated by a need for form and objectivity, by a preference for balance and proportion. And that meant Mozart rather than Beethoven. Sadly, Beethoven's love affair with Goethe's *Faust* remained unrequited and unfulfilled.

Hector Berlioz is the youngest of the three contemporary composers who are often cited to demonstrate Goethe's lack of musical comprehension or his "insensitivity" to modern music. This is not to suggest, however, that Schubert, Beethoven, and Berlioz represent one musical style or background. Each composer has an individual musical language and Goethe reacted to them individually. What they have in common are musical forms that were difficult for the poet to follow or accept: the dominance of music over the word in *Lied* compositions, Beethoven's seemingly unrestrained expressivity, Berlioz's chromaticisms and dissonances, the apparent lack of melody in his music.

In 1829 young Berlioz sent his "Opus I" — *Huit Scènes de Faust, tragédie de Goethe, traduites par Gérard, composées par H. B. Œuvre 1er*[19] — to Goethe, approaching the famed author, just as Schubert had, with words of modesty and veneration: "Although firmly intending never to mix my poor harmonies with your sublime verse, the temptation gradually grew so strong, the charm so violent, that I wrote music to several scenes almost in spite of myself."[20] Goethe, not knowing what to do with these

---

[18] Cf. *The Beethoven Companion*, eds. Thomas K. Scherman and Louis Biancolli (New York: Doubleday, 1972), pp. 1128 ff. We find Beethoven's last written references to *Faust* in one of his "Konversationshefte." In early April 1823 we find the following exchange recorded between him and his friend Dr. Johann Bühler: "Bühler: 'And the oratorio for Boston?' Beethoven: 'The trouble is that I'm not writing what I would like to write. I'm writing for money which I need. But it doesn't mean that I'm only writing for money. Once this period is over I hope to finally compose what for me and for art is above everything — Faust.'" The reference to the Boston oratorio concerns a commission by the Handel and Haydn Society of Boston; cf. Anton Schindler, *Biographie von Ludwig van Beethoven* (Bonn: Karl Glöckner, 1949), p. 270.

[19] The eight scenes are: King in Thule, Easter Chant, Peasant Dance, Ballet of Sylphs, the Song of the Rat, the Song of the Flea, Margaret's Song, the Serenade of Mephisto. The orchestration ranges from full orchestra to solo guitar (in the Serenade of Mephisto).

[20] Quoted in *Hector Berlioz. New Edition of the Complete Works* (Kassel, London, New York: Bärenreiter, 1970) V, viii.

"peculiar looking notes," (GZB III, 163), sent the manuscript to Zelter with a request for advice. The friend responded with unusual severity:

> Certain people can show their presence of mind and their interest only by coughing, snorting, croaking and spitting. Mr. Hector Berlioz seems to be one of these. The sulphurous smell of Mephisto attracts him and so he has to sneeze and spit like a cat, so that all the instruments in the orchestra get into action and haunt us — only he never comes near Faust (GZB III, 169f., June 21, 1829).

(We must keep in mind, however, that Zelter was not alone with his harsh criticism of Berlioz's early work. One French reviewer in *La Revue Musicale* speaks of Berlioz's "weird, twisted shapes; unresolved harmonies without cadences; effects, always effects... Is there no idea of melody in M. Berlioz's head?"[21] We also know that Berlioz himself was so dissatisfied with this early composition that he tried, later on, to destroy all copies he could find.)

As in the case of Schubert, Goethe never sent an answer to the French composer who, fortunately for us, was undaunted and created from these eight scenes one of the most powerful secular oratories, *The Damnation of Faust* (Opus XXIV, 1846).

The actual facts in this case may not be as one-sided as some critics would have them. Max Friedlaender, musicologist and Goethe scholar, provided us with an interesting note indicating that Goethe may not have been in complete agreement with Zelter's devastating criticism of Berlioz's original *Faust* music. Friedlaender quotes from a letter written by Eckermann to Ferdinand Hiller stating that the poet had received Berlioz's composition and tried to read it — "suchte die Noten mit den Augen zu lesen." Goethe, reports Eckermann, not only expressed a desire to hear this music, but fully intended to answer the composer's letter which he thought to be courteous and graceful.[22]

Friedlaender further points out that the "Sérénade de Mephistophélès," one of the numbers in the *Huit Scènes* as well as in *La Damnation de Faust*, is the most significant and successful number of the eight scenes in the composition. The original score is set for voice and guitar and even though Berlioz's instructions say that it should be played with vigor and impertinence — "effronterie" — neither the music itself nor the composer's annotations justify Zelter's diatribe against the composer.[23] Goethe might well have enjoyed Mephisto's serenade. At any rate, his reaction to Berlioz seems to have been more open-minded

---

[21] Quoted in *Hector Berlioz. New Edition*, V, ix.

[22] Max Friedlaender, I, 136.

[23] Max Friedlaender, (1916) II, 239.

than Zelter's. It is a pity that he did not follow his own natural inclination.

In summing up this chapter, several interesting points emerge, points characteristic of Goethe's way of musical thinking and, to a degree, of his personality. Goethe's musical attitudes, we find, are uneven. At times he allows himself to be swayed in his musical judgment, at other times he exhibits an astounding tenacity in sticking to his own ideas. The latter is particularly true when scientific matters are involved as evidenced in his unyielding position about the minor third. (It is a common place in Goethe scholarship that the poet became extremely sensitive when any of his scientific theories were doubted.) Even Zelter, friend of many years and a professional musician, had to give in — if only to keep peace. Another important point is Goethe's idea that all sounds, including minor and chromatic scales, are gifts of nature and descendents of one musical archetype. At least one modern musician agrees with him: Leonard Bernstein. Speaking about these very issues in the Norton Lectures at Harvard University, the musician asserted that musical language is both monogenetic and universal. It can be (like Chomsky's "innate grammatical competence" that Bernstein used as a point of departure) operative and constructive in as many different ways as there are different cultures, but there is only one fundamental beginning:

> *All* music — whether folk, pop, symphonic, modal, tonal, atonal, polytonal, microtonal, well-tempered or ill-tempered, music from the distant past or the immediate future — all of it has a common origin in the universal phenomenon of the harmonic series. And that is our case for musical monogenesis, to say nothing of innateness.[24]

Herr Geheimrat Goethe, had he sat in the Harvard audience, would have vigorously applauded on both counts: the monogenesis and the innateness of music.

But perhaps most significant for our understanding of Goethe's musical thinking is that Goethe's much belabored and maligned attitude towards composers of the "new" music is a logical outgrowth of his theoretical conceptions of sound. His position in music is consistent with his "Ganzheits-Denken" and his ideas of "natural law," of which Hermann von Helmholtz spoke in a well known lecture: "What Goethe looked for was the natural law of all phenomena, that was always his

----

[24] Leonard Bernstein, *The Unanswered Question* (Cambridge: Harvard University Press, 1976), p. 33.

main concern."[25] Goethe's preference for composers of the *style galant* as well as Classicism was, in fact, more than a matter of musical taste. It is a manifestation of his belief that there is a universal harmony and that art should imitate and reflect that harmony. Underneath his stubborn insistence that *Lied* compositions be strophic and regulated rather than through-composed lies his deep conviction that each work of art, no matter how small, must be self-contained and melodious and thereby reflect the universal harmony and order.

[25] Hermann von Helmholtz, "Über Goethe's naturwissenschaftliche Arbeiten," in *Vorträge und Reden* (Braunschweig: Friedrich Vieweg und Sohn, 1884), "Nachschrift," p. 24.

3

Music in Goethe's Writing

TWO ASPECTS OF GOETHE'S RELATIONSHIP to music stand out with uncontested certainty: the intrinsic euphony of his verse and the frequent use of music in his plays and narratives. Music as a poetic element and device is nearly always present in Goethe's creative writing. We hear it in the poet's early lyrics and we hear it still in the final scenes of *Faust*. Let us first consider the euphony of his poetry.

"Of all great poets," writes Willi Schuh in the "Preface" of his *Goethe-Vertonungen*, "none has influenced creative musicians more deeply and lastingly than Goethe." And he goes on: "Since 1769, when Bernhard Breitkopf composed the first songs by Goethe, who was then a student at Leipzig, approximately two thousand composers have set works by Goethe to music."[1] Schuh lists 767 works by Goethe that were set to music at one time or another; some entries ("Sah ein Knab' ein Röslein stehn" and "Der du vom Himmel bist") are cataloged with two hundred different compositions. Another report published in 1912 in the *Börsenblatt für den deutschen Buchhandel* puts the overall count of musical compositions of works by Goethe at 2,660.[2] Naturally, the number has increased since. "Goethe," wrote the musicologist Hermann Abert, "constitutes a decisive turning point not only in the poetic but also in the

---

[1] Willi Schuh, *Goethe-Vertonungen. Ein Verzeichnis* (Zurich: Artemis Verlag, 1952), p. 5.

[2] Quoted by Edwin H. Zeydel, *Goethe, the Lyrist* (Chapel Hill: The University of North Carolina Press, 1955), p. 174.

musical life of the art song... One could base a history of the German *Lied* solely on the relationship of the various composers to Goethe."[3]

The question is, what has made Goethe's lyrics so alluring to musicians; what is the common denominator that attracted such different composers as Karl Friedrich Zelter and Hector Berlioz, Anna Amalia of Weimar and Charles Ives of 58th Street, New York City?[4] One answer that has found consensus among many musicians comes from none other than Ludwig van Beethoven. When Bettina von Arnim visited the composer in Vienna in the spring of 1810, he explained to her that Goethe's poems attracted him because they harbored within them the "secret of harmony:"

> Goethe's poems have great power over me, not only through their content, but also through their rhythm. This language, which seems designed by spirits for a higher order and which carries already the secret of harmony within itself, excites and exalts me to write music." — "...ich werde gestimmt und aufgeregt zum Komponieren durch diese Sprache, die wie durch Geister zu höherer Ordnung sich aufbaut und das Geheimnis der Harmonien schon in sich trägt.[5]

Johannes Brahms and Max Reger went still further. Goethe's poems, they found, were so perfect that no music could improve them — "they are so complete," mused Brahms, "music has nothing to add." — "Die sind alle so fertig, da kann man mit Musik nicht an."[6]

---

[3] Hermann Abert, *Goethe und die Musik*, p. 107.

[4] Charles Ives composed Goethe's "Über allen Gipfeln ist Ruh," which he entitled "Ilmenau," in 1901. It is a sublimely tranquil piece of music and in stark contrast to his residence of the time: noisy 58th Street in New York City. The song is printed in Charles E. Ives, *Ilmenau* (Over all the treetops) (New York: Peer International Corp., 1952).

[5] Bettina von Arnim, "Goethes Briefwechsel mit einem Kind," *Sämtliche Werke* (Berlin: Im Propyläen Verlag, 1920) III, 457.

[6] The quotation comes from the diary of Georg Henschel (later Sir George Henschel), a baritone and conductor (in 1881 appointed as the first conductor of the Boston Symphony Orchestra). He was also a good friend of Johannes Brahms. Henschel wrote: "Wir unterhielten uns dann über Schubert und seine Kompositionen Goethescher Gedichte. Da sagte Brahms: 'Die letzte Strophe des Schubertschen Suleika-Liedes 'Was bedeutet die Bewegung?' ist die einzige Stelle, wo ich mir sagen muß, daß Goethesche Worte durch die Musik wirklich noch gehoben worden sind. Sonst kann ich das von keinem anderen Goetheschen Gedichte behaupten. Die sind alle so fertig, da kann man mit Musik nicht an.'" Quoted by Max Kalbeck, *Johannes Brahms* (Berlin: Verlag der Deutschen Brahms-Gesellschaft, 1910) III, 87. Siegbert Prawer, quoting Elsa Reger (Max Reger's widow), gives us an example from that composer: "When Reger felt the urge to write *Lieder*, he would turn to me and say: 'Find me some text, dear!' Then I would go and fetch my Goethe. If I then would read a poem to him or put it on

What Brahms and Beethoven sensed in Goethe's lyrics and what attracted hundreds of other composers, including Schubert and Berlioz, was precisely that innate harmony of which Beethoven spoke, the "Sprachmusik" or euphony that makes many of Goethe's verses sound as if they were born with a melody inside them. Anyone who has ever recited a Goethe poem aloud can hear that inner melody, whether the poem is from the poet's earlier years, a time of exuberance, or whether it is a verse of more measured tone from his Weimar Classicism, or perhaps a plaintive folksong from Goethe's late period:

> Wie herrlich leuchtet
> Mir die Natur!
> Wie glänzt die Sonne!
> Wie lacht die Flur! (HA I, 30)

(How splendid is the brightness / of Nature around me! / How the sun shines, / how the fields laugh!)[7]

> Füllest wieder Busch und Tal
> Still mit Nebelglanz,
> Lösest endlich auch einmal
> Meine Seele ganz (HA I, 129).

(Silently, once more, you fill / the bushes and the valley with misty radiance, / and at last, too, you bring complete peace to my soul.)

> Es ist ein Schnee gefallen,
> Denn es ist noch nicht Zeit,
> Daß von den Blümlein allen,
> Daß von den Blümlein allen
> Wir werden hoch erfreut (HA I, 372).

(There has been a fall of snow, / for it is still too soon, / for all the flowers, / for all the flowers / to gladden our hearts.)

At times it seems as if Goethe's verses consist of nothing but beautiful sound, gentle echoes reverberating between nature and the human soul, between the poet and the realm of ultimate peace:

his desk, he would say: 'Wonderful — but this tells us everything already, what can I possibly add in my composition? ... I find Goethe's poems so perfect that nothing more can be said about them.'" S.S. Prawer, *Lieder* (Penguin Books, 1964), p. 13.

[7] The prose renderings of these poems are from David Luke, *Goethe: Selected Verse with an Introduction and Prose Translations* (Baltimore: Penguin Books, 1964), pp. 7, 52, 226. The following poetic rendition of Goethe's "Wandrers Nachtlied" by Longfellow can be found in *The Permanent Goethe*, ed. Thomas Mann (New York: The Dial Press, 1948), p. 16.

Wandrers Nachtlied

Über allen Gipfeln
Ist Ruh,
In allen Wipfeln
Spürest du
Kaum einen Hauch;
Die Vögelein schweigen im Walde.
Warte nur, balde
Ruhest du auch (HA I, 142).

Wandrer's Night-Song

O'er all the hill-tops
Is quiet now,
In all the tree tops
Hearest thou
Hardly a breath;
The birds are asleep in the trees:
Wait; soon like these
Thou too shalt rest.

(Translation by Henry Wadsworth
Longfellow)

Elizabeth Wilkinson, the distinguished English Germanist, described the phonetic quality of this extraordinary little poem with great sensitivity and eloquence:

> *Über allen Gipfeln / Ist Ruh.* In the long *u* of *Ruh* and in the ensuing pause we detect the perfect stillness that descends upon nature with the coming of twilight. *In allen Wipfeln / Spürest du / Kaum einen Hauch.* The gentle expiration of breath in *Hauch*, and the echoing *auch* of the last line, have often been compared to that last sighing of the wind as it dies away in the trees. While the indispensable syllable *e* in *Vögelein* and *Walde* makes the sixth line a lilting lullaby....[8]

Goethe's poetic euphony was often noted and praised by his musician friends, especially Zelter, but also by the Romantics. Friedrich Schlegel, for instance, predicted in his review of *Goethes Werke* (Cotta edition of 1806) that the poet's ballads and songs, such as "Der König in Thule" and

---

[8] Elizabeth M. Wilkinson, "Goethe's Poetry," *German Life and Letters*, N.S., 2, (1949) 316-329. The article is partially reprinted in HA I, 533-534.

"Erlkönig," would remain alive and popular for centuries to come, they would retain their freshness "im lebendigen Munde des Gesanges."[9]

Goethe himself was well aware of the effect of his poetry, but he also knew that not all of his verses were euphonious, nor were they meant to be. A number of scholars, however, maintain that Goethe regarded euphony and singability as criteria for poetic quality, and they cite the following verse in support of their argument.[10] The modest little poem is entitled "An Lina" and the middle stanza reads like this:

> Laß die Saiten rasch erklingen
> Und dann sieh' in's Buch hinein:
> Nur nicht lesen! immer singen!
> Und ein jedes Blatt ist Dein
> (WA 1: I, 104).

(Let the strings be quickly sounded / And then look into your [song] book: / Don't just read! Always sing! / And you can call each page your own.)

I do not contest the claim that Goethe liked to have his poems set to music and sung, but I do want to caution against accepting the one poetic line "Nur nicht lesen! immer singen!" as universal truth and motto standing authoritatively over all of Goethe's poetry. Goethe did not think all his poems were singable or melodious. His remarks to Zelter concerning some of the poems in his *West-östlicher Divan* make that quite clear: "I looked over my Oriental Divan," he wrote in May 1815 to his friend, "in order to select a poem for you [to set to music], but I became aware how much this kind of poetry tends to be reflective — "wie diese Dichtungsart zur Reflexion hintreibt" — I found nothing singable" (GZB I, 430f.). Goethe enumerated three reasons why some of the *Divan* poems were, in his judgment, not appropriate for musical composition: their "oriental" reflective nature, their cyclical construction, and their sonnet-like design (GZB I, 457).[11] Goethe, in other words, differentiated between "Gedankenlyrik" and emotive, lyrical forms, between formal, rational constructs and expressions of the heart. Only the latter were, as far as he was concerned, suitable for music and singing.

---

[9] *Friedrich Schlegel, Kritische Schriften*, ed. Wolfdietrich Rasch (Munich: Carl Hanser, 1964), p. 294.

[10] K. Mitchells, for instance, writes: "Goethe was not content with his *Lieder* being merely read, but meant them to be sung." Cf. "'Nur nicht lesen! Immer singen!': Goethe's 'Lieder' into Schubert Lieder," *Publications of the English Goethe Society*, N.S., 44 (1974), p. 63.

[11] I am grateful to Rodney Dennis, Houghton Library, Harvard University, for bringing these Zelter quotations to my attention.

The euphonious and onomatopœic qualities of Goethe's verses are often the product of unconscious lyrical powers. The use of music as a dramatic vehicle by Goethe the playwright, is by necessity more deliberate, more conscious of a desired dramatic effect. We find such conscious employment of music in nearly all of Goethe's plays, from *Götz von Berlichingen* (1773) to *Faust, Part Two* (1831), and, of course, in Goethe's texts for the music theater, from the *Singspiel Erwin und Elmire* (1775) to the neo-Baroque opera *Des Epimenides Erwachen* (1816).

One of the most fascinating but little known dramatic pieces specifically written for music, or perhaps better, as music, is his *Concerto dramatico* (1773), humorously subtitled: *Composta dal Sgr. Dottore Flaminio detto Panurgo secondo*. It is a miniature concerto written for words, an attempt to create "verbal music," which is to say: to imitate tempi and musical structures through verbal forms.[12] The play, which is addressed to Goethe's friends at Darmstadt (the circle around Caroline Flachsland where Goethe was known as "the doctor"), was certainly conceived as a verbal spoof, as a poetic finger exercise in fun and games. Yet the little work demonstrates more than mere skill in versification, it shows the young poet's sense of humor and, most of all, his interest in and knowledge of music. Here are three examples from this intriguing little concerto in words:

Cantabile:

Schlafe, mein Kindlein und ruhe Gesund
Pfeift draus ein Windlein, und bellt
            draus ein Hund. (GA IV, 156)

(Sleep, my child, and rest well / Outside the wind whistles and the dog barks.)

Choral:

Erbarm dich unsrer Herre Gott
In aller Noth
In Langerweil und Grillen Noth,
Entzieh uns lieber ein Stückgen Brodt
Kennst deine Kinder o Herre Gott
(GA IV, 157).

---

[12] I am using the designations "word music" and "verbal music" as suggested by Steven Paul Scher in his book *Verbal Music in German Literature* (New Haven: Yale University Press, 1968), pp. 1-12. "Word music," Scher says, is poetry that has phonetic affinity to music, whereas "verbal music" is literature which presents music as its theme or approximates a musical score.

(Have mercy on us, Lord, / who are burdened / with boredom and fads, / let us rather go without bread / you know your children, Lord.)

Presto fugato:

Weiber und Kinder
Zöllner und Sünder
Kritaster, Poeten
Huren Propheten
Dal dilleri du
    Da stehn sie die Laffen
    und gaffen : /:
    Der Herrlichkeit zu
Dum du. dum du.
Dam dim di di du
Dam dim di di du
    Huhu! Huhu!
(GA IV, 160)

(Women and children / toll collectors and sinners / critics, poets / whores and prophets / dal dilleri du / there they stand, the fops / and gape / at the splendor / dum du. dum du. / dam dim di di du / dam dim di di du / huhu! huhu!)

The *Concerto dramatico* is a fairly isolated instance in Goethe's œuvre, he did not continue practicing this kind of "verbal music," but he did regularly employ music in the service of dramatic texts either as songs or as a means to communicate feelings and inner thoughts of his *dramatis personæ*. In his play *Egmont* (1788) we find both: songs (e.g. "Let's beat the drums" or "Joyful / and tearful / to be deep in thoughts") and background music at the end ("Sweet sleep! You are approaching like pure happiness") to underscore the hero's final dream and vision of victory. It was, in fact, this concluding melodrama that was severely criticized by Friedrich Schiller for being too operatic and not dramatic enough: "In the midst of the truest and most touching situation," he wrote, "we are catapulted by a *salto mortale* into the world of opera in order to visualize a dream."[13] Not surprisingly, the very element that had disturbed Schiller attracted Beethoven. When writing his music for *Egmont*, op. 84, he could draw on musical energy already present in Goethe's text. The composer perceived the poet's intentions perfectly: his melodrama and triumphant symphony at the end stirringly portray

---

[13] Schiller's review, "Über Egmont, Trauerspiel," appeared in 1788. Cf. *Schillers Sämtliche Werke* (Munich and Leipzig: Georg Müller Verlag, 1912) IV, 190.

Egmont's final vision. Goethe, it is clear, was less concerned with dramatic verisimilitude or structural logic than with representing outer and inner, visible and invisible aspects of life. Psychic communications were more important to him and closer to his own sense of human reality than the canons of dramatic development. And to convey these inner truths, Goethe often resorted to music.

Faust, Part One and *Part Two*, Goethe's great metaphysical drama and perhaps the most complex stage play in German, is also the richest in musical forms. It has been observed more than once that no other play by Goethe contains as many stage directions and references to music.[14] And, with the possible exception of one or two plays by Shakespeare, no drama has inspired more musical compositions. Goethe's play literally bursts with music. According to stage directions at least twenty-five scenes require some kind of musical accompaniment — not including any incidental music one might wish to propose. Some of these scenes are of considerable length and dramatic import, e.g. the Easter scene in "Night," "Auerbach's Wine Cellar," "Walpurgisnight," the masquerade in "Spacious Hall," parts of the "Helena Act," and, most of all, the grand finale of *Part Two* which with its "Solo" and "Chorus" sections, its "Gloria" and "Chorus in Excelsis" (an earlier version of the "Chorus Mysticus") seems closer to a requiem mass than to a bona fide drama. The forms and types of music called for in the play vary extensively. Individual songs range from simple folk tunes, such as the beggar's "Good gentlemen and lovely ladies" and Gretchen's "King in Thule," to highly emotional expressions, such as "My peace is gone" and "My mother, the whore." Background music ranges from wild and dissonant chords required for the "Witch's Kitchen" or the "Brocken" scenes to festive sounds and stately minuets in "Carnival," from the martial trumpets of Faust's military exploits to a tender pastoral in "Arcadia."

Music also serves to portray the inner state of being in some dramatic figures. Gretchen is in this respect the most "musically" endowed character. She reveals her innermost being as well as her evolving tragedy completely in the songs she sings, which range from innocence to love, to guilt, to tragedy and madness: "There was a king in Thule," "My peace is gone," "Incline, Thou rich in grief," "My mother, the whore / who smothered me." Unlike Gretchen, Faust, the restless intellectual, does not convey his essence in song; he is a cerebral rather than a musical character, but he is often surrounded by whispering and enchanting spirits, now lulling him to sleep, now rejuvenating his soul and spirit. Music is everywhere in the play. It weaves melodious links between

---

[14] Jürg Cotti, *Die Musik in Goethes "Faust"* (Winterthur: Verlag Keller, 1957), p. 41. Cf. also Hermann Fähnrich, "Goethes Musikanschauung in seiner Fausttragödie — die Erfüllung und Vollendung seiner Opernreform." *Goethe*, N. F. 25 (1963), 250-263.

heaven and earth, preparing Faust's redemption and carrying his soul aloft.

Goethe was aware of the musical potential of the *Faust* drama, especially of sections in *Faust, Part Two* which he himself identified as operatic in nature (Eckermann January 29, 1827). He also talked about composers for the play: Wolfgang Amadeus Mozart, who, of course, was long dead by then, Giacomo Meyerbeer, and Franz Karl Eberwein. He even specified Mozart's *Don Giovanni* as a possible model for his Faustian opera: "The music would have to be in the character of *Don Giovanni;* Mozart ought to have composed Faust!" (Eckermann February 12, 1829). But *Faust* is so multifarious a drama that it is difficult to imagine one single musical structure to encompass the entire play. It seems more realistic to think in terms of musical cycles or sequences (monodramas, for instance),[15] or to adapt *Part One* of the drama as an independent libretto, as a number of nineteenth-century composers have done, and treat *Part Two* separately. Be that as it may, one thing is certain: Goethe's *Faust* is one of the richest sources of and for music. It has been argued, in fact, that Goethe's broad and varied uses of music in *Faust* is as significant a contribution to the musico-literary field as is Beethoven's introduction of the human voice into the symphony.[16] The statement appears excessive, yet it serves to highlight the musical wealth of Goethe's drama, the importance of music as dramatic characterization, and its natural integration with the text. And we are becoming aware of yet another fact: Goethe tended to use music not only to express inner states of being but to indicate spiritual and metaphysical transformation. In *Faust,* as well as in other writings, Goethe used music as a link between the soul of the individual and the universe.

Proserpina, a small and melancholic stage work concerning the fate of the Queen of the Underworld, appears at first glance insignificant compared to the musical richness of *Faust.* But it is in this little monodrama — Goethe wrote it in 1776 inspired by the monodramas of Jean Jacques Rousseau and Georg Benda — that we find his most concentrated fusion of drama and music. The stage play was rescued from oblivion in 1815 by Franz Karl Eberwein, court musician and Goethe's "Hauskapellmeister," who revised the little piece for the Weimar stage and furnished it with a new musical score. The play was an instant success. It became so popular, even outside Weimar, that Goethe decided to write some guidelines for its staging — "to clarify the idea of the entire piece" (WA 1: XL, 107). What Goethe set forth in these notes are

---

[15] This is in analogy to Harold Jantz's suggestion of *Faust* as a series of monodramas. Cf. Harold Jantz, *The Form of Faust* (Baltimore: The Johns Hopkins University Press, 1978): see "Monodrama and Polydrama," pp. 127-134.

[16] Hermann Fähnrich, "Goethes Musikanschauung...," p. 259.

recommendations that go far beyond the theatrical welfare of this little piece, they are, in fact, documentations of his ideas and visions of the neo-Classical music theater. This kind of theater, Goethe argued, must be modest in scope, delicate in balance, and integrated in its artistry. He enumerated all the elements that he considered essential for a good performance: decoration, recitation, declamation, dance, costumes, music for monologues, music for gestures and body movements. All these theatrical ingredients were to be fused into one harmonious *Gesamtkunstwerk* of imagery, sound, and movement. At the end of his article Goethe pointed to a theater that is not only complete and graceful, but sparing in its means: "We must give praise to the restraint of the composer [Karl Eberwein] who sought not to produce himself but to further the performance through a chaste economy of means" — "mit keuscher Sparsamkeit" (WA 1: XL, 118; also GZB I, 429f.).

The key to Goethe's monodrama, the essence of his neo-Classical ideal, is balance and proportion. In the staging of *Proserpina* as well as in Goethe's annotations to the play, we encounter a most important concept of Goethe's thinking. It is a concept that gives us an essential link not only to his own Classicism but to the Classical music of the period, especially the music of Mozart. Wye Jamison Allanbrook has shown in a recent and significant study that the Viennese masters and particularly Mozart aimed in their music at a "harmonious coincidence of the elements of music."[17] Dance and rhythmic gestures, Allanbrook says, are essential features of Mozart's Classical diction. Goethe's idea of integrating gesture, dance, and words into one total dramatic expression derives from the same aesthetic impulse. It is the wish of creating theater in which all the elements are fitted, proportioned, and balanced to attain a "beautiful whole" — "ein schönes Ganzes." The latter quotation is from Goethe's "Prolog" of May 7, 1791, spoken on stage of the Weimar "Hoftheater" when he was inaugurated as its director. It is the same creed that Mozart had already realized in his music.

> Allein bedenken wir, daß Harmonie
> Des ganzen Spiels allein verdienen kann
> Von euch gelobt zu werden, daß ein
>   jeder
> Mit jedem stimmen, alle miteinander
> Ein schönes Ganzes vor euch stellen
>   sollen.
> (WA 1: XIII, 155).

---

[17] Wye Jamison Allanbrook, *Rhythmic Gesture in Mozart.* (Chicago and London: University of Chicago Press, 1983), p. 326.

(Let us consider that only harmony / of the entire play deserves / your praise, that everyone / should be in tune with everyone, that all together / should endeavor to bring before you a beautiful whole.)

The prose work that comes closest to *Faust* in sheer abundance of musical materials is *Wilhelm Meisters Lehrjahre*. The entire spectrum of Goethe's musical interest unfolds in the course of the novel: "word music," poems as songs, scenes described as oratorios with hidden choruses (Mignon's funeral, for instance), dances, and theater. And in Serlo, one of the major figures in the novel, Goethe gave us a fairly accurate portrait of himself and his attitude to music:

> Without himself possessing genius for music, or playing on any instrument, Serlo could rightly prize the value of the art: he failed not, as often as he could, to enjoy this pleasure, which cannot be compared with any other. He held a concert once a week; and now, with Mignon, the harper, and Laertes, who was not unskillful on the violin, he had formed a very curious domestic band — "eine wunderliche kleine Hauskapelle..." (*Wilhelm Meister's Apprenticeship*, Book Five, Chapter One; Thomas Carlyle Translation).

When the novel first appeared it was published with musical notes for eight songs composed by Johann Friedrich Reichardt. Jack Stein comments:

> In view of Goethe's often expressed convictions about the close bond between lyric poetry and music, the presence of the Reichardt melodies in the first edition should come as no surprise. What is in fact surprising is that no edition which has appeared since that time has retained these melodies.[18]

True, Reichardt's melodies have not endured. Today, when we wish to hear the poignant songs of Mignon or the harper, we may well prefer to listen to the renderings of Schubert or Hugo Wolf. What has endured, however, is the intrinsic musico-poetic texture of these poems, the "Sprachmusik" of songs like Mignon's "Do you know the land where the lemons blossom?" or the harper's "Who gives himself to solitude is soon alone."

Wilhelm Meisters Lehrjahre is an educational novel; it is about Wilhelm's individual development and about the need for rational guidance in the world. Music is an essential part of Wilhelm's education — as it will be for his son Felix in the subsequent *Wanderjahre*. Wilhelm

---

[18] Jack M. Stein, "Musical Settings of the Songs from *Wilhelm Meister*," *Comparative Literature*, 22 (1970), 125.

listens to music, he discourses on it, he is affected by it, but, as is true of Faust, music is not an intimate part of him. Mignon, on the other hand, this mystical being who for a time enters Wilhelm's life, is all music, dance, and poetry. She cannot survive in Wilhelm's rational, enlightened society, but while she lives, she fills that world with a sense of poetry and song, she brings to Enlightenment a feeling of mystery and wonder. Mignon is the most enigmatic figure created by Goethe, she and the harper affected the Romantic writers and composers deeply; and their impact was due in no small measure to the intrinsic musicality of their beings.

When *Die Wahlverwandtschaften*, Goethe's greatest and most tragic novel, appeared in 1809, Karl Friedrich Zelter instantly and spontaneously compared it with the symphonies of Joseph Haydn. The novel's clarity of diction, he wrote to the author, — "eine Schreibart, welche wie das klare Element beschaffen ist" (GZB I, 245) — was similar to the idiom of the Austrian composer. Zelter was right. Goethe's language in the novel is precise and balanced, the structure clear and symmetrical, his literary diction and grammar comparable to the musical language of Haydn. But the power of the novel does not derive solely from its structure; it derives from the interaction between content and structure, between human passions and the author's stylistic controls. Today, with a better understanding of the dark side of Goethe's novel, and a better understanding of the tragic aspects of Mozart's music, we might choose Mozart rather than Haydn as a musical analogue. Not that Haydn's music, particularly his late masses, is without passion, but it is in Mozart's late instrumental music that we find a most fitting parallel to Goethe's artistic design. When Leonard Bernstein described Mozart's G Minor Symphony, K. 550, as a "work of utmost passion utterly controlled,"[19] he not only described the essence of Mozart's Classical diction, but, equally fitting, Goethe's artistic mode of *Die Wahlverwandtschaften*.

Perhaps the most intriguing musical aspect in the novel presents itself less in an analogy with the music of Haydn or Mozart, but in a scene at the beginning of the book (Part One, Chapter Eight). The four main characters, Baron Eduard, Baronesse Charlotte, Ottilie, and the Captain, gather for an evening of conversation and music-making. On the surface it is a light-hearted get-together of four cultivated friends, but this evening of talk, reading, and *Hausmusik* reveals more than skills in rhetoric and musicianship. We are given an opportunity, courtesy of the author, to witness the birth of a major theme in the novel: the illicit and ultimately destructive love affair between Ottilie and the Baron. The first communicaton of the fated lovers occurs through music, in the pair's

[19] Leonard Bernstein, *The Unanswered Question*, p. 39.

ensemble playing. Ottilie and the Baron completely harmonize with their instruments (piano and flute); their playing is more intimate and more natural than the instrumental efforts between the Baron and the Baronesse. Not that Ottilie and Baron Eduard engage in flawless music-making, quite the contrary, the Baron remains an erratic performer to the point of distorting the score. What is important, however, is that Ottilie accompanies Eduard with complete empathy, forming with him "a new living whole."

The scene reveals Goethe's remarkable understanding of music as a vehicle and transmitter of psychic messages, as an art form that can communicate from heart to heart. Ottilie and the Baron are shown in psychic harmony through the medium of music before they are rationally aware of their adulterous passion. What Goethe depicted here poetically, Roger Sessions described in our own time musicologically: "Music goes ... to the energies which animate our psychic life... It reproduces for us the most intimate essence, the tempo and the energy, of our spiritual being."[20]

Ottilie is the most sensitive and the most musical being in the novel. She will die as a result of her excess of feelings; and she will join other such figures in Goethe's literary realm: Egmont, Gretchen, Mignon, all figures dear to the author but too vulnerable to live. They are characters who communicate their innermost being in dreams, songs, and in affinity with music, but they cannot survive their passions and the harsh realities of life.

Hugo von Hofmannsthal referred to Goethe's *Märchen* (1795) as an "interior opera" — "eine innere Oper."[21] This is neither a definition of a fairy tale nor of opera, but it is an intriguingly apt description of Goethe's mythic tale. In a fashion akin to opera, Goethe mixes the logical with the irrational, specific de-notations (as in a musical score) with their abstract potential of fantasy and sound. Goethe himself had likened poetic imagination to the nature of musical sound. Fairy tale fantasy, he observed, must be free and unfettered; it must liberate itself from specific object identification and engage our imagination like music — "Sie [die Märchenphantasie] muß sich... an keinen Gegenstand hängen, ...sie soll, wenn sie Kunstwerke hervorbringt, nur wie eine Musik auf uns selbst spielen" (WA 1: XVIII, 223f.).

---

[20] Roger Sessions, "The Composer and His Message," in *Roger Sessions on Music. Collected Essays*, ed. Edward T. Cone (Princeton: Princeton University Press, 1979), p. 19.

[21] Hugo von Hofmannsthal, "Einleitung zu einem Band von Goethes Werken, enthaltend die Singspiele und Opern," *Gesammelte Werke. Prosa IV* (Frankfurt: S. Fischer Verlag, 1955), p. 174f.

What appears musical about this fairy tale is the free play between two basic components, reason and fantasy, the element of "law" ("das Gesetzliche") and the element of imagination. The river, the ferryman, the snake, even the giant in the story, all follow certain natural laws and destinies. They live within an ordered world. But it is a world in danger of rigidity, if not petrification. To move it from a state of numbness ("Erstarrung") to vivaciousness ("Lebendigkeit"), fantasy and love are needed. Not love as passion, but love as altruism; love must not rule but enlighten, and that is more — "Die Liebe herrscht nicht, aber sie bildet, und das ist mehr" (WA 1: XVIII, 268). "Law" and "love" function in this fairy tale like point and counterpoint, like intertwining melodies producing an "inner music," which, says Hofmannsthal, will speak to us "thousandfold," "as if a symphony flowed by and filled our soul completely".[22]

Hofmannsthal also speaks of the "Glockenspiel" harmony that reigns between the earthly and divine powers in Goethe's *Märchen*. And with that he points to another well-known fairy tale: *Die Zauberflöte*. Goethe had produced Mozart's opera for the Weimar stage in January 1794, just one year before he wrote his own fairy tale. It appears that not only the spirit of Mozart's and Schikaneder's work found an echo in Goethe's story, but some of its thematic constellations as well. The similarities between the opera and the fairy tale are too numerous to be accidental. Both works present utopian themes with fairy tale motifs. They speak of hidden temples and promised kingdoms, they depict forces of enlightenment (Sarastro / the old man with the lamp) and forces of darkness (Queen of the Night / the shadow of the giant). Elements of fire and water, ancient symbols of purification, play as incisive a role in the two works as do the metamorphoses of snakes. And at the center of each lies a common theme: a young prince in search of an unknown beloved, a search that will result in a reconciliation of the elements and a rejuvenation of the world.

Das Märchen belongs to Goethe's "Magic Flute" stories, works directly or indirectly inspired by Mozart's *Zauberflöte*. His most explicit effort is, of course, the attempted sequel to the Mozart — Schikaneder opera, but there is one final narrative in this vein, one that comes late in his life: the marvelous little tale called *Novelle*.

Novelle is a symbolic tale (begun in 1797, finished in 1828) that concerns itself, as so often in Goethe's writings, with the mastery of passion — both personal and political.[23] Honorio, the young and fiery

---

[22] Hofmannsthal, *Prosa IV*, 175.

[23] On the political aspects of Goethe's novella, especially with reference to the French revolution, see Dieter Borchmeyer, *Höfische Gesellschaft und Französische Revolution bei Goethe* (Kronberg/Ts.: Athenäum Verlag, 1977), p. 333-350.

lover, must learn to control his impetuous nature — and indeed he does. His victory over himself is depicted at the end through a young boy who is singing and playing the flute while a lion is resting at his feet. The image derives from the ancient legends of Orpheus and Androcles as well as from the *Arabian Nights*.[24] It is used here to signify an archetypal situation: the conquest of animal nature through innocence and music. In his "Conversations with Eckermann" Goethe talked at length about the novella and its meaning. He wanted to show, he said, that the raw state of humankind can and should be overcome. Reality must be transformed through love and gentleness — "durch Liebe und Frömmigkeit" — to a higher and more perfect state of being. "After all," Goethe queried, "what is reality in itself?" The greater value of existence lies not in our lower but in our heightened self. To depict this process of heightening, Goethe employed the image of the boy with the peacable lion and the song. "I needed an idealized conclusion," Goethe said to Eckermann, "so I had to end it lyrically, indeed, I had to conclude with a song" (Eckermann January 18, 1827).

But Goethe was not yet finished. He ended his conversation with a metaphor to explicate the metaphor: story and song in the novella relate to each other like plant and flower — "a green plant which... finally grows a flower." It is Goethe's way of saying — and he said it in many different ways — that all things are related to each other, are "parts of the whole:" passion and self-sacrifice, writing and the blossoming of nature. All is growth toward a higher form of life, transcendence of our animal nature. Poetry and music can lead us beyond ourselves, art can help us — and once again we hear the sounds of Mozart's *Zauberflöte* in the background — to become more fulfilled, more complete, and wiser.

In a recent essay on Goethe's modes of aesthetic theory, Victor Lange concluded that it is not Goethe's "theory of the arts but the achievement of his poetry and his fiction that was to survive in the later climate of modernism."[25] Lange's argument is entirely applicable to Goethe's musical thinking and writing. Here, too, it is not the theories, not Goethe's scientific and aesthetic suppositions that endured, but the

[24] Katharina Mommsen makes this reference to the *Arabian Nights* in the "Nachwort" of her edition: *Goethe Novellen* (Frankfurt: Insel Taschenbuch, 1979), p. 287.

[25] Victor Lange, "Art and Literature," in *Goethezeit. Studien zur Erkenntnis und Rezeption Goethes und seiner Zeitgenossen. Festschrift für Stuart Atkins*, ed. Gerhart Hoffmeister (Bern: Francke Verlag, 1981), p. 175.

"word music" of his verse, the charm of his "musical" figures, his use of music as a psychic vehicle and universal link. Goethe as a musical theorist seems oriented toward the past, but as a musical writer he embraced the future, establishing himself as one of the foremost writers in the field of literature and music. The seeming ambivalence between Goethe the theorist and Goethe the writer does not represent a schism in his work. Rather it is akin to the major and minor scales in music, which the poet perceived as polarities of one organic unit. Ultimately Goethe's aesthetic (Platonic) rationalism in music and his psychological need and love for music were united in some of his late poems, most prominently in the poem "Reconciliation" — "Aussöhnung" — from *Trilogie der Leidenschaft*. The poem represents reconciliation of the aging poet with himself and, more abstractly, reconciliation of individual anguish with the eternal harmonies through the power of music:

> Da schwebt hervor Musik mit Engelschwingen,
> Verflicht zu Millionen: Tön' um Töne,
> Des Menschen Wesen durch und durch zu dringen,
> Zu überfüllen ihn mit ew'ger Schöne:
> Das Auge netzt sich, fühlt im höhern Sehnen
> Den Götterwert der Töne wie der Tränen
> (HA I, 386).

(But now, on wings of angels, music comes forth and rises, / making a million notes intertwine, / penetrating our innermost being, / filling us to overflowing with eternal beauty: / the eyes fill with moisture and we feel with sublime longing, / the divine gift of music and tears.)[26]

The poem reflects Goethe's emotional upheaval over Ulrike von Levetzow, his late love, and his admiration for Maria Szymanowska, the Polish pianist. But it is not an expression of anguish, it is an expression of reconciliation — effected by music. From *Werther* to *Novelle* Goethe invoked the Orphean powers to quell his heroes' passions. In "Aussöhnung" the magic is directed at himself: music soothes all personal pain. In a letter to Zelter, written at the same time, Goethe repeated this theme once more in the image of an unfolding fist; it renders his belief even more personal, visual, and powerful:

And now the most marvelous thing of all! The voice of Milder [the singer Anna Milder-Hauptmann], the rich sound of Szymanowska, even the public performances of the local military band, have opened me up as one

---

[26] Parts of the English prose translation are by David Luke, *Goethe*, p. 317; parts are my own.

amicably unfolds a clenched fist." — "Wie man eine geballte Faust freundlich flach läßt" (GZB II, 219; August 24, 1823).[27]

The composer whose music came closest to Goethe's theoretical and practical ideals, was Wolfgang Amadeus Mozart. The music of Mozart contains all the elements that fulfilled the poet's philosophical, scientific, and personal requirements of art: clear structures, specificity of diction, controlled language without sacrificing individual expression. Mozart's music conveys completeness and "Gestalt" in each composition. The elements of *buffa* and *seria*, of dance and human anguish, are all present and proportionately represented. It is this balance that provides the basis for Goethe's artistic affinity with Mozart.

[27] The image of the opening fist was punctiliously recreated by Thomas Mann in his novella *Death in Venice*. Mann, in fact, conceived the novella initially as the story of the aging Goethe and the eighteen-year old Ulrike von Levetzow.

Part Two:

Goethe and Mozart

4

Common Myths and Images

"NEXT TUESDAY," WROTE KARL FRIEDRICH ZELTER in April 1815 from Berlin to Goethe in Weimar, "we will perform Mozart's 'Requiem' in our *Singakademie*... Why can't I be so fortunate as to have you and Mozart in the audience" (GZB I, 423). "You and Mozart" — Zelter, the knowledgeable and sensitive musician, had long felt what generations of artists and historians would discover over and over again, namely that a strong artistic bond exists between Goethe and Mozart, that the two artists were close not only in time and culture, but in their aesthetic dispositions and the manifestations of their art.

Goethe did not respond to Zelter's affectionate hint, but there can be no doubt that he was pleased by the friend's association, for his own understanding of Mozart's music and his admiration for the composer had steadily grown since he first heard Mozart's *Die Entführung aus dem Serail* in 1785 in Weimar. In his later years, especially in his "Conversations with Eckermann," the poet reflected on Mozart and his art with the greatest of admiration, indeed, with a veneration that he reserved for very few, notably Shakespeare, Raphael, and Napoleon. The composer had become a symbolic, even a mythical figure in Goethe's mind, "a miracle which cannot be explained" (Eckermann Feb. 14, 1831), a "higher nature" unequaled and unreachable in his art — "Mozart... als etwas Unerreichbares in der Musik" (Eckermann Dec. 6, 1829) — and, indeed, one of those rare beings who are "divinely endowed" and can serve as proof of God's benevolent presence in the world (Eckermann March 11, 1832).

Once, after recording Goethe's high-minded reflections on Shakespeare and Mozart, Eckermann added, *sotto voce*: "I thought to

myself that the *dæmons* had intended something similar with Goethe —
[he is] too alluring not to be emulated and too great to be reached"
(Eckermann Dec. 6, 1829). Eckermann's secret wish is both charming and
significant. For it is here, in the thoughts and comments of Goethe's
devoted friends, in Zelter's dream of seeing his two favorite artists side
by side in his beloved *Singakademie*, in Eckermann's private conviction
that his master belonged among the immortals, that an association was
born, a vision of artistic relatedness between Goethe and Mozart which,
to some degree, has endured to the present day.

The following verse from about the middle of the nineteenth century,
entitled "Parallel Lines," typifies this mostly German-Austrian trend of
casting Goethe and Mozart into one common cultural mold and literary
image:

> Der Mozart und der Goethe
> Aus philiströser Nacht
> Schufen die Morgenröte
> Und glühende Tagespracht.[1]

(Mozart and Goethe / from narrow-minded darkness / created dawn /
and the glowing splendor of the day.)

Theme and style of this modest little verse are simple and direct:
Goethe and Mozart are portrayed as liberators of art from the shackles of
the philistines, as heralds and guardians of a promising new age. Similar
themes and perceptions continue throughout the century, but not without
variations: sometimes the two artists serve as inspiration to a younger
generation, as in Julius Bierbaum's sentimental poem, "Rosen, Goethe,
Mozart,"[2] and sometimes they are called upon to exemplify the Classical
tradition of artistic restraint, as in Emanuel Geibel's panegyric verse that
he wrote into the guestbook of the Salzburg *Mozarteum* in 1877:

> Mag die Welt vom einfach Schönen
> Sich für kurze Zeit entwöhnen,
> Nimmer trägt sie's auf die Dauer,
> Schnöder Unnatur zu fröhnen.
>
> Auf den Gipfel strebt sie heimwärts,
> Den die echten Lorbeern krönen,
> Und mit Wonne lauscht sie wieder,

---

[1] The poem is by Karl Enslin and appeared in the *Frankfurter Konversationsblatt*,
Nr. 22, 1856. It is quoted with these and other "Goethe-Mozart" references by
Paul Nettl, *Goethe und Mozart. Eine Betrachtung*, pp. 38-39.

[2] Quoted in *Zweihundert Jahre Liebe zu Mozart* (an anthology), ed. Ludwig Kusche
(Munich: Süddeutscher Verlag, 1956), p. 57.

Goethes Liedern, Mozarts Tönen![3]

(Even if the world abandons for a time / the simply beautiful / it will not indulge for long / in the unnatural. // The world will return homeward, / to the place of true laurels, / and will listen with joy once again, / to Goethe's songs and Mozart's music!)

Readers of more recent German fiction will be most familiar with Hermann Hesse's portrayal of Goethe and Mozart as a pair of immortals in his novel *Der Steppenwolf*. The two artists are conjured up as judges of our modern (i.e. 1920s) world and its civilization in the psychedelic dreams of Harry Haller, the novel's protagonist. The two immortals laugh scornfully at our cultural presumptions and technological frustrations. Harry Haller, such is their message, must learn to laugh, to love, and to live. Goethe advises him to "struggle against death," and Mozart tells him "You are to live and to learn to laugh."[4] The novel ends in hope rather than despair, for Goethe and Mozart help Harry Haller to overcome the alienating and destructive effects of modern technology, they teach him to live.

These various depictions of Goethe and Mozart are conscious literary creations. But not all associations of the two artists are as direct and obvious; at times the common references are subtle, hidden, or implied, at times perhaps unintended.

Eduard Mörike, for instance, wrote a fictional account of Mozart's historic trip to Prague that the composer undertook in 1787 to conduct the first performance of *Don Giovanni*. The charming and imaginative novella, entitled *Mozart auf der Reise nach Prag* (1856), was written in homage to the admired composer, and Goethe's name is nowhere mentioned in the text. Yet, according to the research of Hartmut Kaiser, the story contains a number of allusions to another famous journey: Goethe's journey to Italy. Dates, names, places, which appear in Goethe's travel log, reappear in Mörike's novella.[5] Mörike, a subtle and ingenius writer, may well have

---

[3] *Zweihundert Jahre Liebe zu Mozart*, p. 44. Geibel's poem was directed against the heavy Wagner cult of the time which is not without irony because Wagner himself was a great admirer of Goethe and Mozart (especially *Faust* and *Don Giovanni*).

[4] Hermann Hesse, *Steppenwolf*, trsl. Basil Creighton (New York: Holt, Rinehart & Winston, 1963), pp. 110 and 246.

[5] Hartmut Kaiser speaks of "indubitible allusions to the 'Italian Journey'" in his article "Betrachtungen zu den neapolitanischen Wasserspielen in Mörikes Mozartnovelle," *Jahrbuch des Freien Deutschen Hochstifts 1977*, pp. 383-392. Kaiser devotes an entire chapter to comparisons with Goethe's *Italian Journey*. It is of some interest in this connection that both Goethe and Mozart travelled through

been prompted by the coincidence in time of Goethe's and Mozart's historical trips — Mozart traveled in 1787, Goethe between 1786 and 1788. But it is equally possible that the reference is unconscious and that "parallel lines" were not intended. Even so, it is fascinating to observe that Mörike, in paying tribute to Mozart, may have, wittingly or unwittingly, paid tribute to Goethe as well.

Franz Grillparzer presents an even subtler case. The dramatist, who honored Mozart on the occasion of the composer's fiftieth year of death, did so in words and ideas that seem to have come directly from Goethe's poetic and philosophical workshop:

Zu Mozarts Feier

Nennt ihr ihn groß? er war es durch die
    Grenze.
Was er getan und was er sich versagt,
Wiegt gleich schwer in der Schale seines
    Ruhms.

. . . .

Das Reich der Kunst ist eine zweite Welt,
Doch wesenhaft und wirklich wie die
    erste,
Und alles Wirkliche gehorcht dem Maß.[6]

(You call him great? He was so by observing limits. / What he did and what he shunned / is equally important for his fame. // The realm of art is a second world, / but as essential and real as the other, / and all reality is subject to the law of moderation.)

If we did not know the title of this poem, we might be tempted to conclude that the Austrian writer, known for his admiration of Goethe, was honoring the Weimar poet rather than the Viennese composer, paraphrasing perhaps the poet's famous sonnet, "Natur und Kunst" — "Nature and Art:"... "None proves a master but by limitations / And only law can set us free" (HA I, 245).

The artistic similarities between Goethe and Mozart, especially in their Classical diction, led numerous nineteenth-century European poets and intellectuals into a conscious or subconscious identification of the two.

Italy (Mozart sixteen years before Goethe) along approximately identical routes which included: Venice, Mantua, Florence, Rome, Naples, etc.

[6] Franz Grillparzer, *Sämtliche Werke* (Munich: Carl Hanser, 1960) I, 283-85.

Some of them drew on the two artists as if on a common source of inspiration: Carl Gustav Carus, Christian D. Grabbe, Felix Mendelssohn-Bartholdy, Joseph von Eichendorff, Robert Schumann, Søren Kierkegaard, Franz Liszt, Richard Wagner, Gottfried Keller, Hermann von Helmholtz, Theodor Fontane *et al.*

Associations of Goethe and Mozart, as well as the inspirational effect of their work and heritage, continued well into our own century. Hugo von Hofmannsthal not only related Goethe and Mozart in matters of form — "Beethoven is the rhetoric of our soul, Wagner is its feeling, Schumann perhaps its thinking; but Mozart is more, he is form. That places him next to Goethe and Shakespeare,"[7] — but he acknowledged the two, as did Hermann Hesse, as his artistic forebears. His fairy tale *Die Frau ohne Schatten*, to cite but one work, was inspired by both Goethe's *Märchen* and Mozart's *Die Zauberflöte*. Other modern writers from James Joyce to Hubert Fichte established their own creative ties to the two Classical artists.[8] By and large, however, the literary interest in Goethe and Mozart shifted during this time from the realm of the poets to the province of the scholars. Literary historians and musicologists began to engage in scholarly comparisons of the two artists, comparing their artistic languages, their aesthetic views, and some of their individual works, notably *Faust* and *Don Giovanni*. Recent research has continually pointed in this direction, namely that Goethe and Mozart were highly compatable artists and that among the great composers of his time, Mozart was the most "congenial composer for Goethe."[9] "Goethe and Mozart belong together" — "Goethe und Mozart gehören für unser Gefühl zusammen" — wrote Emil Staiger in a recent essay on the two artists, "they are closely associated in our minds, even more so than Goethe and Raphael, or Goethe and Shakespeare."[10]

[7] Hugo von Hofmannsthal, "Die Mozart-Zentenarfeier in Salzburg," *Gesammelte Werke. Prosa I*, 45.

[8] For James Joyce's relationship to Goethe see Henry Hatfield, "The Walpurgis Night: Theme and Variations," *Journal of European Studies*, 13 (1983) 63-64. Hubert Fichte's novel, *Versuch über die Pubertät* (Frankfurt: Fischer Taschenbuch, 1982), is the most recent fiction, as far as I know, in which Goethe and Mozart appear as references, although Mozart more than Goethe.

[9] See Wolfgang Leppmann, *The German Image of Goethe* (Oxford: At the Clarendon Press, 1961), p. 94; also Friedrich Blume, *Goethe und Musik* (Kassel: Bärenreiter, 1948), p. 11.

[10] Emil Staiger, "Goethe und Mozart," in Staiger, *Musik und Dichtung*, p. 45.

Biographical misconceptions in the history of famous men and women are no rarity. In the case of Goethe and Mozart, misconceptions have been frequent and tenacious. The enduring effect of their works has given impetus to interpretations of their lives and works that often reflect more the emotional or cultural needs of the observer (indeed of entire generations) than the biographical facts of the artists. One such misconception, which has affected Goethe and Mozart in equal measure, is their designation as "Olympians," divinely inspired, serene but detached beings who would weave their artistic spell from beyond all human toil and misery. As Karl Viëtor observed: "Mozart was thought of as a light-hearted favorite of the gods; Goethe as a sublime Olympian who, like a god, was superior to the dark destinies which make the life of man bleak and dreary."[11]

In Goethe's case the legendizing began early, long before his death. Of the many factors that account for the poet's rapid immortalization, I will mention only one: Johann Peter Eckermann, Goethe's faithful scribe and secretary in his last ten years. Perhaps more than any other single individual or element, Eckermann promulgated the myth of Goethe as a higher being, a favorite of the gods. His description of Goethe, one day after the poet's demise, gives a good indication of his idealizing bent:

> Lying on his back he rested as if in sleep. His noble face expressed peace and firmness. The mighty brow seemed to harbor some lingering thoughts... The body lay naked... I was overwhelmed by the divine beauty of his limbs... nowhere a trace of fat or gauntness and decay. A perfect human being lay before me in great beauty... (Eckermann March, 1832).

Thus Johann Peter Eckermann. Reality, however, was different. Goethe's final days were not serene, but filled with physical pain and a wrenching life-and-death struggle. Dr. Carl Vogel, the court physician who attended Goethe during his last hours, left the following account of the ailing and dying man:

> His features were distorted, the face ashen, the eyes deep in lead-pale sockets, they were listless, dull; and they expressed a ghastly fear of dying. The body was like ice and was dripping with perspiration, one could hardly feel the unusually quick and hard pulse; the abdomen was terribly bloated, the thirst unbearable.[12]

---

[11] Karl Viëtor, *Goethe. The Poet*, trsl. Moses Hadas (Cambridge: Harvard University Press, 1949), p. 180.

[12] Quoted by Peter Wapnewski, "Goethe: Todesgedenken," *Die Zeit*, Nr. 12, March 1982, "Feuilleton," p. 7. Wapnewski goes on to say: "Es ist... Eckermanns Bericht Teil jener Legende, die er selber mitbegründet hat. Der Vollkommenheits-Legende vom Olympier, vom Liebling der Götter — jener Legende, die dem Klassiker und Dichterfürsten wenig Menschliches mehr ließ."

What difference in the two perspectives! We know, of course, that death smoothes over many a trace of agony, but we also know that Goethe in his later years was rather overweight, and that he suffered from aching bones that made his appearance stiff and awkward. Eckermann obviously did not wish to take note of any physical blemishes or describe any signs of final struggle. His description is an apotheosis, a romanticized legend for posterity, not an accurate account.

Legends arose just as promptly in the life and death of Wolfgang Amadeus Mozart, indeed, they spread and multiplied more rapidly than in Goethe's case. The composer's young age at the time of his death (he was but thirty-five), rumors of his poisoning by Antonio Salieri or the Freemasons, the absence of an identifiable grave, and the quickly growing fame of *Die Zauberflöte* were all elements that fed the legend. The early biographers contributed their share as well. Even the stern and moralizing Friedrich Schlichtegroll referred to Mozart in his *Nekrolog* as a "higher being," just as Georg Nikolaus von Nissen, Constanze Mozart's second husband, repeatedly spoke of the maestro as a miraculous artist, "the loftiest spirit ever to be found in the world of music."[13] Goethe himself contributed decisively, along with several Romantic writers (especially E.T.A. Hoffmann), to the composer's "divinization." In the last recorded conversation with his secretary (March 11, 1832), Goethe spoke of Mozart not only as one who was "divinely inspired," but who was (like Shakespeare and Raphael) one of those "higher beings" who by their very existence prove the presence and the workings of God in the world:

> Let anybody only try, with human will and human power, to produce something that may be compared with the creations that bear the names of *Mozart, Raphael,* or *Shakespeare.* I know very well that these noble beings are not the only ones, and that innumerable excellent geniuses have worked in every province of art, and produced things as perfect. But if they were as great as those, they rose above ordinary human nature, and in the same proportion were as divinely endowed as they.
>
> And after all what does it all come to? God did not retire to rest after the well-known six days of creation, but is constantly active as on the first. It would have been for Him a poor occupation to compose this heavy world out of simple elements, and to keep it rolling in the sunbeams from year to year, if He had not had the plan of founding a nursery for a world of

---

[13] Friedrich Schlichtegroll, *Mozarts Leben* in *Documenta Musicologica* (Kassel: Bärenreiter Verlag, 1974). This is a facsimile reprint of Schlichtegroll's *Nekrolog auf das Jahr 1791* (Gotha, 1793). Schlichtegroll wrote: "... eben dieser immer zerstreute, immer tändelnde Mensch schien ein ganz anderes, schien ein höheres Wesen zu werden, sobald er sich an das Klavier setzte" (p. 31). Cf. also Georg Nikolaus von Nissen, *Biographie W. A. Mozarts* (Leipzig: Breitkopf und Härtel, 1828, rpt. Hildesheim: Georg Olms Verlag, 1972), p. 695.

spirits upon this material basis. So He is now constantly active in higher
natures to attract the lower ones.[14]

Needless to say, reality, the daily circumstances of life, were a good
deal less "miraculous" or "Olympian" for both Goethe and Mozart than
their admirers would have it. In fact, few artists have drawn the inner
substance of their art from so deep a personal and intrinsically human
well as have Goethe and Mozart, and few artists have portrayed the
human condition with a greater penchant for truth and objectivity.
"Mozart's art is the deepest and most sublime expression of all that is
human, that is of this world, of the entire world," writes Wolfgang
Hildesheimer. "It contains the entire range of everything human."[15] And
the poet Richard Dehmel addressed the issue of Goethe's "Olympianism"
head-on in a famous essay, "Der Olympier Goethe:" "Where he [Goethe]
reveals his innermost being, we see an unfathomable despair unable to
cope with life... It means to belittle Goethe to call him Olympian."[16]
Goethe's own assessment in this regard is well known:

> I have always been thought of as one especially favored by good fortune;
> indeed, I do not want to complain and berate the course of my life. Yet, in
> essence, life has been nothing but toil and work, and I can say that in my
> seventy-five years I have not experienced four weeks of real enjoyment —
> "keine vier Wochen eigentliches Behagen...". It has been the endless
> rolling of a heavy stone which had to be lifted again and again
> (Eckermann January 27, 1824).

A considerable portion of Goethe's and Mozart's art and much of their
private testimony attest to the fact that the two artists experienced a
multitude of non-Olympian events. Underneath the often rigidly
controlled exterior of their art we find thoughts of bitterness and fear,
experiences of isolation and coldness. It is common knowledge that
Goethe, for all his fame and fortune, had few real friends. Wilhelm von
Humboldt wrote to his wife Caroline in 1812 that Goethe felt terribly
alone and that he had confided to him that with two exceptions —

---

[14] This quotation is from Part III of the *Conversations with Eckermann* containing
conversations which are in part reconstructed from notations made by Frederic
Soret and published twelve years after Goethe's death. They are nevertheless
presumed to be authentic utterances of Goethe's, even though Julius Petersen
gives them a low reliability rating in his *Die Entstehung der Eckermannschen
Gespräche und ihre Glaubwürdigkeit* (Frankfurt: Verlag Moritz Diesterweg, 1925), p.
141-43. I am quoting here from *Conversations with Eckermann*, trsl. John Oxenford
(London: G. Bell and Sons, 1875, rpt. San Francisco: North Point Press, 1984), p.
343.

[15] Wolfgang Hildesheimer, *Betrachtungen über Mozart* (Pfullingen: Günter Neske,
1963), p. 7.

[16] Richard Dehmel, "Der Olympier Goethe," *Gesammelte Werke* (Berlin: S. Fischer
Verlag, 1913) III, 138 and 139.

Humboldt being one — there was no one in Germany with whom he could speak freely.[17] Goethe often remarked on the envy and jealousy that surrounded him in Weimar and elsewhere, the hatred he had to endure. "They all send their regards," he wrote mockingly but with a chilling ring, "yet they hate my guts" — "Sie lassen mich alle grüßen / Und hassen mich bis in Tod."[18] Once Goethe observed, characterizing a situation reminiscent of the intrigues surrounding Mozart in Vienna: "I am well aware that there are many who think of me as a thorn in their flesh; they would all be glad to be rid of me, and since they cannot touch my talent, they try to take it out on my character" (Eckermann March 14, 1830). To his friend Zelter he wrote so pessimistically about his greatest gift, poetic writing, that we have to reach for testimonies from our own time, perhaps Thomas Mann's depictions of the "cursed artist," to find a suitable comparison: "If talent were not so dreadfully predetermined by one's nature, one would have to consider oneself a fool to keep burdening oneself with a lifetime of pain and hardship" — "Wenn der Mensch nicht von Natur zu seinem Talent verdammt wäre..." (GZB III, 23). Such undercurrents of pessimism run through Goethe's entire life. They are present in his œuvre from *Werther* to *Die Wahlverwandtschaften* and have found their most powerful and devastating expression in Faust's curse on life and human hopefulness just before his wager with the devil. Indeed, Gottfried Benn claimed Goethe as one of those "great spirits of Western civilization" who saw their main task in constantly overcoming their own nihilism.[19] Benn's formulation may be extreme, but it is not without foundation.

Mozart's situation was not too different. At the end of his short life he probably could have, much like Goethe, counted the truly happy moments he had experienced on the fingers of one hand. Underneath the seemingly cheerful surface of his music we find some harsh and baneful elements: melancholy, sadness, tension. "If people could see into my heart, I should almost feel ashamed," he wrote on September 30, 1790, from Frankfurt, where he attended (with little financial success) the

[17] *Wilhelm und Caroline Humboldt in ihren Briefen*, ed. Anna von Sydow (Berlin: Ernst Siegfried Mittler, 1910) IV, 8-9.

[18] These lines are from a poem which Goethe had omitted from his *West-östlicher Divan*. The poem begins: "Mit der Deutschen Freundschaft/Hat's keine Not/..." (WA 1, VI, 282).

[19] Gottfried Benn, *Briefe an F. W. Oelze 1932-1945* (Frankfurt: Fischer Taschenbuch Verlag, 1979) I, 165. Benn writes: "Ich komme endlich dahinter, daß *alle* großen Geister der weißen Rasse seit 500 Jahren die eigentliche innere Aufgabe darin erblickten, ihren Nihilismus zu bekämpfen und zu verschleiern. Dürer, Goethe, Beethoven, Balzac, alle!"

coronation of Leopold II. "To me everything is cold — cold as ice."[20] (Mozart was in Frankfurt from September 28 to October 16. On October 15 he performed his piano concertos No. 19, K. 459 and No. 26, "The Coronation Concerto," K. 537; a second concert did not materialize). Ten months later, shortly before his death, Mozart wrote to Constanze, who was as usual taking the baths at Baden (a health spa about 25 km. from Vienna):

> ...You cannot imagine how I have been aching for you all this long while. I can't describe what I have been feeling — a kind of emptiness, which hurts me dreadfully — a kind of longing, which is never satisfied, which never ceases, and which persists, nay rather increases daily. When I think how merry we were together at Baden — like children — and what sad, weary hours I am spending here!... If I go to the piano and sing something out of my opera [*Die Zauberflöte*], I have to stop at once, for this stirs my emotions too deeply. Basta! (LM July 7, 1791)

Mozart never used his compositions as vehicles for private sentiments; his music is based on musical logic, not emotions. Still, we can perceive tension arising from many of these compositions, often expressed through chromaticisms, which, as Leo Schrade pointed out (especially with reference to the D Minor Quartet, K. 421), often "frightened the contemporaries."[21] We hear tense and foreboding undercurrents running through the entire *Don Giovanni*, from the opening bars of the overture to the Commendatore's chilling "Di rider finirai pria dell' aurora." — "Your laughter will be silent before morning." We hear tense, disharmonic, and brooding sounds in the G Minor Quintet, K. 516, the G Minor Symphony, K. 550, and the pain-evoking Adagio of the A Major Piano Concerto, K. 488.

These sounds can well be interpreted as suppressed anguish translated into art. Leo Schrade contends that some of these Mozartian compositions lead us right to the edge of an emotional abyss (the D Major Quartet, K. 499, the Andante of the F Major, K. 590), which he felt Mozart avoided only through "the strength and magic" of his style.[22] The French poet Pierre Jean Jouve came to a similar assessment of Mozart's art:

> It should not be supposed that the mozartian idea was always that of catharsis, or of ascent towards the light as in *The Magic Flute*. No, there is far more variety, human truth, despair and *error* in Mozart's divine outpourings. Strong analogy with the pitiless onward movement of Shakespeare. In the Symphony in E flat [Symphony No. 39, K. 543], the

---

[20] Letter of September 30, 1790; *The Letters of Mozart and His Family*, ed. Emily Anderson, 3rd ed. (New York: W. W. Norton, 1985), p. 943. This edition will be cited hereafter as LM plus the date of the letter.

[21] Leo Schrade, *W. A. Mozart* (Bern: Francke Verlag, 1964), p. 130.

[22] Leo Schrade, *W. A. Mozart*, p. 130.

dissonance-filled Menuetto (according to the modern interpretation) is like the tense advance of an angry demon. *Don Giovanni*, which is so entirely Demoniac a work, abounds with the strangest instances. Don Juan's great aria about wine, women and the dance, expresses black destruction by means of a radiant gaiety. In a vigorous and solemn recitative, set against the graceful festive minuet, Leporello invites the Masks to enter and at the same time invites Death.[23]

While Mozart's music is not lacking in tragic potential, it is not tragic in its essence or intent. Mozart's music formalizes and harmonizes all constituent elements, even emotions arising from passion and bitterness. The composer never indulged in sentiment or self-pity in his music, and his compositions, no matter how technically complex, affect us as orderly, soothing, and inspiring. Mozart had nothing else in mind. "Passions, whether violent or not," he wrote to his father in 1781, "must never be expressed to the point of exciting disgust, and as music, even in the most terrible situations, must never offend the ear, but must please the listener, or in other words, must never cease to be music..." (LM Sept. 26, 1781). Mozart aimed at agreeable effects in his compositions, and he usually attained them, even in times of personal disarray, disillusionment, and what he himself called "emptiness."

Goethe's and Mozart's "Olympianism" — if indeed such a designation is useful and appropriate — requires a great deal of qualification. It certainly does not mean detachment from individual agony and personal toil; it does not mean distant serenity. What appears to be serene and harmonious in Goethe's and Mozart's art is but the measure of success in excluding the ugly, the chaotic, and the all-too-human. "The main thing is to learn how to control yourself," Goethe contemplated. "If I were to let myself go without restraint, I think I would have it in me to destroy myself and everything around me" (Eckermann March 21, 1830). But he also said: "I want to preserve and to build" — "Ich möchte erhalten und aufbauen" (Eckermann March 17, 1830). Instead of destroying himself, he let Werther, his youthful *alter ego* be destroyed. Goethe, to paraphrase Leo Schrade's earlier comment about Mozart, saved himself through his art, through form. Writing furthered his conciliatoriness, and in the end he sent Faust, his greatest sinner, to heaven rather than to hell.

Wolfgang Amadeus Mozart wrote his final masterpiece, *Die Zauber-flöte*, K. 620, in the depth of financial woes and artistic isolation. The grand opera, which opened on September 30, 1791 in an old, ramshackle suburban theater outside of Vienna, is the musical fairy tale of the Enlightenment — "The rays of sunshine will vanquish the night" — "Die Strahlen der Sonne vertreiben die Nacht." It is a fairy tale not only for children; textually and musically it is a serious work, a work of high

---

[23] Pierre Jean Jouve, "The Present Greatness of Mozart," *Horizon*, 1 (1940), 89.

idealism and ethical intent. But its seriousness is a "golden seriousness,"[24] permeated with earthiness, humor, and charm. It is art directed towards reconciliation rather than an expounding of personal afflictions.

Not all biographical facts and not all popular conceptions of Goethe and Mozart fostered a common image of the two artists. After all, there were some obvious differences in the lives of the two artists. Goethe came from a prestigious Frankfurt family. His father was an independent, well-to-do jurist with the impressive title "Imperial Councillor without Portfolio," while his mother was the daughter of Johann Wolfgang Textor, the Chief Magistrate of the City of Frankfurt. The boy grew up in a sheltered and cultured environment where he was encouraged at an early age to explore and develop his natural talents. He never experienced any kind of economic hardship, not in his childhood, and not later in his life.

Mozart, on the other hand, never knew financial security. His father, Leopold Mozart, earned a modest income as a court musician and "Vizekapellmeister" of the Archbishop of Salzburg, and Wolfgang himself began to contribute to the household coffer at the tender age of six. Instead of enjoying the warmth and protection of a stable home, which we assume to be beneficial for a child, he went on concert tours with his parents and his sister "Nannerl," displaying his extraordinary talents to curious audiences from Vienna to Paris and London.

The difference between Goethe and Mozart in family background and financial security became even more pronounced at the end of their lives. Goethe lived to be eighty-three and had become in the course of his long and fruitful life the undisputed poet laureate of the German language. He was known and honored throughout the civilized world. Napoleon urged him to come to Paris, the King of Bavaria re-routed a journey just to visit him in Weimar, and from England came a golden pendant inscribed "From Friends in England to the German Master" (among the distinguished inscribers: Sir Walter Scott, Thomas Carlyle, John Lockhart; GZB III, 458f.). And there are other, more concrete signs of Goethe's prominence. In the last years of his life he negotiated a contract with the German publishing house Cotta to produce a sixty-volume complete edition of his works, *Vollständige Ausgabe letzter Hand* (published between 1827 and 1842), for 72,500 *Thaler* in royalties, the highest sum of money

[24] Friedrich Nietzsche, "Nietzsche contra Wagner," *Gesammelte Werke* (Munich: Musarion Verlag, 1926) XVII, 282.

ever paid to a German author up to that time. When he died, Goethe left a bank account of 30,000 *Thaler*, his stately "Haus am Frauenplan" in Weimar, and valuable art and mineral collections.[25] On March 26, 1832, he was laid to rest in the *Fürstengruft* at Weimar, the official burial place of the House of Sachsen-Weimar-Eisenach.

By contrast, Mozart died at the age of thirty-five; he died penniless and left debts amounting to 3,000 *Gulden*.[26] He was buried on December 7, 1791, in St. Marx, a cemetery on the outskirts of Vienna. Moreover, for lack of money he was interred in a pauper's grave whose exact location has never been determined. The last three years of his life saw him constantly in need of money, often borrowing from friends and acquaintances. Best known and most poignant are his letters to Michael Puchberg, a Viennese merchant and fellow Mason in the "Lodge of Charity." These letters are among the most painful evidence of the depressing reality in which Mozart's life came to an untimely end. One example will suffice:

> Dear Friend and Brother,
> Whereas I felt tolerably well yesterday, I am absolutely wretched to-day. I could not sleep all night for pain. I must have got overheated yesterday from walking so much and then without knowing it have caught a chill. Picture yourself my condition — ill and consumed with worries and anxieties. Such a state quite definitely prevents me from recovering. In a week or a fortnight I shall be better off — certainly — but at present I am in want! Can you not help me out with a trifle? The smallest sum would be very welcome just now. You would, for the moment at least, bring peace of mind to your trusted friend, servant and brother.
> W.A. Mozart (LM Aug. 14, 1790).

Naturally, the question comes to mind again and again: what happened in the life of the composer to bring about such dire circumstances? After all, Mozart had enjoyed brilliant successes in earlier years, both as a pianist and as a composer. His piano concertos Nos. 11, 12, and 13 (K. 413, 414, 415) had met with rousing and lucrative success; in 1782 alone he gave twelve concerts in the *Augarten* (a garden restaurant in the old Imperial park), in 1784 he was engaged for twenty-two subscription concerts, and the audiences in Prague had cheered his *Figaro* and *Don Giovanni* in January and October of 1787. But suddenly Mozart's popularity came to an end. Audiences and patrons alike were

---

[25] See Ernst Beutler, "Das Goethesche Familienvermögen von 1687 - 1885," in *Essays um Goethe* (Wiesbaden: Dieterich'sche Verlagsbuchhandlung, 1946), p. 230. It is difficult to assess the approximate equivalent value of 30,000 Thaler in today's currency. But it is certainly upwards of DM 100,000.

[26] Uwe Kraemer, "Wer hat Mozart verhungern lassen?" *Musica*, 30 (1976), 211.

withholding their favors, and within two years Mozart was close to being ignored in Vienna. Even his music was falling on deaf ears. In 1788 he offered his G Minor Quintet, K. 516, for subscription, but nobody signed up. He extended the subscription to 1789; still no one came forth to support the composer or his music. In March 1791 Mozart offered to play his latest (and as it turned out his last) piano concerto, the Concerto No. 27 in B flat, K. 595, in an "Akademie" (public subscription concert). But he was unable to attract an audience of his own and had to settle for a spot in the "Akademie" of the clarinetist Joseph Bähr (March 4, 1791).[27]

It is not surprising, therefore, that a legend grew of Mozart, the divinely gifted musician, who in the end was cruelly neglected by his friends and abandoned by a fickle society, that in contrast to the famed poet in Weimar, Mozart never received the recognition or the rewards he deserved. But most Mozart biographers no longer believe that to be true. Uwe Kraemer, for instance, informs us in a fascinating essay, "Who Let Mozart Starve to Death?," that Mozart's income was by and large very good, at times even excellent. At the height of his career he earned as a composer and performing artist approximately 12,000 *Gulden* a year, an extraordinary amount of money judging by the fact that a chief surgeon at the general hospital in Vienna (*Allgemeines Krankenspital*) received about one tenth of that: 1,200 *Gulden* a year.[28] Even towards the end of his life (1790, for instance), Mozart earned an income of 2,000 *Gulden*, markedly down from previous years, but by no means a starvation salary.

One popular and insistent rumor has it that Wolfgang and Constanze Mozart were not exactly models of frugality. Wolfgang liked fancy clothes and servants; Constanze, who was frequently pregnant, spent much time and money in spas around Vienna. Friedrich Schlichtegroll, Mozart's first biographer, is also the first to make some mention of the maestro's nonchalance in fiscal matters: "He [Mozart] never learned to govern himself; he had no sense for domestic order, for a proper use of money, for self-control and reasonable choices in his pleasures."[29] The unreasonable pleasures that the stern Mr. Schlichtegroll alludes to included, from all we know, gambling. It seems that Wolfgang Amadeus was very fond of gambling and billiard playing — and not always to his profit. Franz von Destouches, a contemporary musician quoted by

---

[27] Otto Erich Deutsch, *Mozart. Die Dokumente seines Lebens*, p. 339.

[28] Uwe Kraemer, "Wer hat Mozart verhungern lassen?" p. 204.

[29] Friedrich Schlichtegroll, *Mozarts Leben*, pp. 30, 33. One cannot help but wonder whether Schlichtegroll's references to Mozart's "easy" life-style were the reason why Constanze bought up and destroyed the 600 copies of Schlichtegroll's booklet when it appeared in Graz, Austria, in 1794.

Kraemer, had this to say on the subject: "Mozart was a passionate billiard player and he played poorly. The arrival of a famous billiard player in Vienna could intrigue him more than a famous musician. He played for high stakes and played the whole night through."[30]

Whatever Mozart's skills as a billiard player — and the accuracy of Destouches' statement has been seriously questioned[31] — the truth of the matter is that we do not know the exact state of Mozart's affairs, financial or otherwise. There is not enough evidence for making definite assertions.[32] One thing we do know: the composer was unable to live within his means no matter how good or bad his income. Partly because of it he became increasingly nervous and irritable during the last three years of his life and began to show signs of physical — but not creative! — deterioration. He continued to desire company, but the company, says Wolfgang Hildesheimer, may well have shied away from him. He looked neglected and unkempt and may well have repelled some of his friends by his disorderly appearance. "Would we have felt comfortable in his company?" Hildesheimer queries pointedly.[33] Kraemer, too, argues that Mozart's growing isolation had its causes less in the changing taste of a fickle public than in a growing wariness among Mozart's patrons of being "held up" for money. After all, says Kraemer, Mozart still received honoraria from Prague, Dresden, and Berlin, but in Vienna, where he lived, he had become "persona non grata."[34]

One interesting fact emerges with some clarity from this sea of biographical confusion: there was no large discrepancy in income and potential wealth between Goethe and Mozart. Even here, where popular imagination had created a gulf between the two — the affluent Goethe, the poverty-stricken Mozart — the two artists were much closer than has been assumed for a long time. Both had rather high incomes; they may well have been the two best paid artists of their time — at least during certain periods of their lives. The real difference between them was one of

---

[30] Kraemer, p. 209.

[31] Wolfgang Hildesheimer, for instance, says that these reports are highly unreliable. See Hildesheimer, *Mozart*, p. 266.

[32] The English Mozart biographer Francis Carr writes: "... we are ignorant of the true state of Mozart's financial position at this time, and of the real nature of his relationship with Constanze. The sudden paucity of Mozart's letters written in the last three years of his life indicates that many may have been destroyed by Constanze." Francis Carr, *Mozart and Constanze* (London: John Murray Ltd., 1983), p. 83.

[33] Hildesheimer, pp. 281-282.

[34] Kraemer, p. 211.

attitude towards money: Mozart was a spendthrift, whereas Goethe administered his income with the characteristic circumspection of someone born to affluence. Goethe was a fiscal pragmatist, though not a penny pincher. He maintained firm and beneficial relationships with the Court of Weimar all his life (he had no reason to shun the Duke's patronage), and he knew how to protect himself from his fellow citizens, especially from those who would needlessly consume his time and energy. Because of it some of his contemporaries describe him as vain, egotistical, unfeeling, and, indeed, to a degree, he was. He cultivated that posture as a shield and means for his survival. "I often feel like a shipwrecked man," he confided to Eckermann, "who reaches for a plank just big enough to support one person. This one person will save himself while all others pitifully drown" (Eckermann February 10, 1830).

Mozart, by comparison, was much more vulnerable. Had he been fortunate enough to find the kind of patron and friend that Goethe had found in the Duke of Weimar, he might have flourished rather than succumbed so quickly. But that, of course, is speculation. As it was, he felt nothing but contempt for his patron and superior, Count Hieronymus Colleredo, the Archbishop of Salzburg: "I hate the Archbishop to madness" — "ich hasse den Erzbischof bis zur raserey" (LM May 9, 1781). After he quit the "safety" of his employment in favor of freedom and freelancing in Vienna, he was ecstatic: "I am no longer so unfortunate as to be in Salzburg services. To-day is a happy day for me" (LM May 9, 1781). However, after six or seven short years of phenomenal success, Mozart's life and daily circumstances deteriorated to the level described earlier: his income shrank, as did his personal and artistic appeal to the public. We know much less about Mozart, about his feelings and private thoughts, than we know about Goethe. Mozart as a person is not as visible in his works as is Goethe; not even his letters allow us easy access to his private life. But one thing seems quite certain: in contrast to Goethe, Mozart was not a "survivor," he paid little heed to the possibility of an early shipwreck. And when it came, it found him helpless.

5

Wunderkinder in Frankfurt

ON A LATE AFTERNOON IN AUGUST 1763, Johann Caspar Goethe took his two offspring, the fourteen-year old Johann Wolfgang and his younger sister Cornelia, to one of the most acclaimed musical events of the year: the appearance of a seven-year old musical prodigy from Salzburg who would perform, according to the advertisement, spectacular feats on the piano and the violin and play compositions of his own.[1] The wunderkind was Wolfgang Amadeus Mozart en route with his family to Paris and London and scheduled to give, together with his sister "Nannerl," one performance in the Imperial City of Frankfurt. The

---

[1] There is some disagreement as to the exact date when the Goethe family attended the concert. Ernst Beutler says without hesitation: "Es war am Donnerstag, dem 25. August 1763, im 'Scharfischen Saal' hinter der Liebfrauenkirche gewesen." Ernst Beutler, "Begegnung mit Mozart," in *Essays um Goethe* (Wiesbaden: Dieterich'sche Verlagsbuchhandlung, 1946), p. 241. The Insel edition of *Goethes Leben und Werk in Daten und Bildern*, eds. Gajek and Götting (Frankfurt, 1966), p. 13, gives the same date: "Aug. 25: Goethe hört ein Konzert des siebenjährigen Mozart." On the other hand, Otto Erich Deutsch and others think it might have been the first Frankfurt performance on the 18th of August, since Goethe's father shows an entry in his household book relating to the purchase of tickets on that day: "4 Gulden, 7 Kreuzer pro concerto musicali duorum infantium." Cf. *Mozart. Briefe und Aufzeichnungen. Gesamtausgabe*, eds. W.A. Bauer and O.E. Deutsch, Band V: Commentary I/II, p.76. Max Morris, too, gives August 18th as the day of Goethe's visit. Cf. *Der junge Goethe*, VI, 14 and 15.

concert had been announced for the evening of August 18th.[2] When it
turned out to be a success, Leopold Mozart, father and manager of the
two young artists, wasted no time in arranging three additional
performances for August 22, 25, and 30,[3] even though his initial
"Avertissement" in the *Wochentliche Frankfurter Frag- und Anzeigungs-
Nachrichten* had claimed that there would be time for only one such
concert in Frankfurt. The announcement of the children's final
appearance in that city on the Main river is worth quoting in full:

> The general admiration aroused in the soul of every listener by the skill,
> never before either seen or heard to such a degree, of the two children of
> the Kapellmeister to the Court of Salzburg, Herr Leopold Mozart, has
> already entailed a three-fold repetition of the concert planned for one
> single occasion. Indeed, this general admiration and the request of several
> great connoisseurs and amateurs is the cause of the concert (which,
> however, will quite definitely be the last) today, Tuesday, 30 Aug., in
> Scharf's Hall on the Liebfrauenberg, at 6 o'clock in the evening; where the
> girl, who is in her twelfth year, and the boy, who is in his seventh, will not
> only play on the harpsichord or fortepiano, the former performing the
> most difficult pieces by the greatest masters; but the boy will also play a
> concerto on the violin, accompany symphonies on the clavier, completely
> cover the manual or keyboard of the clavier, and play on the cloth as well
> as though he had the keyboard under his eyes; he will further most
> accurately name from a distance any notes that may be sounded for him
> either singly or in chords, on the clavier or on every imaginable instrument
> including bells, glasses and clocks. Lastly he will improvise out of his
> head, not only on the pianoforte but also on an organ (as long as one
> wishes to listen and in all keys, even the most difficult, that may be named
> for him), in order to show that he also understands the art of playing the
> pianoforte. Admission, a small Thaler per person. Tickets to be had at the
> Golden Lion.[4]

---

[2] The announcement appeared on the 16th of August 1763 in the *Wochentliche
Frankfurter Frag- und Anzeigungs- Nachrichten*. It is reprinted in Otto Erich
Deutsch, *Mozart. Die Dokumente seines Lebens* (Kassel: Bärenreiter, 1961), p. 25.

[3] There was also some confusion as to whether the Mozarts gave four or five
concerts in Frankfurt, and on what days. Some of the confusion stemmed from
Leopold Mozart himself, who wrote on August 20th to Hagenauer in Salzburg:
"We gave our concert on the 10th. It went off splendidly. On the 22nd and also
on the 25th or 26th we are repeating it." But the reference to the 10th was clearly
an error on the part of Leopold that was corrected in the most recent, the 1985
Norton edition, of the letters. Cf. LM Aug. 20, 1763. It is agreed now that the
Mozart children gave four *public* performances in Frankfurt: the 18th, 22nd, 25th,
and 30th of August 1763. Cf. Joseph Heinz Eibl: *Mozart. Die Dokumente seines
Lebens. Addenda und Corrigenda* (Kassel: Bärenreiter, 1978), p.6.

[4] The original announcement is reprinted in Maria Belli (geb. Gontard), *Leben in
Frankfurt am Main. Auszüge der Frag- und Anzeigensnachrichten* (Frankfurt, 1850) V,
25-26. I am following here largely the translation of the announcement in Otto

Mozart at the Age of Six

If this announcement smacks a bit of a circus atmosphere and fairground barking, we must keep in mind that such boisterous advertisements were by no means uncommon in the eighteenth century, even in the field of the arts. Neither musical nor theatrical events were announced or carried out with quite the sobriety and graveness that we attach to them today. But whatever the style of the "Avertissement," for the young artists themselves it was serious business. Unfortunately we have no program notes for these performances and Leopold Mozart, for all his praising of "Wolferl" and "Nannerl" as prodigious performers, rarely gives any information about the music they played. Leopold's elaborate letters concern themselves much more with income, expenses, and potential patrons than with the young artists' repertoire. We do not know, therefore, specifically what young Goethe heard that evening in Scharf's Hall on the Liebfrauenberg. Yet, if we allow ourselves to indulge a little in speculation we may be able to reconstruct the event and the excitement of the performance.

First of all, we have Goethe's own testimony. To be sure this is not a fresh and immediate impression, rather it comes from the memory of the seventy-eight-year old. Eckermann recorded on February 3, 1830: "Dined with Goethe. We spoke of Mozart. Goethe said, 'I saw him as a seven-year old boy, when he gave a concert on his way through. I myself was fourteen years old and I have a vivid recollection of the little man with his wig and dagger.'" Characteristically, Goethe, the "Augenmensch," remembered the young artist's visual effects and not his pianistic abilities or any part of the program. Still, the recollection was accurate, for there is indeed a painting showing Mozart as a young boy in a gold-embroidered courtly costume complete with wig and dagger, a suit he had received as a gift from the Empress Maria Theresa the year before when he performed in Schönbrunn castle. The painting has been attributed to Pietro Antonio Lorenzoni and dates from 1763, the very year in which young Mozart made his debut in Frankfurt.[5] The Imperial gift had become the boy's standard concert uniform, and he wore it when Goethe saw him.

We have no direct description of performance style and mannerisms of young Wolfgang Amadeus in any of the Frankfurt concerts, but we do have a fairly detailed account from the Englishman Daines Barrington who observed and described the boy less than a year later in London. Mr. Barrington had been rather skeptical about the wunderkind's advertised age and abilities. Leopold Mozart not only produced proof of Wolfgang's

---

Erich Deutsch, *Mozart. A Documentary Biography*, trs. Eric Blom (Stanford: Stanford University Press, 1965), pp. 24-25.

[5] *Mozart and his World in Contemporary Pictures*, ed. Otto Erich Deutsch (Kassel: Bärenreiter Verlag, 1961), p. 3.

birth date but provided an opportunity for Mr. Barrington to interview the child and test his musical skills. The boy passed with flying colors. Mr. Barrington not only proclaimed Wolfgang Amadeus a genius, but he proceeded to publish his findings in the *Philosophical Transactions* of the *Royal Society of London*. Here are two excerpts from Daines Barrington's ten-page report attesting to young Mozart's musical qualities as well as his habits as a performer:

Account of a very remarkable young Musician

I carried to him a manuscript duet, which was composed by an English gentleman to some favourite words in Metastasio's opera of Demofoonte.

The whole score was in five parts, viz. accompaniments for a first and second violin, the two vocal parts, and a base [sic]... My intention in carrying with me this manuscript composition, was to have an irrefragable proof of his abilities, as a player at sight, it being absolutely impossible that he could have ever seen the music before.

The score was no sooner put upon his desk, than he began to play the symphony in a most masterly manner... His father, who took the under part in this duet, was once or twice out, though the passages were not more difficult than those in the upper one; on which occasion the son looked back with some anger, pointing out to him his mistakes and setting him right....

Finding that he was in humour, as it were inspired, I then desired him to compose a *Song of Rage*, such as might be proper for the opera stage.

The boy again looked back with much archness, and began five or six lines of a jargon recitative proper to precede a *Song of Anger*... and in the middle of it, he had worked himself up to such a pitch, that he beat his harpsichord like a person possessed, rising sometimes in his chair.[6]

It is not difficult to surmise from this and other descriptions with what eagerness and energy, with what control and precision young Mozart met whatever challenge was put before him, how much self-assurance and pride he brought to his performances. No doubt it was this kind of musicianship and personal charm that attracted crowds in Frankfurt and elsewhere. And even though he did not elaborate on it, we can assume that the fourteen-year old Goethe keenly observed and admired young Mozart's professional stance.

In regard to works performed by the young musician, again we must speculate a bit. But here too we can come fairly close to reality by looking at the compositions young Mozart wrote and played during the preceding and succeeding months. There is, for instance, the "Allegro in

---

[6] "Account of a very remarkable young Musician," *Philosophical Transactions. The Royal Society of London* (London: Printed for Lockyer Davis, 1771) LX (For the year 1770), pp. 56 and 60.

C Major," K. 9a, a small but spirited piano piece that Wolfgang composed in the summer of 1763, just before the big concert tour.[7] The "Allegro" serves as an excellent indicator of the pianistic technique and dexterity of the seven-year old, in fact, it seems ideally suited for encores and may well have served as such. Then there are the four Parisian Sonatas, K. 6-9, and the six trios for harpsichord, violin (or flute), and cello, K. 10-15, the latter dedicated to Queen Charlotte of England.[8] These sonatas and trios, even though printed more than a year after the visit to Frankfurt, were probably conceived and performed during the concert tour of 1763. We know from public announcements that Wolfgang had such pieces in his repertoire:

> After that the public will be transported to complete astonishment upon seeing a lad of six sitting before a piano and hearing him perform not only sonatas, trios, concerti, which he performs with vigor — "mannhaft" — and not with childish playfulness, but also hearing him improvise by the hour, now playing cantabile, now with full chords... (Augsburg newspaper, summer 1763).[9]

A good portion of the concerts was reserved for young Mozart's greatest and most advertised gift: improvisations. The scope of this ability is perhaps best reflected in the so-called "London Notebook" (Erich Schenk calls it the "Chelsea-Notenbuch"),[10] a compositional sketch book into which the boy scribbled more than forty compositions while his father lay ill in Chelsea, England. As the children were not allowed to practice during this time, young Wolfgang reached for quill and notebook, and composed. He wrote his first symphony (K. 16) in Chelsea and he wrote the short pieces for the notebook. These latter compositions are particularly remarkable. They are not only rich in forms, e.g. minuets, allegros, contredances, andantes, etc., but they were written largely without the benefit of Leopold's supervision and finishing touches. In fact, some of them are sufficiently improvisational that they express more accurately than other early works the boy's creative spontaneity and inventiveness. Some pieces, such as the "Andante in B flat Major" (Henle, p. 143), can charm the listener with sheer melodiousness, others, such as

---

[7] *W.A. Mozart. Klavierstücke.* Urtext. (Munich: G. Henle Verlag, 1974), p. 11. Also Walter Klien: *Mozart. The Complete Piano Music* (Vox SVBX 5407), vol. II.

[8] Hanns Dennerlein, *Der unbekannte Mozart* (Leipzig: Breitkopf und Härtel, 1951), pp. 8-13 and *Wolfgang Amadeus Mozart. Sonaten KV 10-15* (Archive Production 2533 135).

[9] Quoted by Erich Schenk, *Mozart, sein Leben—seine Welt* (Vienna, Munich: Amalthea Verlag, 1955), p. 80.

[10] Erich Schenk, *Mozart*, p. 117.

KV Anh. 109b Nr. 7 (15r)

the "Sonata Movement in G Minor" (Henle, p. 116) or the "Andante in G Minor" (Henle, p. 120),[11] convey great rhythmic intensity.

It is no less interesting to contemplate which contemporary composers young Mozart might have had in his repertoire. One of the first names that comes to mind is that of Georg ChristophWagenseil. Wolfgang had been memorizing and playing pieces by the Viennese master since the age of four. He played Wagenseil in a recital for Maria Theresa in 1762 (in the composer's presence), and again in London for King George and Queen Charlotte.Wagenseil, it seems, was a favorite of the Mozarts and his name may well have shown up in the Frankfurt performance. Other masters mentioned in Leopold's letters and Wolfgang's notebooks before Frankfurt are Carl Philipp Emanuel Bach, Georg Philipp Telemann, Johann Adolf Hasse, and Carl Heinrich Graun. A few months after Frankfurt, in Paris, George Frederic Handel, Johann Schobert, and Johann Eckard were added to the list, and in London Wolfgang would play

[11] Wolfgang Amadeus Mozart, *The London Sketchbook*, in *Klavierstücke* (Henle, 1974), pp. 106-147. See also *The Musical Heritage Society*, MHS 1760.

works by Johann Christian Bach and Karl Friedrich Abel.[12] Naturally, when he played in Frankfurt, the young pianist did not yet have the sophistication and ingenuity that he developed so rapidly a few months later in Paris and London, but his pianistic abilities must have been of a high caliber even then. Whatever he performed in Frankfurt, works by Wagenseil, Telemann, Graun, perhaps a violin piece by Giuseppe Tartini or by his father, he played with greatest musicianship and poise.

Such, approximately, were the sights and sounds young Johann Wolfgang Goethe was treated to as he sat in the audience with his father and sister listening to the little musician from Salzburg. We might ask: was this one of the rare moments in history where the paths of two wunderkinder crossed, where one wunderkind watched another one at work? Yes and no! Opinions differ as to whether young Goethe can be considered a child prodigy. Karl Viëtor, a Goethe scholar, does not favor such a view: "Youthful prodigies," he wrote, "familiar in the history of music, are rarely possible in literature. Creative literature is the most spiritual of the arts and demands high intellectual maturity for attainments beyond mere virtuosity of form."[13] Indeed, one of the essential differences between the two arts is that literature depends to a much greater degree than music on specific signification, on verbal definition and exact meaning. The writer would seem to require, initially at least, greater intellectual comprehension than the musician. Certainly this is one of the reasons why Goethe was much less dazzling in his accomplishments as a child than Mozart, and why Goethe's genius must be seen, as the psychoanalyst Kurt Robert Eissler points out, more in the totality of his work and life than in the accomplishments of any given work or period. Eissler writes:

> Like Mozart, Goethe exhibits an immense productivity. In Mozart, whose life is in some respects an even greater puzzle to the psychologist, the genius quality manifests itself at a surprisingly early age, when the personality has barely begun to reveal its basic structure. This precocity Goethe does not share. In him, the earliest hints that betray objectively the approach of genius occur in late puberty. But from then on a stream of creativity pours forth that is breath-taking, and the mere record of what was created, done and accomplished makes one marvel how so much could find its place in one life.[14]

---

[12] See *Mozart. Briefe. Gesamtausgabe*, I, 61, 151; V, 44. Also: Georg Nikolaus von Nissen, *Biographie W.A. Mozarts*, p. 30. Erich Schenk, *Mozart.*, pp. 47-48. Hanns Dennerlein, *Der unbekannte Mozart.*, p. 8.

[13] Karl Viëtor, *Goethe. The Poet*, p. 4.

[14] Kurt R. Eissler, *Goethe: A Psychoanalytic Study 1775-1786* (Detroit: Wayne State University Press, 1963) I, xxxi f.

Yet, Goethe's mental faculties, his power to learn and to retain, as well as his linguistic abilities, were uncommonly developed even before puberty. At age seven he wrote three Latin-German dialogues that not only show an astounding command of Latin grammar, but also reveal a sufficient sense of poetic promise to induce his biographer Albert Bielschowsky to devote over three pages to these school-boy exercises.[15] At age nine Goethe had read his way into Racine and Molière in the original; he had begun to study Greek, English, and Hebrew, and he had written a fairy tale. "It is a precocious lad who presents himself here as one who rapidly consumes all the education offered to him" comments Max Morris in his edition of *Der junge Goethe*.[16] Indeed, looking at Goethe's early exercise book, especially his language studies gathered under the heading of *Labores Juveniles* (Max Morris, vol. I), one cannot help but marvel at the workload and the mental agility of this eight- and nine-year old, who could write a Biblical text in four languages.

At the time of young Mozart's visit to Frankfurt, Goethe had written scores of poems, several plays, and at least one epic. And shortly afterwards he attempted, according to a note for his sister, a comic opera in the style of Terence: "j'avois composé l'Opera comique La sposa rapita et bien d'autres choses."[17] Certainly, for the teen-aged Johann Wolfgang this was a time of experimentation, a time for learning, growing, and preparing. But we can observe from the beginning the same significant pattern of development that is evident in Mozart: after a brief period of searching and emulating, the poet finds his own creative voice swiftly and unerringly. Goethe had, like Mozart, an extremely quick and engrossing mind; often he surpassed his literary models in the very process of imitating them. His verbal ingenuity, which is so akin to Mozart's gift for musical invention, carried him swiftly past anacreontic and Rococo poetry into the most remarkable poetical efflorescence of his career and perhaps in all of German literature: the "Sesenheim Songs," the drama *Götz von Berlichingen*, and the epistolary novel that spread his fame throughout the world, *The Sufferings of Young Werther*. The intensity of emotion, the passions, and the psychological realism conveyed in these early works, must have been simmering and building within him long before he could fashion the words that gave form to these feelings. It is a process of "damming up," as Heinrich Henel called it: "Without this

---

[15] Albert Bielschowsky, *Goethe. Sein Leben und seine Werke* (Munich: C.H. Beck'sche Verlagsbuchhandlung, 1911) I, 33-35.

[16] Max Morris, *Der junge Goethe*, I, vi.

[17] Hans John, *Goethe und die Musik* (Langensalza: H. Beyer und Söhne, 1927), p. 36.

damming up of his creative power, Goethe could not have become a poet."[18]

When Goethe's creative powers were beginning to emerge, young Mozart was already showering the courts and cities of Europe with his musical gifts. Whether or not we think of both these extraordinary talents as wunderkinder is not important. Regardless of their outward accomplishments at that moment, they were both poised at the threshold of an immense artistic productivity that would soon catapult them into fame and immortality. The historic moment in Frankfurt passed without immediate consequences. Still, in the history of the arts, especially in Goethe studies, it is a moment of charm, fascination, even sober reflection: the young Frankfurt patrician watching intently the dazzling little artist in his aristocratic attire, observer and observed so far apart, yet inwardly even then such kindred spirits.

[18] Heinrich Henel, "Der junge Goethe," *Monatshefte*, 41 (1949), 142.

6

The Abduction in Weimar

IN AN ATTEMPT TO BOLSTER THE SPORADIC and faltering efforts of the
local amateur theater, Carl August, Duke of Sachsen-Weimar, invited the
acting troupe of Giuseppe Bellomo to his capital city of Weimar. Bellomo,
who had been performing near Dresden,[1] came with his company and
moved into the *Redoutensaal*, an old building opposite the ducal palace,
which had been refurbished in 1780 to house the new court theater.[2]
Bellomo opened on January 1, 1784 with Friedrich Gotter's *Marianne*, a
bourgeois tragedy in three acts, and, in general, surprised the staid and
sleepy community of six thousand with a rather brisk pace of new
performances. Comedies, light operas, *Singspiele*, and a modest number of
tragedies were staged in rapid succession; even Shakespeare made his
first appearance in Weimar under Bellomo's direction. *Hamlet, King Lear,*
and *Macbeth* were all performed in 1785 and apparently with great
success.[3] Goethe reported later (in a speech intended for the
Freitagsgesellschaft, a weekly science colloquium) that between 1784 and
1795 over four hundred new works had been launched at the Weimar

---

[1] According to Julius Wahle, *Das Weimarer Hoftheater* (Weimar: Verlag der
Goethe-Gesellschaft, 1892), p. 16, Bellomo's troupe had played last "im
Linkeschen Bad zu Dresden."

[2] Marvin Carlson, *Goethe and the Weimar Theater* (Ithaca: Cornell University Press,
1978), pp. 38 and 39.

[3] For a detailed account of Bellomo's repertoire see Carlson, *Goethe and the
Weimar Theater*, pp. 48-50.

theater.[4] Yet, in spite of these commendable efforts, Bellomo did not find favor with the Weimar court and theater public, and when he received an invitation in 1790 to move his company to Graz, Austria, no one in Weimar strenuously objected. A new acting company was founded and Goethe himself was appointed the general director of the new Ducal Court Theater. He opened on April 5, 1791 with August Wilhelm Iffland's *Die Jäger* and concluded his tenure on April 7, 1817 with Beethoven's *Fidelio.*[5]

Giuseppe Bellomo may not have satisfied the taste and expectations of Weimar high society, but, wittingly or unwittingly, he played a major role in the musical education of Johann Wolfgang Goethe. In September 1785 Bellomo staged a performance of Mozart's *Die Entführung aus dem Serail*, an event that proved to have a significant effect on Goethe's artistic relationship to Mozart and probably to music in general. For over twenty years Goethe had not given much thought to Mozart and his music. Not that he had neglected music altogether: he had gone to the French *opéra comique* in Frankfurt, and he had been inspired by the German *Singspiel* in Leipzig. Mozart, however, seems to have been far from his mind. But now, after Bellomo's production of *Die Entführung*, Mozart's name began to appear with some frequency and regularity in Goethe's letters and diaries. Indeed, *Die Entführung* rekindled Goethe's awareness of the composer and became a point of departure for Goethe's gradual recognition of Mozart as a musical and dramatic genius.

Goethe's path to Mozart was not without struggle, however. On December 22, 1785, the poet wrote to Philipp Christoph Kayser, the young musician he had met ten years earlier in Frankfurt:

> Not long ago *Die Entführung aus dem Serail* was performed here. Everybody was in favor of the music. The first time I saw it, the performance was rather mediocre, the text is very poor and the music, too, did not really impress me. The second performance I saw was so bad I walked out. But the play remained in the repertoire and everyone kept praising the music. When it was given for the fifth time, I went to see it once more. They acted and sang better than before, I distanced myself from the text and understood now why I had come to such a different judgment from the rest of the audience (WA 4: VII, 143).

Goethe, it appears, had problems with Mozart's *Singspiel*. The question is whether these problems were strictly of an aesthetic nature, as

---

[4] "Über die verschiedenen Zweige der hiesigen Tätigkeit," a report concerning the cultural activities in Weimar during the preceding decade (WA 1: LIII, 182).

[5] The opening date and work are mentioned by Johannes Höffner, *Goethe und das Weimarer Hoftheater* (Weimar: Gustav Kiepenheuer, 1913), p. 26f. Apparently, the regular "Spielplan" did not start until May 19th and featured *Lilla, una cosa rara* by Martin y Solar. See also Alfred Orel, *Goethe als Operndirektor* (Bregenz: Eugen Russ Verlag, 1949), pp. 115 and 162.

his letter seems to indicate, or whether there were also personal reasons that kept him from embracing Mozart's work.

First of all we have, as Goethe himself says, the poor quality of the text. Even though the libretto of *Die Entführung* is not any worse than the average German theater text of the time, one finds it hard to disagree with the poet on this point. The play, published in Leipzig in 1781 under the title of *Belmont und Constanze, oder die Entführung aus dem Serail*, "Eine Operette in drey Akten,"[6] had been adapted from various French and English sources by Christoph Friedrich Bretzner to serve as a libretto for an operetta by the *Singspiel* composer Johann André. Bretzner's play was set in Turkey, a favored eighteenth-century stage locale, and featured the popular Enlightenment theme of divided lovers and generous (i.e. "noble savage") despots. Mozart and his librettist, Gottlieb Stephanie,[7] had made several changes in Bretzner's text, increasing, for instance, Osmin's role and singing part and, in general, tightening the structure of the play by correlating action, *personæ dramatis*, and the music to form a coherent music drama. "The whole story is being altered," Mozart wrote to his father on September 26, 1781, in a detailed account of his work — "and to tell the truth, at my own request" (LM Sept. 26, 1781).

Mozart was so eager to improve the play dramaturgically that he began altering it musically before Stephanie had a chance to rewrite the text. In general, however, Stephanie did not make as many changes as Mozart's letter to his father implies.[8] The most significant addition in the first scene is Osmin's aria: "By the Prophet's beard, I swear it" — "Drum, beim Barte des Propheten," which shifts the emphasis in that scene from Belmont to Osmin. The other major change comes at the end of the *Singspiel*. In Bretzner's text Belmont turns out to be Selim Pasha's own son; in the Mozart-Stephanie version Belmont is the son of Selim's arch-

---

[6] (Leipzig: bey Carl Friedrich Schneider, 1781). For a detailed discussion of Bretzner's text in relation to Mozart's libretto consult Otto Jahn, *W.A. Mozart*, 5th rev. ed., Hermann Abert (Leipzig: Breitkopf und Härtel, 1919), I, 931-973. For an account of the English predecessors of the play see Edward J. Dent, *Mozart's Operas*, p. 71; for the "Turkish" tradition on the eighteenth-century stage check William Mann, "Mozart alla Turca," *Opera News*, 44 (1980), 14-16.

[7] Stephanie der Jüngere also wrote the libretto for Mozart's *Der Schauspieldirektor* as well as the popular comic opera *Der Apotheker und der Doktor* (a Goethe favorite) with music by Karl Ditters von Dittersdorf.

[8] Bretzner's play contains many of the numbers which we generally identify with Mozart's *Singspiel*, e.g. "Wer ein Liebchen hat gefunden" (Act I), "O wie ängstlich, o wie feurig" (Act I), "Marsch! Marsch! Marsch!" (Act I), "Durch Zärtlichkeit und Schmeicheln" (Act II), "Traurigkeit ward mir zum Loose" (Act II), "Vivat Bacchus!" (Act II), "Im Mohrenland gefangen war" (Act III), "Ach, mit freudigem Entzücken" (Act III). A copy of Bretzner's play can be found in the Austrian National Library in Vienna.

enemy, the Commander of Oran. This change increases both the tension in the play and the ultimate humaneness of the pasha.

Christoph Friedrich Bretzner did not like any of this. He wrote an indignant letter to a Leipzig newspaper in which he protested vigorously against such mistreatment of his play:

> A certain person by the name of Mozart, in Vienna, has had the audacity to misuse my drama *Belmont und Constanze* as an opera-text. I hereby protest most solemnly against this infringement of my rights and reserve the right to take further measures.
>   Christoph Friedrich Bretzner,
>   author of *Das Räuschchen*.[9]

There is no evidence that any "further measures" were taken or, for that matter, could have been taken. But it is also clear that Stephanie had not substantially improved the literary quality of the piece. The new libretto had gained in dramatic quality — Mozart had seen to that — but the text as a whole remained flat and uninspired, "the very worst" that Mozart "ever set to music," as Edward Dent contends.[10] We might find Dent's judgment a bit harsh, but Goethe would probably have agreed with it. After all, it was the "poor" quality of the libretto which, according to the letter, had interfered with his appreciation of Mozart's music. And we know how difficult it was for him to separate text and music in an opera, how little he could enjoy one if he thought the other was of lesser quality. Once he mockingly berated his dinner guests who were discussing text and music of Rossini's *Mosé in Egitto*: "I do not understand you, how you can divide *sujet* and music and enjoy the one without the other... I marvel at your nature, how your ears are capable of listening to beautiful sounds while your most powerful sense, your eye, is tormented by the most absurd happenings" (Eckermann October 7, 1828).

A second reason for Goethe's initial difficulties with Mozart's *Singspiel* was — again we read it in his letter — the music itself. This may seem somewhat odd to us today, but we must take into account that Goethe was accustomed to compositions of the *style galant* and small ensembles. We have no evidence that Mozart's music ever affected him adversely, yet the relatively large sound and rich orchestration of *Die Entführung*, which includes bass drum, cymbals, triangle, and piccolo to produce exotic (i.e. "Turkish") coloration, was something new and unfamiliar. *Die Entführung* is scored for fifteen instruments, as is *Die Zauberflöte*. By

---

[9] Quoted by Alfred Einstein in *Mozart, His Character, His Work*, pp. 455-456. Otto Erich Deutsch, *Mozart — Die Dokumente seines Lebens*, p. 187, lists this quotation as from 1782 and adds: "Das Datum dieses Protestes ist noch unbekannt. Er fand sich in den *Leipziger Zeitungen*."

[10] Dent, *Mozart's Operas*, p. 87.

comparison, Joseph Haydn's comic opera *L'Infedeltà Delusa* is scored for seven, and his *Il Mondo della Luna* for eight instruments. Haydn's scoring is much more typical of what Goethe was accustomed to and liked.

Nor was Goethe alone with his preference of simple sound. One of the reviewers of *Die Entführung* in Baron von Knigge's *Dramaturgische Blätter* of 1788 conveyed some points of criticism — after a performance of *Die Entführung* in Hannover — that might well have been written by Goethe himself:

> The composer is too loquacious with the wind instruments. Instead of using them to underline a special part of a melody, and to support the harmonic whole, they often darkly color the whole orchestral palette and confuse it; they swallow up a beautiful, simple song and disturb the singer in performance.[11]

And the Austrian monarch, Joseph II, supposedly remarked to maestro Mozart after the first performance of *Die Entführung* on July 16, 1782 in Vienna: "Too beautiful for our ears, and far too many notes, my dear Mozart," to which the composer allegedly replied: "Exactly as many, Your Majesty, as are needed."[12] Even if this exchange is entirely anecdotal, it does contain a kernel of truth. For it is true that in contrast to our modern sensibilities, Mozart's contemporaries often perceived his music as "heavy," obscure, and difficult. Mozart's quartets, wrote one reviewer in *Cramers Magazin der Musik*, "are too well seasoned" — what palate can endure that for long?[13] *Die Entführung* in particular contains a variety of musical innovations that make Goethe's uneasiness at least understandable. As Alfred Einstein observed:

> This orchestra speaks a new language, new also as regards dynamics, which are here of infinitely fine gradations. The whole work marks the complete emergence of Mozart's personality as a dramatic composer. He had taken extreme pains with it: none of his other opera scores is so full of deletions, condensations, and alterations as *Die Entführung*; for none of them did he require so long a time — almost a full year.[14]

Mozart was aware that he was creating new and special effects in his music, designed not only to create an oriental atmosphere, but also to convey a broad range of human emotions, such as anger, fear, humor,

---

[11] Quoted by H.C. Robbins Landon in "Mozart on the Eighteenth Century Stage," *High Fidelity*, 15 (1965), 64. The complete review can be found in Deutsch, *Dokumente*, p. 287.

[12] Einstein, *Mozart*, p. 458.

[13] Quoted by Wolfgang Hildesheimer, *Mozart*, p. 202.

[14] Einstein, *Mozart*, p. 459.

wit, and the palpitations of a loving heart. In the previously quoted letter of September 26, 1781 to his father, Mozart writes:

> Let me now turn to Belmonte's aria in A major, 'O wie ängstlich, o wie feurig.' Would you like to know how I have expressed it — and even indicated his throbbing heart? By the two violins playing octaves. This is the favorite aria of all those who have heard it, and it is mine also. I wrote it expressly to suit Adamberger's voice. You see the trembling — the faltering — you see how his throbbing breast begins to swell, this I have expressed by a *crescendo*. You hear the whispering and the sighing — which I have indicated by the first violin with mutes and a flute playing in unison.

The "throbbing heart," the "whispering and sighing" — the rendering of human feelings in musical language was an exciting venture of creativity for Mozart. For Goethe, however, such individualization of musical sound was new and unaccustomed. Ironically, he who just a decade earlier had introduced a similar enlivening process into German poetry, could only gradually get used to personal expressions in the other arts.

In all fairness to Goethe, let it be said that *Die Entführung* is a difficult and uneven work. It is a fascinating and enormously colorful creation, rich in musical ideas, alive with humor and individuality, and all of it is brilliantly rendered by an exciting orchestration. But Mozart had not yet found the precision style of his later years, and several of his arias suffer from excessive length and technical difficulties. For instance, Osmin's aria "Solche hergelaufne Laffen," Belmonte's "O wie ängstlich, o wie feurig," Constanze's "Traurigkeit ward mir zum Lose," as well as "Martern aller Arten," are all long and repetitive arias; the last number in particular has been characterized as more suitable for the concert stage than for the theater.[15] These arias are a challenge even for first-rate singers. Vienna was blessed with good voices and Mozart, when composing his music, did not have to be concerned with the technical limitations of his singers. (In fact, the most difficult arias in *Die Entführung* were written for specific singers: Osmin's part for Ludwig Fischer, a basso profundo, Belmonte for the tenor Valentin Joseph Adamberger, Constanze for the soprano Caterina Cavalieri). But Weimar was another story. Not that the Court Theater was without talents, quality, and tradition, but it was, after all, a provincial theater with limited means. It therefore employed, as was customary throughout Germany, actors who could also sing, rather than well-trained professional singers. Marvin Carlson gives the following interesting account of role-casting practices at the Weimar theater:

> The actors were hired according to traditional specialties and performed, as was the custom, in both spoken and musical theatre. Thus one actress played leading romantic roles and sang first and second operatic roles,

---

[15] Dent, *Mozart's Operas*, p. 77.

another played lovers and bravura roles in operettas, a third played heroines and mothers and danced, a fourth played confidantes and comic mothers in operettas, and so on.[16]

Goethe undoubtedly witnessed a performance of *Die Entführung* that was not exactly a model of perfection. And when we read his later reminiscences of these early days of the Weimar theater, we realize that such suppositions are not entirely off the mark. In a small essay, a sort of memorandum for the Duke, entitled "On the Separation of Stageplays and Operas," written in 1808, Goethe reflects: "We will all remember the wife of Director Bellomo, who for years presented leading romantic roles — "Die ersten Liebhaberinnen" — with a barely tolerable voice, an unmistakable South German accent, and an inconspicuous appearance" (WA 1: LIII, 268).

An uninspired text, the novelty of the music, lengthy arias, a questionable performance — given these odds, it would have required a very patient and favorably disposed listener to have an enjoyable first night at the opera. But it is doubtful that Goethe was in any mood to be either patient or favorably disposed. Indeed, he may well have been deliberately critical and captious, for it is no secret that he had his own ambitions for writing *Singspiele*. He had written five such texts between 1775 and 1785: *Erwin und Elmire* (1775), *Claudine von Villa Bella* (1776), *Lila* (partial publication 1777), *Die Fischerin* (1780), and *Jery und Bätely* (written 1780, published 1790). During his stay in Italy and prompted by Kayser's music for *Egmont*, Goethe revised his *Singspiele*. In his *Italian Journey* he wrote:

> The arrival of Kayser, who had brought with him his overture to *Egmont*, revived an old interest in music which now turned me, both from inclination and necessity, more and more towards the musical theatre.
>
> In Germany, they were waiting for *Erwin und Elmire* and *Claudine von Villa Bella*, but, as a result of my work on *Egmont*, I had become so much stricter in my standards that I could not bring myself to send them off in their original form. I was very fond of many of the songs which bore witness to so many foolish but happy hours, and to the pain and sorrow to which rash, impetuous youth will always be exposed. But the prose dialogue was too reminiscent of French operettas. Though I shall always remember the latter kindly, since they were the first to introduce cheerful melody into our theatre, they no longer satisfied me. Having become an Italian citizen [sic: i. e. having become rather Italian in my tastes], I wanted the arias to be linked by declamatory recitative. I revised both operettas along these lines and they have since enjoyed some popularity (IJ 416-417).

In spite of Goethe's attempts to change his *Singspiele* and to reform the entire genre, his taste remained by and large within the boundaries of neo-Classical aesthetics, favoring simple plots, simple musical

---

[16] Carlson, *Goethe and the Weimar Theater*, p. 48.

accompaniments, and simple orchestration. In other words, he continued the type of *Singspiel* espoused by his friend Christoph Martin Wieland, who suggested in his "Versuch über das deutsche *Singspiel*" that the "plot be as simple as possible... and be confined to as few people as possible."[17] Just before Bellomo's performance of Mozart's *Die Entführung* in Weimar, Goethe had begun to write yet another such "simple" *Singspiel*, entitled *Scherz, List und Rache*,[18] for which Kayser was composing the music. This *Singspiel*, a fast-paced Enlightenment farce about greed and deception, was doomed from the beginning, and none other than Mozart helped carry it to an early grave. "*Die Entführung aus dem Serail*," Goethe freely admitted in his *Italian Journey*, "put an end to all our hopes, and the piece we had worked on so hard was never heard of again in the theatre" (IJ 418).

What Goethe expressed here in his "Retrospect" (IJ 416-422) may well have had its beginning in Weimar years earlier. As he sat in the Court Theater and listened to *Die Entführung* for the first time, he may well have realized darkly that Mozart's new *Singspiel* was better than any of the *Singspiele* he himself had produced. Mozart had already arrived at the point of dramatic and musical integration that Goethe was beginning to advocate. This vague awareness of Mozart's superiority may well have disturbed the poet subconsciously, it may have even prejudiced his initial judgment of Mozart's *Singspiel*.

Ultimately, however, Goethe could not resist the charm and power of Mozart's *Entführung*. After he became Director of the Weimar Court Theater, the play appeared immediately in the repertoire (it was first performed on October 1, 1791) and was staged forty-nine times during Goethe's stewardship of the theater. In 1808 Goethe noted that *Die Entführung* had made a real impact on the theatrical and musical world, an impact "im höheren Sinne" as he put it, meaning not as popular entertainment, but as an artistic experience and accomplishment of "higher" significance (WA 1: LIII, 268).

---

[17] *Wielands Gesammelte Schriften*, ed. Preußische Akademie der Wissenschaften (Berlin: Weidmannsche Buchhandlung, 1928): 1: XIV, 91. This is a point that Charles Rosen emphasizes: "Goethe's ideals were much the same as Wieland's: the latter (one of the few authors Mozart is known to have admired) wrote in his essay on the German *Singspiel* that 'the greatest possible simplicity of plan is proper and essential to the *Singspiel*. Action cannot be sung!' It was, of course, just this point that Mozart was so triumphantly to prove wrong." Rosen, *The Classical Style*, p. 177.

[18] The text was first published in Goethe's *Schriften* (Leipzig: Göschen, 1790), VII. It is commonly held that Kayser did not finish the composition. In a letter to Zelter, May 4, 1814, Goethe indicates that Kayser completed the overture and the first act: "Was ich senden werde, ist die Ouvertüre und der erste Akt von 'Scherz, List und Rache,' das er[Kayser] ganz komponiert hat. Ich gedenke sein jetzt, da ich meine italienische Reise bearbeite" (GZB I, 390).

Once Goethe had overcome his initial skepticism and reluctance, there was so much for him to enjoy and admire in this Viennese *Singspiel*. Blonde's arias "Durch Zärtlichkeit und Schmeicheln" and "Welche Wonne, welche Lust," for instance, are exactly what Goethe liked in music: hearty melodies with a folksong-like simplicity and a crisp strophic setting. And who can resist for long Osmin's "poison-and-dagger" shenanigans or his "Vivat Bacchus" conviviality, communicated as they are by a music of wit, mockery, and infectious humor. Yet, in the final analysis, it may well have been the serious elements in the play, the themes of self-restraint and forgiveness, which received Goethe's closest attention. Pasha Selim, the barbarian king, reveals himself as a noble and magnanimous ruler. He controls his emotions and subdues his urge for revenge by allowing the four captives, Constanze, Belmonte, Blonde, and Pedrillo, to return to their homeland, even though he desires the beautiful Constanze, and Belmonte, her lover, turns out to be the son of his worst enemy. When the freed and happy lovers join their voices in a concluding quartet, "Nichts ist häßlicher als die Rache," they intone not only a favorite theme of the Enlightenment, one which Mozart so splendidly recreated in Sarastro's aria "In diesen heil'gen Hallen, kennt man die Rache nicht," but they touch on something very close to Goethe's heart: self-control and individual restraint. Goethe himself had begun to dramatize this theme in his play *Iphigenie auf Tauris* (begun in 1779 and published in 1787; Goethe had written at least two versions of the play when he saw *Die Entführung* in 1785).[19] Thoas, the barbarian king in Goethe's play, overcomes, much like Pasha Selim in *Die Entführung*, his personal desires and his feelings of anger and revenge to spare the lives of the captive Greeks. He allows them to leave the island and bids them farewell, even Iphigenia, whom he had hoped to win as his queen. Dieter Borchmeyer writes:

> Thoas, whose self-mastery alone assures the happy ending of [Goethe's] drama, remains a lone and isolated figure on the barbaric island, robbed of his one happiness: Iphigenia's presence... Similarly lonely is Selim Bassa at the end of Mozart's *Entführung*. Indeed, in as much as he was given but a speaking role, he is even excluded from the final hymn to humanity and benefaction.

[19] See *Iphigenie*, Prosafassung von 1778 and *Iphigenie*, Zweite Prosafassung. GA VI, 102-147 and VI, 148-212.

Borchmeyer goes on to relate this theme of the renunciation of personal happiness for the sake of others to Mozart's *Titus* and Lessing's *Nathan the Wise*.[20]

The parallels in Goethe's *Iphigenie auf Tauris* and Mozart's *Die Entführung aus dem Serail* are striking: both works depict generous and humane despots; both present heroines, Iphigenia and Constanze (Pamina, too, belongs here), who possess similar personal and dramatic characteristics: strength, steadfastness, incorruptibility. And while Thoas and Iphigenia are cut from a much finer poetic cloth than either Bassa Selim or Constanze (or Sarastro and Pamina), theme and dramatic constellations are too much alike for Goethe not to have noticed. In fact, the recognition of these elements may well have contributed to Goethe's initial problems with Mozart's *Singspiel*.

Whatever the objective or subjective reasons for Goethe's difficulties, he soon overcame them. He overcame the effects of technical shortcomings in the Weimar performance and, what is more, he overcame his own prejudice. He recognized that Mozart had composed a *Singspiel* more powerful and effective than what he and his composers had created and he did something rather uncharacteristic: he bowed before the younger artist and within a relatively short period of time became one of Mozart's greatest admirers. As Director of the Weimar Court Theater he performed and promoted Mozart's operas and later, long after Mozart's death, he turned to the composer and his music again and again in appreciation, artistic association, and complete wonderment.

---

[20] Dieter Borchmeyer, "'Ganz verteufelt human.' Über Mozarts Titus," in *Ludwigsburger Schloßfestspiele. Almanach 1983*, p. 69.

7

Faust and Don Giovanni

> Eckermann to Goethe: "I don't give up hope of seeing the proper music come along for Faust." "It's quite impossible," said Goethe, "all these repulsive, odious, and terrifying matters that would have to be included, at least in parts of it, are not in the style of the time. The music would have to be in the character of Don Giovanni; Mozart ought to have composed Faust! Meyerbeer might be able to do it, but he is not going to get involved in anything like this. He is too busy with the Italian theater."

THE ABOVE CONVERSATION TOOK PLACE BETWEEN Goethe and Eckermann on February 12, 1829. It is one of the most explicit exchanges between the poet and his scribe on the subject of *Faust* and music, particularly *Faust* and Mozart's *Don Giovanni*. Two years earlier Goethe had referred to sections of the "Helena Act" in *Faust, Part Two* as being "operatic" in nature: "The first part [of Act III] requires first-rate tragic actors, just as later on, in the operatic portion, the parts must be sung by the best male and female singers" (Eckermann January 29, 1827). Both these conversations as well as a number of design features in the *Faust* drama itself suggest that Goethe consciously conceived these segments of *Faust* as music drama. Yet, it is also evident that he had become somewhat skeptical about any "modern" composer being able to write the appropriate music for the play. Only two musical dramatists would have been up to the task in his opinion: Mozart, dead for almost forty years, and Meyerbeer, who was very much alive, but occupied with his own operas in Paris.

It may strike us a bit puzzling today to find Giacomo Meyerbeer so prominently linked with the name of Wolfgang Amadeus Mozart. We must remember, though, that in the 1820s and 30s Meyerbeer was a highly successful composer and a rising star in the world of music theater. His opera *Il Crociato in Egitto*, first performed in Venice in 1824, followed by performances in London and Paris in 1825, was hailed both by audiences and critics as great and powerful music theater. Heinrich Heine would later, in a review of *Les Hugenots*, call the composer "the greatest living contrapuntist, the greatest musical artist." In fact, in the same review the poet compared the composer with Goethe himself: "He [Meyerbeer] offers new melodies, extraordinary melodies, not in anarchic profusion, but rather *where* he wants them and *when* he wants them... his artistic sensibilities have, therefore, quite rightly been compared... to Goethe's."[1] Meyerbeer's musical language, which Heine and other critics found comparable to Goethe's literary style, (i.e. precise structures and strict auctorial controls), are elements of composition that Goethe had always admired in Mozart's music. It is quite possible that Goethe was attracted to Meyerbeer for the same reason: controlled musical diction, measured style, harmonious expressions.

But there is at least one other reason for Goethe's appreciation of Giacomo Meyerbeer. The German-born musician — his original name was Jakob Liebmann Meyer Beer — had received his musical training in Berlin, in part under the tutelage of Goethe's friend Karl Friedrich Zelter, and he had gone to Italy for his apprenticeship and first professional experience. Quite apart from the personal connection with Zelter, Goethe undoubtedly found the combination of Northern precision and Southern mellifluousness in his music highly appealing. When Eckermann once exclaimed about the "Helena Act:" "The act would provide occasion for great variety and splendor in costuming and staging... If only a great composer would take it in hand," Goethe replied: "It would have to be one like Meyerbeer who has lived in Italy for a time and so combines his German nature with Italian style and manner" (Eckermann January 29, 1827).

No less striking and challenging is Goethe's remark that the various kinds of ugliness in his *Faust* drama, "all those repulsive, odious, and terrifying matters" (Faust's ruthlessness? Mephisto's cynicism?), were not in the taste of the time, i.e. the early nineteenth century, and were

---

[1] Heinrich Heine, *Werke und Briefe*, ed. Hans Kaufmann (Berlin: Aufbau Verlag, 1961) V, 380. Heine wrote quite frequently about Meyerbeer and not always favorably. Once he referred to the successful composer as the "musical millionaire," II, 384; in another poem he called him a musical hack: "den Musikverderber, den Meyerbeer" II, 380.

therefore problematic for composers and audiences alike. Earlier in the same conversation Goethe had referred to a remark by Zelter, according to which one of his singers had ruined a performance of *The Messiah* in Berlin because of weak and sentimental singing. Goethe added: "Painters, scientists, sculptors, musicians, poets, they are all with few exceptions, weak — "alles schwach" — and the masses are no better" (Eckermann February 12, 1829). It is from this vantage point that we must understand his judgment of contemporary composers in relation to his *Faust* drama. Goethe dreaded mushy artistry. He looked for a defined and specific musical syntax, for clear and consistent key structures, complete cadences. He shied away from music that indulged in excessive modulations and a blurring of form. Charles Gounod, in his commentary on Mozart's *Don Giovanni*, unintentionally summarized Goethe's feelings about such modern, often Romantic composers perhaps better than Goethe himself could have done:

> It is, too often, the absence or poverty of ideas which leads to that abuse of modulation so frequent in a multitude of modern compositions. Tonal unity is dreaded as a weakness, and composers launch out into endless harmonic digressions, the inevitable result being most wearisome monotony.[2]

Goethe desired for his Faust the kind of music that Mozart had wrought for Don Juan, the legendary Spanish nobleman, a music that could properly accomodate metaphysical dread and human anguish, immoral as well as dæmonic elements, without surrendering to dissonant and disjointed expressions and without sentimentalizing its subject. "Goethe sensed in Mozart's music the same dæmonic quality that connects *Don Giovanni* with *Faust*," comments Leo Schrade,[3] and one is tempted to add: Goethe sensed in *Don Giovanni* the same magnificent and vital contradictions that characterize his Faust figure: damnable desires and personal irresistability, hybris and arrogance, but also vitality, excitement, and self-assertion. Mozart's and Da Ponte's stage world presents a veritable kaleidoscope of moods and scenes; laughter and tears follow each other in rapid succession, while seduction and defiance, natural and supernatural events are often roped into one and the same visual image. But all of these diverse expressions, all polarities and incongruities, issue from one organic musical design: Mozart's musical universe, which encompasses all manifestations of earth, heaven, and hell. And in spite of immoral happenings, chromatic tensions, and ominous sounding trombones, the overall effect of Mozart's music in *Don Giovanni* has a positive spiritual effect and is pleasing to the ear. It is an

---

[2] Charles Gounod, *Mozart's Don Giovanni*, trsl., Windeyer Clark and J.T. Hutchinson (New York: Da Capo Press, 3rd edition, 1970), p. 57.

[3] Leo Schrade, *W.A. Mozart*, p. 159.

art that "confronts us with the terror of underworld flames," as Geoffrey Clive wrote, without cancelling the beautiful. It is creativity "on the edge of profound nihilism,"[4] yet ultimately affirmative, harmonious, and encouraging. The same can be said of Goethe's *Faust*. Indeed, it may well be that Goethe was one of the first to recognize this essential truth and commonality in both of these extraordinary works.

Faust and Don Juan, two figures born of legend and history, had created a tradition of their own long before Goethe and Mozart lifted the two transgressors into archetypal prominence, long before Mozart and Da Ponte shifted the Don Juan tradition "from the proper interest of Latin Europe and Catholic morality...to the proper interest of Northern, Faustian philosophy."[5] Once these shifts and changes had occurred, comparisons and analogies of the two "overreachers" were only a matter of time. And what time could be more propitious for such pairing than the early nineteenth century, a period given to awe and speculation about uncommon individuals. Three writers in particular, E.T.A. Hoffmann, Christian D. Grabbe, and Søren Kierkegaard, created literary associations between Faust and Don Juan that influenced German thinking and writing about the two legendary heroes throughout the century.

E.T.A. Hoffmann's major contribution to the literature on Mozart's *Don Giovanni* was his idea that the irresistible Don had actually seduced Donna Anna in her chambers. Don Giovanni, when he first appears on stage, had just consummated his evil designs and was now trying to make his escape. He had kindled, so the Romantic author, Donna Anna's passion and filled her heart with "supreme enjoyment." But after killing her father and abandoning her, Donna Anna's passion turned to a "fire of destructive hatred."[6]

No less imaginative is Hoffmann's description of Don Juan as a Faustian quester.[7] His association of the two legendary figures is more by

---

[4] Geoffrey Clive, *The Romantic Enlightenment* (New York: Meridian Books, 1960), pp. 45, 46, and 55.

[5] Julian Rushton, *W.A. Mozart: Don Giovanni* (Cambridge: Cambridge University Press, 1981), p. 6 f.

[6] E. T. A. Hoffmann, " Don Juan" in *German Stories*, ed. Harry Steinhauer (New York: Bantam Books, 1964), p. 65.

[7] Rushton, *W.A. Mozart: Don Giovanni*, p. 73, writes: "E.T.A. Hoffmann interpreted the hero's game as a Faustian striving for the unattainable perfection in Woman."

implication than by actual comparison. Still, contemporary as well as subsequent readers of his short story *Don Juan* (first published in the *Allgemeine musikalische Zeitung*, 1813) were almost invited to draw parallels between his Don Juan figure and Goethe's *Faust*, of which *Part One* had appeared just five years earlier. The following text, taken from Hoffmann's tale, could easily be read as the story of Faust:

> But this is the horrible result of the Fall, that the Evil One retained the power of lying in wait for man and setting wicked snares for him even in his striving for the highest in which he expresses his divine nature. This conflict between divine and demonic powers creates the concept of life, just as triumphant victory creates that of life beyond.[8]

Perhaps the best known literary work that unites the two legendary figures in one setting is Christian Dietrich Grabbe's *Don Juan und Faust: Eine Tragödie* (1829).[9] Grabbe, a young, ambitious German playwright, retained much of the literary heritage of his two protagonists: the Spanish seducer tends toward carnal pleasures and Faust, the German "dreamer of God," seeks metaphysical fulfillments. Both lust, however, after Donna Anna, and they litter the stage with victims in pursuit of their unsavory intentions. Don Juan kills the Governor, Donna Anna's father, and Don Ottavio, her fiancé, while Faust murders Donna Anna, who had fallen in love with the Don and was terrified of the sinister Faust. But the "Black Knight," an emissary from hell, has the final move: he takes both Faust and Don Juan. The play is not without vitality and ingenuity, but it hardly fulfills the ambition of its author to eclipse in one brilliant stroke two of the world's masterpieces: Goethe's *Faust* and Mozart's *Don Giovanni*.

The third writer to influence nineteenth-century perceptions of Don Juan and Faust is the Danish philosopher Søren Kierkegaard. His primary object of deliberation was Don Juan, not Faust. Mozart's *Don Giovanni* fascinated him as the consummate artistic expression of the erotic. But inevitably the philosopher was drawn into comparisons between Don Juan and Faust. Not that he attempted to equate the two characters. Faust, in the philosopher's conception, is primarily "idea" born of history, Don Juan is the "life-principle" conceived in music.

> What I really mean will perhaps be best understood if I show the difference in connection with a related idea. Goethe's *Faust* is a genuinely classical production, but the idea is a historical idea, and hence every notable historical era will have its own *Faust*. *Faust* has language as its medium, and since this is a far more concrete medium, it follows on this ground also, that several works of the same kind are conceivable. *Don Juan*, on the other hand, will always stand alone by itself, in the same sense

---

[8] "Don Juan," ed. Steinhauer, p. 61.

[9] Christian Dietrich Grabbe, *Don Juan und Faust* (Stuttgart: Reclam, 1963).

that the Greek sculptures are classics.... There can, of course, be a number of classical musical works, but there will never be more than the one work of which it is possible to say that the idea is absolutely musical, so that the music does not appear as an accompaniment, but reveals its own innermost essence in revealing the idea. It is for this reason that Mozart stands highest among the Immortals through his *Don Juan*.[10]

Clearly, Kierkegaard assigns Mozart's *Don Giovanni* and Goethe's *Faust* to different aesthetic and affective realms, but he keeps relating one to the other throughout his essay. And in one significant aspect he even perceives them as united, as brothers-in-arms; he sees them as two great and haughty individualists, as mythic heroes, challenging the heavens and defying all social and moral systems:

Faust and Don Juan are the Titans and giants of the Middle Ages, who in the supercilious haughtiness of their endeavors are not different from those of older times, except that they stand in isolation, not forming a union of forces with which unitedly to storm the heavens, but here all the power is concentrated in the single individual.[11]

As time went on, Faust and Don Giovanni were frequently seen, portrayed, and interpreted as a pair, mostly by German writers and composers. (There are, however, instances in other literatures where similar associations and allusions occur, e.g. Théophile Gautier's *La Comédie de la Morte* and Igor Strawinsky's *The Rake's Progress*; Leo Weinstein's "Catalogue of Don Juan Versions" also includes a French motion picture: *Don Juan et Faust* by Marcel L'Herbier, 1922).[12] On occasion the associations of the two transgressors went so far that they assumed each others' characteristics and attributes,[13] but by and large Faust and Don Juan appeared, when compared, either as rebels against a common cause, "against the laws of God and Society,"[14] or as related psychological archetypes: "Faust plus Don Juan could... be equated with

---

[10] Søren Kierkegaard, *Either/Or* (Princeton: Princeton University Press, 1959) I, 55-56.

[11] Kierkegaard, *Either/Or*, I, 89.

[12] Leo Weinstein, *The Metamorphoses of Don Juan* (New York: AMS Press, 1967), p. 213.

[13] J.W. Smeed discusses some of these features in a chapter on "Faust and Don Juan" in *Faust in Literature* (London: Oxford University Press, 1975), pp. 161-196.

[14] This quotation is from Alfons Rosenberg, *Don Giovanni* (Munich: Prestel Verlag, 1968), p. 11. Rosenberg opens his first chapter with a discussion of Faust in relation to Don Juan.

Everyman," or more specifically, "Mozart's *Don Giovanni* is the 'Faust' of the senses, Goethe's *Faust* is the 'Don Giovanni' of the intellect."[15]

Goethe became acquainted with Mozart's *Don Giovanni* not as a literary historian, critic, or opera buff, but as the director and regisseur of the Ducal Court Theater in Weimar. The following memorandum, "Notes on Don Juan," dictated by him on December 28, 1797, gives us some indication of his concerns about a proper staging of the opera:

(1)   Leporello, if he uses a book rather than a scroll, should not carry the book under his arm when entering the scene, but should fetch it before his aria from behind the scene as if getting it from a tavern.

(2)   In the final scene of the first act the three masks should not exit through the garden as we must assume that the gate is locked; rather they should come out from the exact same wing where they had entered at Leporello's invitation.

(3)   In the second act, when the stage is in darkness, exact instructions must be given as to when the servants should enter with torches and how long they should stay; yesterday some scenes were inappropriately played in the dark.

(4)   The same is true of the first act. Donna Anna and Don Gussman [Don Ottavio] should not be left in darkness after the body of the Governor has been carried away, a third stage hand is needed with a light.

(5)   The bailiff ["Der Gerichtsbote"], who comes to Don Juan, should carry a small, white staff with him.

[15] Smeed, *Faust in Literature*, quotes these statements by Carl Helbig and Ernst Lert, pp. 161 and 195. Other important comparisons and analyses of Faust and Don Juan can be found in E.M. Butler, *The Fortunes of Faust* (Cambridge: At the University Press, 1952). Butler not only has a lengthy introductory essay on "Faust and Don Juan," but also a very useful "Chronological Survey" (xi) of the two characters. One of the more recent studies of the two figures is by Hans Mayer, *Doktor Faust und Don Juan* (Frankfurt: Suhrkamp Verlag, 1979). And we find a brief but excellent discussion in Chapter IX, " Don Juan and Faust," in Leo Weinstein, *The Metamorphoses of Don Juan*, and in Georgi W. Tschitscherin, *Mozart: Eine Studie* (Leipzig: Deutscher Verlag für Musik, 1975), pp. 115 and 150.

(6)   The table must be removed quickly at the end so that the
        circle of evil spirits will not be broken.

(7)   Also the chains need to be painted and care should be
        taken to mix sufficient glue into the paint so that the red
        color will stick.[16]

If Goethe was dissatisfied with the performance of December 27, 1797,
to which he is referring in these notes, he made no mention of it two days
later in a letter to Friedrich Schiller in which Mozart's *Don Juan* figures
prominently. Schiller had written to Goethe concerning opera as a
dramatic genre. Modern tragedy, Schiller had suggested, might benefit
from the opera because the latter permitted more imaginative use of
staging and design; opera required less "slavish imitation of nature" than
did traditional (Aristotelian) drama.[17] Previously Schiller had insisted on
a strict separation of the genres (as exemplified in his criticism of
Goethe's *Egmont*), but now he himself was looking to opera as a means to
liberate and rejuvenate the dramatic genre. Goethe was quick to agree
with his friend, and he immediately pointed to the opera that he
considered the most perfect example of what Schiller had in mind:
Mozart's *Don Giovanni.*

> You would have seen your hopes regards opera completely fulfilled in a
> recent performance of Don Juan; granted that this work is unique, and
> since Mozart's death we have lost all prospect of ever seeing its kind
> again. — Ihre Hoffnung, die Sie von der Oper hatten, würden Sie neulich
> in Don Juan auf einen hohen Grad erfüllt gesehen haben, dafür steht aber
> auch dieses Stück ganz isoliert und durch Mozarts Tod ist alle Aussicht
> auf etwas Ähnliches vereitelt.[18]

Goethe's comment to Schiller is but one indication of his admiration
for Mozart's *Don Giovanni.* Time and again he returned to the work in
thought and commentary, musing and philosophizing about the opera.
Once he remarked to the young Arthur Schopenhauer that *Don Giovanni*
was in his judgment a *buffa* piece only on the surface; in its depth, he said,
it was a serious and solemn work, and the music reflected that "dual

---

[16] "Bemerkungen zu Don Juan den 28. Dec., 1797." In *Gesang und Rede, sinniges
Bewegen. Goethe als Theaterleiter*, ed. Jörn Göres (Düsseldorf: Goethe-Museum,
1973), pp. 127-128. The dictation is signed "G." The references to Don Gussman
instead of Don Ottavio and the *Gerichtsbote* at the end are typical of early German
versions of the opera. See also Paul Nettl, "Goethe and Mozart" in *Goethe
Bicentennial Studies*, p. 100, who says that this performance was sung in German
in the "poor translation" by Spiess.

[17] *Der Briefwechsel zwischen Schiller und Goethe*, ed. Emil Staiger (Frankfurt: Insel
Verlag, 1966), p. 529.

[18] *Der Briefwechsel zwischen Schiller und Goethe*, ed. Emil Staiger, p. 530.

character" of the opera very well (GA XXII, 743). Knowingly or unknowingly, Goethe touched here on a problem of definition that has been in the forefront of criticism ever since the opera was first performed in Prague on October 29, 1787. It is a question raised again most recently by Charles Rosen: "Is *Don Giovanni* opera seria or *buffa?*" Mozart, says Rosen, blended elements of both genres so well that the "mixture of genres is no longer noticed today, but it was decidedly remarked upon and often condemned at the end of the eighteenth century."[19] Goethe, so it appears, was not only sensitive to the mixture of genres in Mozart's opera, but found the mix to be excellent. In one of the livelier conversations with his secretary he stressed above all the cohesiveness of Mozart's great work:

It is an altogether base and unacceptable word [composition]... How can anyone say Mozart 'composed' his Don Juan! — Composition! — As if it were a piece of cake or biscuit which one stirs together using eggs, flour, and sugar! It [Don Juan] is an intellectual-spiritual creation — "Eine geistige Schöpfung ist es" — ; the details as well as the work as a whole flow from one spiritual creative center, a process permeated by one breath of life, where the artist did not piece something together by notion or experiment, but followed in his creation the dictates of his dæmonic genius (Eckermann June 27, 1831).

Goethe, as has been noted before, was uncommonly perceptive about Mozart's art. He had an excellent understanding of its inner energy and creative vitality. And certainly, of all Mozart's works, none is more intrinsically imbued with life's energies — and here Goethe's perception closely resembles those of the Romantics — than *Don Giovanni*. In fact, it may be largely attributable to this inner vitality of the work, its creative "breath of life," that the opera has remained so popular for two hundred years. Indeed, *Don Giovanni*'s appeal is closely matched, at least in German-speaking countries, by the continued actuality of Goethe's *Faust*, the other great German stage work that deals with physical and metaphysical adventures, with life's passions and failures, with love, sacrilege, and continuous striving.

A detailed comparison of Goethe's *Faust* and Mozart's *Don Giovanni* would go beyond the scope and purpose of this study. But let us examine three or four aspects common to both works, analogies that we may

[19] Charles Rosen, *The Classical Style*, pp. 321-322.

assume played an important role in Goethe's conscious and unconscious attraction to the opera.

The most obvious parallel is the role of the two protagonists: Faust and Don Giovanni as rebels and "overreachers," legendary heroes who want more than society and religion permit, and who become transgressors of "set limits."[20] To be sure, Faust and Don Giovanni come from different historical and national backgrounds (sixteenth-century Germany and seventeenth-century Spain) and their quests have different aims: Faust seeks forbidden knowledge, Don Giovanni seeks sexual freedom and sexual domination. Yet a common bond exists: they are both individualists violating the moral and religious codes of their times. And particularly in Goethe's and Mozart's versions, they appear as loners and outsiders. It has been observed that other Mozartian figures, such as Count Almaviva and Figaro, are very much part of their environment and social milieu, but Don Giovanni is a solitary figure, one who exploits his surrounding but does not belong to it.[21] The same is true of Goethe's Faust. Many Goethean heroes, e.g. Götz, Werther, Egmont, are intricately tied to their historical and social backgrounds. Faust, however, is aloof and distant; especially in the second part of the drama he exists very much outside of time and space, encompassing in his experiences both the classical and modern worlds, and two thousand years of history. This sense of timelessness and relative isolation of the two characters undoubtedly added to their commonality as well as their elevation to archetypes.

Naturally, there are differences in Goethe's and Mozart's treatment of these legendary figures. Goethe deviated from the Faust tradition; instead of condemning him, he allowed his protagonist to be rescued at the end, whereas Mozart and his librettist Lorenzo da Ponte remained, at least on the surface, faithful to the literary tradition of Don Juan. They sent their hero, to quote the inimitable George Bernard Shaw: "straight down through the floor to eternal torments."[22] But if we look at the Faust literature *before* Goethe — more precisely before Gotthold Ephraim Lessing who was the first to suggest a Faustian redemption — we find especially in the depiction of the final scenes a remarkable closeness between earlier Faust versions and the traditional Don Juan literature.

---

[20] Hans Mayer, *Doktor Faust und Don Juan*, p. 156. Mayer includes both Leporello and Wagner, the protagonists' assistants, in this designation. He calls them "Figuren einer Grenzüberschreitung."

[21] Bernard Williams, "Don Giovanni as an Idea," in Julian Rushton, *W.A. Mozart: Don Giovanni*, p. 87.

[22] George Bernard Shaw, *Music in London, 1890-94* (New York: Wm. H. Wise and Co., 1931) III, 213.

Compare, for instance, the final scene of reckoning in Christopher Marlowe's *Dr. Faustus* with that of Mozart's and Da Ponte's *Don Giovanni*:

Marlowe, *Dr. Faustus*:

My God, my God, look not so
fierce on me!
(*Thunder*) *Enter Devils.*
Adders and serpents, let me
breathe awhile!
Ugly hell, gape not —
come not, Lucifer —
I'll burn my books —
ah, Mephistophilis!
Exeunt with him.

Da Ponte-Mozart, *Don Giovanni*:

Statue: Your hour of doom
is come (Exit).
(Flames appear in all directions. The
    earth trembles.)
Don Giovanni (in desperation):
Fingers of terror clutch at me.
Horrible faces grin at me,
A chasm yawns to swallow me,
A gulf of blazing fire.
Despair commands me utterly,
My bowels melt in agony,
Undying pains await me,
In darkness, ice and fire,
Ah, the darkness! ah the fire!
Ah.[23]

---

[23] The analogy between Marlowe's *Dr. Faustus* and Da Ponte's *Don Giovanni* was pointed out by Conrad L. Osborne, "The Operas of Mozart," *High Fidelity Magazine*, 15 (1965), 72. The quotations are from: Christopher Marlowe, *The Tragical History of Dr. Faustus*, ed. Paul H. Kocher (New York: Meredith Corporation, 1950), p. 61 and *The Great Operas of Mozart* (New York: G. Schirmer, 1962), p. 265.

These depictions of the transgressors' ultimate fate are clearly parallel. And they are not the only scenes or themes where the pre-Goethean Faust tradition shows explicit similarities with the Don Juan legend. The causes and motivations for the two transgressors' death and damnation are equally comparable. In the sixteenth-century chap book, *The History of the Life and Death of Dr. J. Faustus* (published by Johann Spieß in Frankfurt [1587]), the protagonist's pact with Mephistopheles becomes unpardonable only when Faust insists that his sin is greater than God can forgive. Disbelief in God's mercy is the ultimate cause of Faust's doom. Don Juan's fate, too, is sealed not so much by his earlier transgressions, his illicit sex life, or even his killing of the Commendatore, as by his trespasses toward the end. (It is commonly assumed that Gabriel Téllez, better known as Tirso de Molina, fashioned his play *El Burlador de Sevilla y convidado de pièdra* from two different folklore traditions: the Don Juan myth and the legend of the "Stone Guest").[24] And it is in the second part, the drama of the "Stone Guest," that Don Juan commits the critical offense: disturbing and mocking the dead in their graves and refusing to repent. "*Statue*: Kneel and pray God for pardon / His mercy still can save you /... *Don Giovanni*: I scorn him / I defy him! /"[25] This is not to suggest that the theological implications of Faust and Don Giovanni are entirely the same; after all, one comes from a Catholic tradition, the other is presumably Protestant, but there is the underlying common theme of resisting God's mercy. And that is what sends both perpetrators, as has been wittily observed, to neighboring cells below.[26]

Be that as it may. Goethe's changes in the Faust tradition by no means diminish the correspondence between Faust and Don Juan in his and Mozart's dramatizations. The protagonists' haughty individualism, their flagrant disregard of God's and society's laws, remain strong parallels and links.

Faust and Don Giovanni are not the only characters in the dramas that bear comparison. Another pair is Gretchen and Zerlina, two of the most attractive females in eighteenth-century dramatic literature. The marvelous seduction scene early in the opera, with its persuasive melody — "La çi darem la mano" — "Let us take each other's hand" — very much resembles Faust's first encounter with Gretchen: "Mein schönes Fräulein darf ich wagen, / Meinen Arm und Geleit Ihr anzutragen?" — "My fair young lady, may I make free / to offer you my arm and

---

[24] See the chapter on "The Literary Antecedents of Tirso's Don Juan. The Stone Guest Motif," in Gerald E. Wade, *El Burlador de Sevilla y convidado de piedra* (New York: Charles Scribner's Sons, 1969), pp. 36-40.

[25] *The Great Operas of Mozart* (Schirmer), p. 265.

[26] Hans Mayer, *Doktor Faust und Don Juan*, p. 102.

company?"[27] A beguiling melody in the opera, persuasive rhythms and end-rhymes in the play, those are the formal means by which the maidens are quickly conquered. Zerlina and Gretchen are charming, coy, innocent; yet not so innocent as to be impervious to the flattery of a dashing nobleman. Both succumb — with one essential difference: Don Giovanni is foiled in his designs by Donna Elvira, while Faust consummates his lust, and in the process destroys the beloved girl. But both young women have a similar quality and function in their respective drama, they represent basic feminine attraction — "das Ewig-Weibliche" — and they provide thereby powerful incentives in the two heroes' searches for fulfillment.

Another major issue inviting comparison is irony. Forms of irony abound in Goethe's *Faust* and Mozart-da Ponte's *Don Giovanni*. And many of these forms serve similar artistic purposes. Probably the greatest and most obvious irony focuses on the two protagonists, their activities and achievements. We soon discover, for instance, that Don Giovanni constantly fails in the pursuit that gained him fame and happiness: the seduction of women. What we know of his accomplishments in that area (approximately two thousand triumphs), we know from his servant's "catologo." We, the audience, witness nothing but failures, none of the Don's sexual endeavors are crowned with success — not in the course of the opera anyway. A bad day for the Don? I believe not. Rather, I think what we are witnessing is an ironic perspective on the famous seducer. We are given the image of a man who has outlived his own time and reputation. After all, the legend originated in the late Middle Ages, a time when transgressions and sacrileges were the proper domain of the church and its doctrines, a time when violators could expect due and proper punishment. On an eighteenth-century stage, the same violations could hardly be presented with complete naiveté either as an act of history or faith. Humor had long entered the story, and now irony had to make it even more palatable to eighteenth-century audiences.

The ironic conception of Don Giovanni is but one of the ironies in the opera; we can find numerous others, some in Da Ponte's text, most of them in Mozart's music. For instance, when Mozart presents his musical in-jokes at the Don's last supper, including a snatch from his own *Figaro*, he punctures the seventeenth-century ambience of the Don Juan tradition and turns a potential *opera seria* into his own fiction — and into a Romantic play of irony. Even the conclusion of the opera is nothing less than ironic. When the sextet assembles in the *scena ultima* to sing about life without the Don, the music is harmonious and pleasing but devoid of energy and excitement. Life without the Don seems dull, drab, and

---

[27] The English quotations of Goethe's *Faust* are all taken from *Faust*, trsl. Walter Arndt, ed. Cyrus Hamlin (New York: W.W. Norton, 1976). Future references to this edition will appear in the text as *Faust* plus page number.

boring.[28] Don Ottavio and Donna Anna will get married in a year —
maybe; Donna Elvira will enter a nunnery, and the final duet of Zerlina
and Masetto has nothing of the electrifying eroticism that characterized
Zerlina's duet with the Don earlier in the opera. To be sure, the libretto
consigns the culprit to hell and damnation, but Mozart's music tells us
that life without Don Giovanni's wicked charm is frightfully bland. The
evil has been expunged, but so has all pleasure, pain, and excitement.

Faust, like Don Giovanni, belongs to a different era. By the time
Goethe took the story in hand, some two hundred years had passed.
Instead of the tense medieval climate that produced the Faustian rebel,
Goethe's version evolved out of the Enlightenment; instead of a haughty
God-seeker, he gave us the portrait of an eighteenth-century intellectual,
perhaps the tragedy of modern man.[29] Whether we see Faust's quest
ultimately as tragic or optimistic, the means Goethe employed to
demonstrate his hero's course and final hours are replete with irony.
Some of the ironies belong to the very essence of the play:

> How ironic [it is] when just before Mephisto's arrival on the scene Faust
> had come close to the ultimate denial of life, suicide, and, still in the throes
> of deep depression, had cursed life to its innermost core! How ironic that
> Mephisto, the eternal denier of the creation and life's value, has initiated
> Faust's cure and launched his career upwards towards supreme
> affirmation.[30]

Before such affirmation can take place — it is in itself no small parcel
of irony — God has to step in and rescue his protogé, whose quest, fate,
and failings had entangled him in a web of ironies and ambiguities.[31]
What, for example, could be more ironic than the aged Faust standing at
the edge of his utopian construction project, a blind and solitary figure,
mistaking the clanking of spades, with which the devil's workmen are
digging his grave, for the sounds of progress, giving him an illusory
moment of existential meaning for which he is willing to trade his
immortal soul. It is this metaphor of grotesque self-deception, says
Christa Wolf, that affects us moderns, believers in technology and

---

[28] Joseph Kerman says in his *Opera as Drama* (New York: Vintage Books, 1959), p.
122: "It only goes to show how drab life is without the Don."

[29] See Melitta Gerhard, "Faust: die Tragödie des 'neueren Menschen'," in
Jahrbuch des freien deutschen Hochstifts 1978, pp. 160-164.

[30] Alfred Hoelzel, "The Paradoxical Quest: A Study of Faustian Vicissitudes,"
manuscript submitted for publication.

[31] See also Hoelzel's comprehensive article on this issue: "The Conclusion of
Goethe's *Faust*: Ambivalence and Ambiguity," *The German Quarterly*, 55 (1982),
1-12.

creators of atomic bombs, more deeply than anything else.[32] Fortunately for Faust, and most ironically indeed, Mephisto is also caught up in this scheme of ironies, for the devil, who had worked so hard to lead Faust "gently up my alley," had inadvertently furthered the sinner's progress and salvation.

At the end we may well be a bit perplexed by so much relativism, uncertainty, and ambiguity, by such a dupable devil. Of course, we knew from the outset that Faust would be redeemed; no less an authority than the Lord himself has given us that assurance in the "Prologue" of the play. But Goethe's artistry had made us forget that,[33] and Faust had proved himself sufficiently a sinner that we had every reason to fear for his soul. But beyond that we are left, as in Mozart's *Don Giovanni*, with a final irony for the audience, one handed down by the author to those who expected a salient conclusion. Goethe did not leave us with a vision of human greatness and accomplishments, we cannot cull from his drama a reassuring message about the meaning of life. We are left with ambiguities, ironies, and contradictions, signs of human failure but also signs of God's continuing mercy.

In spite of the multitude of negative and even tragic events in *Faust* and *Don Giovanni*, in spite of murders, seductions, arrogance of power, both works exude in the end a positive feeling, they are uplifting rather than shocking or tragic. A major reason for this must be seen in their controlled and balanced form. And here too we find these masterpieces similar and comparable.

Beginning with his Weimar Classicism, Goethe's form-consciousness tended more and more toward proportionateness and wholeness — "Ganzheit" — in all matters of science and creativity. *Faust* was no exception. The lengthy, two-part play is without doubt Goethe's most complicated piece of writing. No other work in German literature contains such diversity in metrical and structural forms. Yet, in essence, it is a simple and concentrated drama. It presents one basic idea, the Faustian quest for knowledge, and this quest, successful or not, takes place within a defined and delimited universe. The hero proceeds from the dark and subjective sphere of the dissatisfied scholar in *Part One* to the wider horizons of *Part Two* which are, as Goethe himself commented, "almost totally lacking in subjectivity; what we have here is a higher, wider, brighter, and less passionate world" (Eckermann February 17, 1831). But the widening gyre and the growing abstractness of the play presented the dramatist with a problem: how to maintain a unified

---

[32] Christa Wolf, *Büchner-Preis-Rede*, Sonderdruck für die Freunde des Luchterhand Verlages, p. 2.

[33] Henry Hatfield, unpublished MS.

design, how not to lose himself or his hero in undefinable cosmic or psychological dimensions. Goethe spoke eloquently about this dilemma:

> You will admit that the conclusion, where the redeemed soul is ushered upwards — "wo es mit der geretteten Seele nach oben geht" — was difficult to write and that I could have, with all these supernatural... events, easily lost myself in vagueness if I had not given my poetic intentions a benevolently limiting form and substance — "eine wohltätig beschränkende Form und Festigkeit" — through sharply delineated figures and images from the Christian church (Eckermann June 6, 1831).

Inner organic unity and outer "form and substance" is what Goethe wanted most for his *Faust* drama, and this is exactly what he perceived as the compositional principle of *Don Giovanni*. I have already quoted his own words on this matter: "How can anyone say Mozart 'composed' his Don Juan... the details as well as the work as a whole flow from one spiritual and creative center" — "aus einem Geiste und Guß" (Eckermann June 20, 1831). And Goethe had perceived correctly. From the awe-inspiring first notes of the overture to the famous minuet at the end of act one (a Goethe favorite) to the mild counterpoints of the finale: the opera is a masterpiece of organic, unifying form.

We know that Mozart experimented with leaving off the *scena ultima*, ending the opera "with Don Giovanni's D-major journey to hell."[34] We also know that Gustav Mahler revived the experiment more than a hundred years later and that some critics, Theodor W. Adorno among them, favored the abridgement.[35] But, fortunately, most musicologists and conductors are agreed that the epilogue is an integral part of the opera, it is neither superfluous nor accidental. The "happy ending" is a balancing of the account, balancing murder, pain, transgression and declaring, not without irony, that the evil is expunged and once again "all's well with the world." Faust's conclusion is not much different. When the sinner's soul is ushered upward by a host of angels to the receiving arms of Gretchen and the Virgin, God is affirming His benevolence in the universal order. All of life's problems and contradictions are, for that moment, lifted into an aesthetic harmony — while real life goes on unabated.

Some such thoughts must have gone through Goethe's mind as he reflected on Mozart's *Don Giovanni* and found the music to be ideal for his *Faust* drama — "the music would have to be in the character of *Don Giovanni*." Mozart's firm, clear, balanced diction and structure would

---

[34] Janos Liebner, *Mozart on the Stage* (New York: Praeger Publishers, 1972), p. 191.

[35] Wolfgang Hildesheimer, *Mozart*, p. 231, writes: "This *scena ultima* of *Don Giovanni* has repeatedly been attacked over the years. Gustav Mahler omitted it in his 1905 production, and Adorno censures Klemperer for not leaving it out of his recording."

have aided Goethe's poetic intent to lift all matters of gravity in *Faust*, all things "repulsive, odious, and terrifying," into the realm of art. For such is the purpose and power of art that it will create a "serious jest" out of seriousness, a play or an opera out of human transgression, frailty, agony. Goethe wistfully declared his *Faust* to be "one of those serious jests." No doubt he thought the same of Mozart's *Don Giovanni*.

Kostümierung zur *Zauberflöte* in Weimar
Watercolor by G. M. Kraus

8

Forms of the Magic Flute: Mozart's Opera and Goethe's Sequel

GOETHE'S INTEREST IN MOZART'S *Don Giovanni* was based on both content and form, on the unity of text and music. His interest in *Die Zauberflöte*, however, seems more narrowly focused on the libretto and its inherent symbolism. What he thought of Mozart's music for that opera has come to us only indirectly and by implication.

We may find this difficult to understand, for while there is universal agreement about the sublimity of Mozart's music in *Die Zauberflöte*, there is serious doubt about the literary quality of its libretto. In fact, we can safely assume that the two-act play, written for the occasion by the German librettist, actor-singer, and theatrical entrepreneur Emanuel Schikaneder,[1] would long be forgotten had not Mozart's music kept it alive. Yet it is equally true that Schikaneder's text has, over the years, intrigued a great number of musicians and critics, moving them, at times, to extreme judgments, such as "there is no better opera text in existence,"[2] and, on the other side of the ledger, "a mere agglomeration of

---

[1] Emanuel (Johann Joseph) Schikaneder was born in Straubing, Bavaria (he himself lists Regensburg), on September 1, 1751 and died in Vienna on September 21, 1812. He was a productive playwright and stage manager; as an actor he played Hamlet and created the role of Papageno. He managed the Freihaus-Theater auf der Wieden where *The Magic Flute* was first performed on September 30, 1791. In 1801 he opened the Theater an der Wien in Vienna.

absurdities,"[3] with the French novelist Stendhal occupying an imaginative middle position:

> The libretto of *die Zauberflöte* conforms exactly to that degree of charming extravagance and light, amusing fantasy which comes so easily to any French writer in search of a facile popularity; but, as we have maintained so often, this type of writing may often be ideal for the requirements of music. Music holds the secret of transforming even the cheap fancies of the vulgarest imagination into conceptions of noble grace and individual genius.[4]

The opinion that probably comes closest to Goethe's own was expressed by Johann Gottfried Herder, Goethe's former mentor and long-time friend. Herder neither ignored the libretto's weak spots, nor did he let them cloud the central issue of the opera, which he saw in the theme of Enlightenment, in the opera's value as educational art: "No matter how clumsily constructed the plot, no matter how poor the choice of words, the content of the play — "der Inhalt der Fabel" — comes through even to the least educated: light is struggling with darkness."[5]

The questions concerning Schikaneder's text, whether it is low-brow, pompous, or simple-minded, whether Mozart's composition of such a literary hodge-podge is truly Mozartian or downright un-Mozartian, these questions are still being asked today. The fact of the matter is that no one, including Goethe, ever denied the existence of dramatic flaws in Schikaneder's libretto. One could easily draw up a sizeable catalogue of textual inconsistencies, ranging from the seemingly unmotivated transformation of the Queen of Night from "motherly" to "destructive" to the realization that Sarastro, the humane and noble priest, is a veritable slave-holder who metes out corporal punishment for disobedience. But whether these flaws in logic are carelessness of design or calculated

---

[2] Hermann W. von Waltershausen, *Die Zauberflöte* (Munich: Bruckmann Verlag, 1920), p. 42f.: "Es gibt kein besseres Opernbuch als die Zauberflöte."

[3] Edward J. Dent, *Mozart's Operas: A Critical Study*, p. 222. Dent goes on to say: "The language of the dialogue is for the most part a ludicrous mixture of theatrical commonplaces and trivial jests, while the versified portions are clumsy doggerel relieved occasionally by passages borrowed from popular Masonic songs."

[4] Stendahl, *Life of Rossini* (New York: The Orion Press, 1970), p. 477.

[5] The article, "Wirkt die Musik auf Denkart und Sitten?," appeared in Herder's journal *Adrastea*. See *Herders Sämmtliche Werke*, ed. Bernhard Suphan (Berlin: Weidmannsche Buchhandlung, 1885), XXIII, 343-46.

contrasts, is a matter of debate.[6] And so is the oft lamented dearth of artistic quality in the libretto. True, it would prove difficult to defend lines such as the following as scintillating poetry: "Schön Mädchen jung und fein, / Viel weißer noch als Kreide!" — "Pretty girls, young and beautiful, / Much whiter yet than chalk!" Yet the text is not without a certain charm and humor, especially when brought to life on stage with a touch of Viennese ad-libbing *commedia dell' arte* style. Even verbal witticisms are not entirely absent, as in the following inquiry about Pamina: "Wo ist sie denn?" "Sie ist von Sinnen." — "Where is she?" "She is out of her mind."

This is not the place to try to resolve the two-hundred year debate about the worth or worthlessness of Schikaneder's libretto, rather let us focus our attention on two irrefutable facts: first, it was this particular libretto, this seemingly awkward crossbreed of fairy tale and Masonic ritual, which served Wolfgang Amadeus Mozart as both text and inspiration to create one of the most enduring magic shows ever composed for the stage; and, second, Goethe was never put off by its incongruities. On the contrary, he found words of praise for the text and its much maligned author. Schikaneder's libretto, he remarked in 1823, was certainly full of "improbabilities and jests — "voller Unwahrscheinlichkeiten und Späße" — that not everyone could understand and appreciate," but, he added, "one must grant the author great ability in achieving dramatic contrasts and grand theatrical effects" (Eckermann April 13, 1823). Goethe, there can be no doubt, was completely charmed by *Die Zauberflöte*. And not by Mozart's music alone, but by the libretto as well. It would be ludicrous to assume that Goethe would have found Schikaneder's text nearly so enticing without Mozart's music. Still, the poet's attraction to the Viennese stage work was in no small measure due to the libretto; his comments on the work, even his efforts to write a sequel, are centered on Schikaneder's text. I shall try, in the following, to explain Goethe's fascination with the opera and identify some points of attraction, themes and textual configurations that, for one reason or another, were likely to have captivated the poet's attention.

The first item on such a list might well be the theatricality of the work, its architecture of contrasts and polarities, its potential for splendid visual effects. Goethe remarked often on the importance of vivid, colorful theater, of "total" theater, especially with regard to his *Faust* drama. Years after *Die Zauberflöte* had first been performed in Weimar he still drew on the opera as a model for possibly staging the "Helena Act" in *Faust, Part Two*:

---

[6] See Hans-Albrecht Koch's excellent article on "Das Textbuch der 'Zauberflöte'," in *Jahrbuch des Freien Deutschen Hochstifts 1969*, pp. 76-120. Koch makes a very credible attempt to "rescue" Schikaneder's libretto by rejecting the "Bruchtheorie."

Everything is concretely visual and will, since it is designed as theater, be well received by the audience. And that's all I ever intended. I will be satisfied if most of the theater-goers enjoy the spectacle; the initiated will not miss the deeper meaning — "Dem Eingeweihten wird zugleich der höhere Sinn nicht entgehen" — just as is the case with *Die Zauberflöte* and other such things (Eckermann January 29, 1827).

"What he dreamed of," wrote Oskar Seidlin in his essay on "Goethe's Magic Flute," "was the combination of intoxicating popular entertainment and highest poetry."[7] Particularly in *Faust, Part Two* Goethe aimed at the kind of grand-style spectacle with contrasting yet ultimately harmonizing effect which he felt Schikaneder had attempted in *Die Zauberflöte*. To be sure, it was Mozart who endowed *Die Zauberflöte* with its "highest poetry," and it was Mozart who moved Goethe to think of opera as the potentially highest form of art. But it was Schikaneder who had supplied the text for this grand spectacle, the drama, the comedy, the visual effects, the Baroque theater with modern stage technology ("Maschinenoper"). All of this fascinated Goethe the poet, dramatist, and theater director.

The second point of attraction for Goethe — we might also call it a point of recognition — is the symbolism prevalent in the work: the confrontation of light and dark and the ancient symbolism of dying and rebirth. The principle of light is embodied by Sarastro, High Priest of Isis and Osiris, the principle of darkness by the Queen of the Night, who has been variably described as "Earthmother" and "Great Mother" commanding the powers of fertility and destruction. Kurt May sees in this thematic symbolism of *Die Zauberflöte* a succinct summation of the struggle of the "divine with the demonic elements in the world," and as such of primary interest to Goethe.[8] Indeed, the struggle between light and darkness, symbolizing the primordial struggle beween good and evil, belongs to the very concept and essence of *Faust*, characterizing in particular Mephistopheles, the emissary from hell who leaves no doubt about hell's eternal challenge to God's power:

> I am but part of the part that was the whole at first,
> Part of the dark which bore itself the light,
> That supercilious light which lately durst
> Dispute the ancient rank and realm to Mother Night.
>   (*Faust*, 33)

Clearly, Sarastro is not God, the Queen of Night not the devil; their confrontation is but a secular reflection of the larger metaphysical

---

[7] Oskar Seidlin, "Goethe's Magic Flute," in *Essays in German and Comparative Literature* (Chapel Hill: North Carolina Press, 1961), p. 58.

[8] Kurt May, "Entwürfe zu Operntexten," in GA VI, 1252.

struggle that takes place in Goethe's drama. Yet the struggles are related. Goethe could not overlook the dramatic, spiritual, and symbolic similarity of his and Schikaneder's principal themes.

Another symbolism well understood by Goethe is Tamino and Pamina's transcendence of fire and water. The theme of death and rebirth occurs at various junctures in Goethe's writings, especially in his late works. It permeates the entire *Faust* drama, we find it as a central idea in *Des Epimenides Erwachen*, in *Das Märchen*, and in the verse drama *Pandora* where Phileros (son of Prometheus) and Epimeleia (daughter of Epimetheus) undergo, much like Tamino and Pamina (and possibly inspired by them) the ordeal of fire and water. Goethe's poetic summation of the topos, and surely his most succinct rendering of the idea it implies, namely the need for human rejuvenation, comes to us in the poem "Selige Sehnsucht" from *West-östlicher Divan*:

> Sagt es niemand, nur den Weisen,
> Weil die Menge gleich verhöhnet,
> Das Lebendge will ich preisen,
> Das nach Flammentod sich sehnet.
> . . . .
> Und so lang du das nicht hast,
> Dieses: Stirb und werde!
> Bist du nur ein trüber Gast
> Auf der dunklen Erde (HA II, 18f.).

> Tell it only to the wise
> For the crowd at once will jeer
> That which is alive I praise,
> That which longs for death by fire.
> . . . .
> Never prompted to that quest:
> Die and dare rebirth!
> You remain a dreary guest
> On our gloomy earth.[9]

Many of these symbolic forms are related to yet another central theme in Schikaneder's libretto, the theme and idea of Freemasonry. *Die Zauber-flöte* has often been interpreted as a stage work informed and shaped by

[9] *Johann Wolfgang von Goethe: Selected Poems*, ed. Christopher Middleton (Boston: Suhrkamp/Insel, 1983), p. 207.

thoughts and images derived from Masonic literature.[10] Mozart was a Freemason, as was Goethe and, most likely, Schikaneder.

Goethe had joined the Weimar Lodge "Amalia" in 1780. In 1808 the Lodge's "Registry of Members" lists him as "Mason, Third Degree,"[11] and even though he was never an avid participant in the brotherhood, he did maintain his membership throughout his life. On June 23, 1830, he celebrated his fiftieth anniversary as a brother of "Amalia" and the Lodge bestowed upon him an honorary membership. Goethe, in appreciation, answered with a poem honoring the brotherhood: "Dem würdigsten Bruderfeste" — "To the Worthiest Celebration of Brotherhood" (GZB III, 305). Given his Masonic background, we may assume that Goethe not only readily comprehended the numerous allusions to Freemasonry in Schikaneder's text, but that these Masonic elements were part of the inspiration for writing a sequel to *Die Zauberflöte*.[12] Paul Nettl points out that Goethe's staging of *Die Zauberflöte* was very exacting with regard to the Masonic rituals mentioned in the text, e.g. at one moment in the Weimar performance Tamino and Pamina were brought on stage with "sacks over their heads" as is tradition in Masonic initiations.[13]

It is not unlikely that Masonic elements also affected Goethe's novel *Wilhelm Meisters Lehrjahre* which appeared one year after Goethe's staging of *The Magic Flute* in Weimar. Wilhelm's guidance by "The Society of the Tower" forms an interesting parallel to the ritualized and controlled education of Tamino in the opera. Goethe's novel weaves, much like Schikaneder's libretto, a curious pattern of rational and mystical elements, Enlightenment ideas and ancient rites of passage. Perhaps most important: both works address the question of human perfectibility and answer it in the affirmative.

Finally, we must include Mozart's music among the possible attractions for Goethe in *Die Zauberflöte*, even though he did not specifically comment on it. From all we know of Goethe's taste in music, the opera was a feast for his ears. We know that Goethe used Papageno's "Ein Mädchen oder Weibchen" for purposes of parody in his "cour

----

[10] For a discussion and bibliography of Freemasonry in relation to *The Magic Flute* see Jaques Chailley, *The Magic Flute, Masonic Opera*, trsl. Herbert Weinstock (New York: A. Knopf, 1971).

[11] Cf. J. Pietsch, *Johann Wolfgang v. Goethe als Freimaurer* (Leipzig: Bruno Zechel, 1880), pp. 20-21.

[12] Oskar Seidlin, "Goethe's Magic Flute," p. 49: "Even a casual reader cannot help noticing that what prompted Goethe's imagination to continue Schikaneder's story was its Masonic elements."

[13] Paul Nettl, *Goethe und Mozart*, p. 17.

d'amour,"[14] and we can assume that "Der Vogelhändler bin ich ja" had cast a similar charm over him. But even Sarastro's big aria "In diesen heil'gen Hallen" most likely pleased the poet, for the aria is strophic and deals with the themes of self-control and humaneness, central to his drama *Iphigenie auf Tauris*.

These are some of the possible reasons for Goethe's fascination with Mozart's and Schikaneder's *Magic Flute*. In the following I will discuss Goethe's staging of the opera at the Ducal Court Theater in Weimar, and his own creative efforts in this direction. But before doing so, I shall review briefly the major literary sources that form the background to Schikaneder's libretto. It may help us understand Goethe's fascination with the play. Schikaneder's text is stitched together from ingredients that come from a common pool of eighteenth-century European literature. Schikaneder drew freely on that pool and, in many ways, so did Goethe.

The libretto of *Die Zauberflöte* consists in the main of two literary traditions: folklore and Masonic writings. Some of these sources are contemporary, some derive from myths of ancient Greece and Egypt, and some (such as the origin of Tamino) prove difficult to trace. Of the texts that have been identified as sources for Schikaneder, two stand out prominently: *Sethos, histoire ou vie tirée des monuments, anecdotes de l'ancienne Egypte traduite d'un manuscript Grec* (Paris, 1731) by Abbé Jean Terrasson, and *Lulu oder die Zauberflöte* by the German eighteenth-century writer J.A. Liebeskind.

Terrasson's novel, translated into German by Matthias Claudius, himself a Freemason, appeared in two volumes as *Geschichte des egyptischen Königs Sethos* between 1777 and 1778.[15] The narrative, which although fiction became widely used as a source book for Freemasonry, relates the story of the Egyptian prince Sethos, a young man of sixteen, who must undergo tests of bravery, endurance, and intelligence. The first such test consists of a bout with a giant serpent, a monster described as "about forty-five feet in length, six feet in diameter,"[16] which the young hero captures alive. For the second trial Sethos descends through a dry well into the subterranean part of a pyramid. Deep within the earth he sees, written across a doorway, the following message:

[14] Frederick W. Sternfeld, *Goethe and Music*, pp. 13-19.

[15] The translation by Matthias Claudius appeared in Breslau (bei Gottlieb Löwe).

[16] *Geschichte des egyptischen Königs Sethos*, I, 135 and I, 155.

Whoever walks this path alone without looking back will be purified by fire, by water, and by air; and if he can overcome his fear of death, he will emerge again from the depth of the earth and see the light and will be priviliged to prepare his soul for the revelations of the mysteries of the Goddess Isis.

This text appears almost verbatim in Schikaneder's libretto of *Die Zauberflöte* in form of a duet sung by the two men in armor:

Whoever wanders on this road of tribulation
Will be cleansed by fire, water, air, and earth;
If he prevails against the fear of death, he soon will
   reach the realm of heaven.
Enlightened he will be in readiness
To dedicate himelf to the mysteries of Isis.
          (Act II, Scene 28).

Sethos enters the gate, walks past blazing fires, over glowing irons, and crosses a dangerous canal. At the end of his perilous journey he emerges from under the triple statue of Isis (here symbolizing wisdom), Osiris (symbolizing benefaction to man), and Horus, the divine child (symbolizing silence).[17] As he emerges, the sun is rising and the High Priest awaits the youth with outstretched arms.

Lulu oder die Zauberflöte is, like *Sethos*, an eighteenth-century creation based on ancient motifs. It is contained in a fairy tale collection entitled *Dschinnistan*, published by Christoph Martin Wieland approximately one year before Mozart and Schikaneder began work on *Die Zauberflöte*.[18] It, too, is the story of a young prince, named Lulu, who loses his way while hunting — "He wanted to slay a lion or tiger with his own hands" — in the forbidden forest of a mysterious queen. "The people called her the radiant fairy" — "die strahlende Fee" — whose gown was whiter than snow and from whose eyes shone light three times brighter than the morning sun. The fairy entreats Lulu to find her daughter, who had been abducted by an evil magician, and to recapture both the maiden and the magic "Fire-Steel," instrument and symbol of her power. The dangerous deed could be successfully undertaken only by a youth who is bold, prudent, and pure. To aid him in his task the fairy hands the prince a magic flute: "Take this flute, it has the power to make each listener love you and it can incite or soothe all passions." In the end, the prince and the

---

[17] These symbolic meanings are indicated in the novel itself; cf. I, 251. The novel also involves the figure of Orpheus who undergoes similar trials and fails to pass. At the very end Sethos withdraws from government and seeks complete privacy.

[18] C.M. Wieland, *Dschinnistan oder auserlesene Feen- und Geister-Mährchen, theils neu erfunden, theils neu übersetzt und umgearbeitet* (Winterthur: bey Heinrich Steiner, 1786-89) III, 298-356. I am quoting from pp. 301, 302, 305.

princess become man and wife, and to assure their eternal happiness the fairy queen destroys the sorcerer's castle with a "Glockenspiel" of silver bells.

Sethos and *Lulu* provided the key ingredients for Schikaneder's text: the Isis and Osiris cult (considered by some to be the origin of Freemasonic symbolism); the serpent, Biblical symbol of evil and chaos that must be overcome; the figure of the mysterious fairy queen with extraordinary powers and magical instruments; and the myth of Orpheus with its rich literary legacy in folklore, where magic flutes, harps, pipes, and horns excercise compelling charms over snakes, dragons, evil spirits, and assorted wicked people.[19] [A quick aside: in Mozart's score of *Die Zauberflöte* the original text in Act I, Scene 1 reads: "Dem grimmigen Löwen zum Opfer erkoren" — "The angry lion will soon devour me." But "Dem grimmigen Löwen" is crossed out and "Der listigen Schlange" — "The cunning snake" — written above it. For some (probably Masonic) reason Mozart and Schikaneder decided, at the last minute, to take out the lion and bring in the snake.][20]

Sethos and *Lulu* were not the only sources for Schikaneder; there were several others, all from the common literary pool.[21] For instance, the motif of the helpful magic instruments also occurs inWieland's Romantic epic *Oberon* (published in *Deutscher Merkur*, 1780) which tells the popular story of Hüon, a young knight, who is sent out by Charlemagne to accomplish an impossible task, and who solves it with the help of Oberon, King of the elves, and a magic horn. Wieland's epic was adapted for the Viennese stage in the form of a *Singspiel* by Sophie Seyler and Carl Gieseke. The latter, it is often assumed, collaborated with Schikaneder on the text of *Die Zauberflöte*.[22]

Two other popular plays must be briefly mentioned as additional sources for Schikaneder: *Lisuart und Dariolette* (1766), an operetta by

[19] Cf. *The Types of the Folktale*, ed. Antti Aarne, trsl. Stith Thompson (Helsinki: Academia Scientiarum Fennica, 1964), pp. 210, 211, 219.

[20] The emendation appears in Mozart's autographed manuscript of *Die Zauberflöte*. Cf. Music collection of the Austrian National Library, catalogue No. M 23/24.

[21] See H.A. Koch, "Das Textbuch der 'Zauberflöte'," for a survey of these and other relevant texts pp. 83-90.

[22] The question whether Johann Georg Metzler, who called himself Carl Ludwig Gieseke, was a co-author of *The Magic Flute* has often been discussed. Today it is generally believed that he did not play a prominent part. Cf. Jacques Chailley, "The Libretto: How Many Authors?" *The Magic Flute, Masonic Opera*, pp. 11-20; and Otto Rommel, *Die Alt-Wiener Volkskomödie* (Vienna: Verlag von Anton Schroll, 1952), pp. 988-990.

Daniel Schiebeler, and *Der Fagottist, oder die Zauberzither* by Joachim Perinet. *Lisuart* derives from Arthurian romances and presents a young knight falling in love with the picture of an abducted maiden, here the daughter of "Ginevra, Königin von England, Witwe des Königs Arthur."[23] The Perinet opera (music by Wenzel Müller) was playing at the Leopoldstädter Theater in Vienna when Mozart and Schikaneder were in the midst of creating their own magic show.[24] Whether by coincidence or by design, Perinet had used the very same fairy tale by Liebeskind which served as source for Schikaneder. We find all the motifs and figures familiar to us from Schikaneder: a young and innocent hero, a fairy queen, the magic instruments, the winning of the princess, and the punishment of the sorcerer. Perinet even has a Papageno figure in the form of the popular "Kaspar," the traditional clown figure of the South German and Austrian stages.

A close comparison of Perinet's and Schikaneder's texts reveals embarrassing similarities, embarrasing even for the eighteenth-century Viennese theater, where originality was rare and magic shows abounded.[25] We know that Mozart saw the show at the Leopoldstädter Theater and was not impressed. On June 12, 1791, he wrote to Constanze, who was vacationing near Baden: "To cheer myself up I went to the Kasperle Theater to see the new opera 'Der Fagottist' which is making such a sensation, but which is shoddy stuff" — "aber gar nichts daran ist" (LM June 12, 1791). Mozart obviously did not feel threatened by Wenzel Müller's music, but whether Schikaneder could face the competition with the same equanimity is not at all clear. It is quite possible, therefore, that he undertook all those changes in the libretto of *Die Zauberflöte* that have inspired much learned discussion ever since: changing the character of the queen from benevolent to vengeful, reducing the role of the original

---

[23] Daniel Schiebeler, *Lisuart und Dariolette oder die Frage und Antwort, eine Operette in zwey Aufzügen* (1766) II: 2, p. 21. Austrian National Library, No. 2.955-A.

[24] Joachim Perinet, *Der Fagottist, oder die Zauberzither. Ein Singspiel in drey Aufzügen* (Vienna: Mathias Andreas Schmidt, 1791), in *Theatralische Sammlung* (Vienna, 1797), theater collection of the Austrian National Library, vol. 262.

[25] The entrance of Perinet's fairy queen is accompanied by the same "thunderclap" that signals the arrival of the Queen of the Night, she emerges from the same "rock gate" and is surrounded by the same "radiant splendor." In Perinet's play she sings in her first aria to the prince and his companion: "Zittert nicht und folget mir" (I:3) which corresponds precisely to the Queen of the Night's "O zittre nicht, mein lieber Sohn!" Perinet employs two little "Genii," Schikaneder has three, but the most intriguing parallel is this: Sidi, the companion of the evil magician sings: "Alles liebet, was da lebet,/Liebe athmet die Natur ..." (III:1) which is very similar indeed to the aria sung by Monostatos, the "Sidi" of The Magic Flute (II:7): "Alles fühlt der Liebe Freuden,/ Schnäbelt, tändelt, herzt und küßt."

villain, perhaps Monostatos, and introducing a positive character, Sarastro, to memorialize Ignaz von Born, a distinguished Austrian Freemason who died that summer.[26]

Irving Singer makes the point that *Die Zauberflöte* is a heightened version of *Die Entführung aus dem Serail*. He relates Sarastro's wisdom to the magnanimity and self-negation of the Turkish Pasha andTamino's and Pamina's journey through death and rebirth to Belmonte's and Constanze's facing of "death together."[27] Singer's argument is both sensible and significant. It not only adds Mozart's own earlier *Singspiel* to the list of possible sources for *Die Zauberflöte* but it also points to two common themes in the two *Singspiele*, self-restraint and spiritualized love, themes very familiar and attractive to Goethe.

Goethe assumed the directorship of the Ducal Court Theater in 1791. Within four years he established a veritable Mozart era in Weimar. He opened the 1791 fall season with *Die Entführung aus dem Serail*, in 1792 he followed with a production of *Don Juan* in German, in 1793 he produced *Die Hochzeit des Figaro* (also in German) and on January 16, 1794, he staged *Die Zauberflöte*. The last work became, in the course of the next twenty years, the most frequently performed stage play at the *Hoftheater*, making Mozart the most frequently performed composer in Weimar at that time.[28] *Die Zauberflöte* had begun an unprecedented conquest of the German stages — unprecedented for Mozart — and Weimar was among the first dozen or so theaters to produce the opera.[29] So when Goethe's

[26] Ignaz von Born, a highly respected figure among Freemasons in Austria (he was born in Transylvania) wrote an influential essay, "Über die Mysterien der Ägypter," in the *Journal für Freimaurer* (Vienna, 1784) I, 15-132. In this essay Born derived Freemasonry from secret brotherhoods in ancient Egypt. Born's death gave rise to the interpretation of *The Magic Flute* as a Masonic opera in his honor and against Maria Theresa who was hostile to the Freemasons.

[27] Irving Singer, *Mozart and Beethoven. The Concept of Love in Their Operas* (Baltimore and London: The Johns Hopkins University Press, 1977), pp. 103-111.

[28] Alfred Orel, *Goethe als Operndirektor*, p. 190. Orel gives the entire "Spielplan" of the Weimar, Lauchstädt, and Erfurt performances, pp. 115-162. See also: Willi Flemming, *Goethe und das Theater seiner Zeit* (Stuttgart: W. Kohlhammer Verlag, 1968), pp. 258-266.

[29] There are numerous references claiming that Weimar was among "the first five places" to stage *The Magic Flute* outside of Vienna. But according to the chronology of performances in *Die Zauberflöte*, ed. Attila Csampai and Dietmar Holland (Hamburg: Rowohlt Taschenbuch Verlag, 1982), p. 269, there were at least fourteen places ahead of Weimar: Prague, Augsburg, Leipzig, Passau,

mother, Katharina Elisabeth Goethe, wrote to her son in November 1793 about the phenomenal success *Die Zauberflöte* was having in Frankfurt (it opened there on August 16, 1793), rehearsals of the opera were already under way in Weimar. Still, Frau Goethe's enthusiastic report very likely added a little impetus to the proceedings at the *Hoftheater*:

> There is nothing new to report, except that *The Magic Flute* was given here eighteen times and the theater was filled to capacity each time... We haven't had a sensation like this ever — "so ein Spektakel hat man hier noch nicht erlebt" — the theater had to open its doors before 4 P.M. and still people are turned away by the hundreds.[30]

Before the opera could go into production at the Court Theater, the *Hofdramaturg*, whose official function it was to read and prepare new plays for the stage, went to work on the libretto. The *Hofdramaturg* was Christian August Vulpius, resident playwright and Goethe's future brother-in-law. And Mr. Vulpius found that substantial alterations were in order before Schikaneder's text could appear before the "delicate ears" of the Weimar audience.[31] So Vulpius attacked Schikaneder's libretto with scissors and glue, changed the two acts of the original opera to three, "smoothed out" the language and purified it "from all nonsense." What resulted was not an improvement, but a "Verschlimmbesserung" of the text. For instance: in the opening scene, when Tamino rushes on stage with the snake in hot pursuit, Vulpius attempted to rationalize Tamino's losing effort by including a reference to his waning strength. But instead of rationality, he added comedy:

Schikaneder:

> Barmherzige Götter! Schon nahet sie
>   sich!
> Ach rettet mich! Ach schützet mich!"
> (Ah, Heavens, have mercy! I see it draw
>   near!
> O rescue me, protect me, save me, rescue
>   me!)

Vulpius:

Budapest, Graz, Brünn, Godesberg, Munich, Warsaw, Dresden, Frankfurt, Linz, Hamburg, Weimar.

[30] *Die Briefe der Frau Rath Goethe*, ed. Albert Köster (Leipzig: Carl Ernst Poeschel, 1904) I, 240-241.

[31] *Die Zauberflöte. Eine Oper in drei Aufzügen*, neu bearbeitet von C.A.Vulpius (Leipzig: bei Johann Samuel Heinsius, 1794), "Vorrede." Other quotations are in the following order: pp. 8, 67, 7/8.

> Wie bin ich ermattet, vom schrecklichen
>   Kampf!
> O welch ein Qualm! O welch ein Dampf!
> (I am so weary from the terrible fight!
>   O what vapors! O what fumes!)

The Queen of Night's second aria, "Der Hölle Rache kocht in meinem Herzen" — "The wrath of Hell is boiling in my bosom," powerfully graphic and succinct in Schikaneder's language, is replaced by a limp and tepid: "Es sterbe der Tirann von deinen Händen!" — "Let the tyrant die from your very hands."

In those areas of the text where Vulpius might have administered some rationalization to good effect, for example in the famous contradictions in plot and characters, he actually made only slight alterations. He made Papageno more self-conscious and Sarastro more communicative, but the essential textual incongruities remain. Goethe, interestingly enough, did not accept all changes suggested by his *Hofdramaturg*. He kept a number of verbal changes, but did not accept the division into three acts. He maintained, in other words, the important polarity of the work. Nor did he accept an alteration of Tamino's Japanese hunting costume, althoughVulpius had thought it a splendid idea to change the dress to an ancient Greek apparel — "Idealisch-griechisch."

If the text of the Weimar *Zauberflöte* turned out to be somewhat questionable, the initial staging of the opera was not exactly a model of perfection either. The opera, which in the course of time inspired some of the greatest artists to first-rate stage designs, did not have an auspicious beginning at the Ducal Theater. At least not in the opinion of one Arthur Schopenhauer who left us these recollections:

> I was there quite often [at the Weimar Court Theater under Goethe's directorship] and saw very good performances. But the decorations were at times woefully inadequate. In The Magic Flute, which after all deserves some beautiful stage scenery because of its attractive theme and splendid music, they put some unstylish little huts on stage with a giant sphinx in the middle. Nothing at all like the beautifully decorated Egyptian temple we are used to seeing on the stage in Frankfurt. And the boys [the three spirits] wore crinolines which made them look like bells rather than winged youths."[32]

We may wonder whether these observations of the philosopher of pessimism were perhaps a trifle too pessimistic. Apparently not. A look at a partial list of expenses incurred by the Court Theater for the staging of *Die Zauberflöte*, a list found in the "Chronicles of the Court Theater,"

---

[32] *Arthur Schopenhauer. Gespräche*, ed. Arthur Hübscher (Stuttgart—Bad Canstadt: Friedrich Frommann, 1971), p. 297.

(*Theaterakten*),[33] convince us that Schopenhauer had not exaggerated. To be sure, the financial outlay recorded here is mainly for repairs, but even so, the total of about 25 Thaler (less than $100) suggests greatest modesty if not frugality in the Weimar staging of *The Magic Flute*:

For *Die Zauberflöte*

To build a transparent temple	10 Thaler	
3 /4 ctr. cardboard at 1 th. 6 gr.	3 th.	18 gr.
Colored paper	3 th.	15 gr.
Reparing 10 palm branches at 3 gr.	1 th.	6 gr.
Making one new palm branch and one horn	1 th.	8 gr.
Making a new little box for bells and padlock	–	8 gr.
Regilding the spears, bows, and arrows and making a new bow		10 gr.
Making two new large birds that move for Papageno's cage	1 th.	8 gr.
New painting of Hell	3 th.	–

Goethe's involvement in the production of the opera was substantial. He directed, staged, and helped with designing. He even contributed a sketch in ink and watercolor for the scenery, depicting the entrance of the Queen of the Night in the first act. But more important are the notes that he dictated during rehearsals. The comments therein reveal Goethe's keen eye as a director, his attention to the smallest detail, and a Classical sense of balance and symmetry in staging:

Notes to *The Magic Flute*:

The transparent decoration showed a tear at the bottom. The *Glockenspiel* needs to be changed.

Demoiselle Maticzek is requested to use a completely white handkerchief; she was using one with a red border.

At the end of the first act Sarastro and Pamina as well as the priests and slaves should not turn to leave ... until the curtain is about to come down.

The [placement of] *Réverbères* [lamps with mirrors] needs to be discussed more...

---

[33] Portions of the "Theaterakten des Weimarer Hoftheaters" are reprinted in the catalogue of the "Ausstellung des Goethe-Museums Düsseldorf." See *Gesang und Rede, sinniges Bewegen. Goethe als Theaterleiter*, ed. Jörn Göres, catalogue editor Christina Kröll (Düsseldorf: Goethe-Museum, 1973). This particular "Rechnung über die Ausstattung zur 'Zauberflöte,' Weimar, 24. Jan. 1795" is reprinted on p. 120. I am quoting here the English translation by Marvin Carlson, *Goethe and the Weimar Theater*, p. 79. The abbreviations th. and gr. mean "Thaler" and "Groschen," standard denominations of the time.

Regards the "Gate of Horrors" ("*Schreckenspforte*") let's do the following: Tamino and Pamina will approach it, a man in armor at either side; then the decoration [transparent curtain] will open; at this point we'll have an attractive grouping in the middle of the stage with the couple clutching each other in terror, while the men in armor remind them of their duty with unmistakable gestures...

The high waterfall was too slow, the water further down is fine.

Can we avoid the clanking noise from the machinery?; it interferes with the sound of the flute. Could the "Gate of Horrors" be shut again after the ordeals of fire and water are over? The Chinese lanterns were not raised high enough ... there was not sufficient light on the last scenes ...

At the end, when the temple of the sun emerges, the priests should stand outside so that all the actors and singers are in readiness for their final entrance. One might arrange it in such a way that two of the boys stand with Pamina at one side, one stands with Tamino at the other, the two priests in red and the priests in blue can be symmetrically placed across the stage.[34]

In spite of the inadequacies of text and staging, *Die Zauberflöte* was performed twelve times in its first half season in Weimar (that is the second half of the 1793/94 winter season) and eleven times during the subsequent summer season in Lauchstädt, Rudolstadt, and Erfurt. It seems that the Weimar production of Mozart's opera was substantiating what one music critic had claimed and extolled about *Die Zauberflöte* as early as 1794, namely that the opera was likely to be successful wherever it was performed, in regular theaters or in temporary shacks — "auf allen Bühnen und Buden" — wherever one could find "one-and-a-half throats, a couple of fiddles, one curtain, and six pieces of stage scenery."[35] Nothing could diminish the attractiveness of that work or the enthusiasm of the audiences who came from all walks of life to see the Schikaneder spectacle and enjoy Mozart's sublime music.

For all the initial success, however, Goethe soon realized that a somewhat more artistic, more unified stage design was desirable in order to realize more fully the potential of *Die Zauberflöte* as theater and as music drama. As early as 1797 he began negotiating with the well-known stage designer Georg Fuentes in Frankfurt, but ultimately he had to settle for a student of Fuentes, the neo-Classicist Friedrich Beuther, who came to Weimar in 1815, bringing with him talent, vision, and energy. Within a

---

[34] These "Bemerkungen zur 'Zauberflöte'" are reprinted in *Goethe als Theaterleiter*, ed. Jörn Göres, p. 159; in A. Orel, *Goethe als Operndirektor*, pp. 78-79; and Willi Reich, *Goethe und die Musik* (Zurich: Ex Libris-Verlag, 1949), pp. 91-92. The translation is mine.

[35] "Über Mozarts Oper Die Zauberflöte," in *Journal des Luxus und der Moden*, ed. F.J. Bertuch and G.M. Kraus (Weimar: Verlag des Industrie-Comptoirs, 1794) IX, 364. Reprinted in *Goethe als Theaterleiter*, ed. Jörn Göres, p. 130.

year Beuther had created thirty-nine new sets, among them a new temple for Goethe's *Iphigenie*, scenes for Schiller's *Wilhelm Tell*, a new hell for *Don Giovanni*, and a variety of scenes for *Die Zauberflöte*: a temple of Isis, rock decorations for the Queen, an Egyptian room, and a Temple of the Sun.[36]

Goethe was enthusiastic about Beuther's Classical designs, but for his own management they came too late. He resigned his post as Director of the Court Theater during the 1816-1817 season, after twenty-five years of intense, often frustrating, often glorious theater life. But Mozart's *Zauberflöte* remained his companion for life. He went to see and hear it again and again. He used the cherished Papageno theme in poems and songs, such as "Wer kauft Liebesgötter?" and "Frühlingsorakel" ("Aber, wenn wir uns genommen, / Werden Pa-pa-papas kommen?" WA 1: I, 41 and 111); and in his old age he listened patiently when his grandson Walther would tell him about the marvellous goings-on in an opera called *Zauberflöte*. But perhaps the most charming tribute to *Die Zauberflöte* — and I think one of the most gracious bows to Mozart — is contained in Goethe's verse epic *Hermann und Dorothea*. The young protagonist, shy and unpolished Hermann, is teased by his sophisticated neighbors for not recognizing the names of Pamina and Tamino, names, after all, nearly as familiar as Adam and Eve. But even more important: by dubbing Hermann with the nickname "Tamino," Goethe calls attention to the parallels in the development of the two young protagonists who grow from adolescence to maturity as chaos and destruction loom in the background.

> When I came in they were giggling, but not at me, I was
>   certain.
> Mina was at the piano, and their old father was present,
> List'ning with joy to the songs of his daughters, quite
>   happy and cheerful.
> I could not understand very much of the text they were
>   singing,
> But I did hear a lot about Pamina, Tamino.
> Naturally I did not want to be silent, so when they had
>   finished
> I asked what was the text, and who were the characters
>   mentioned.
> All were silent at this, but they smiled, and the father
>   responded:
> "Tell me, my friend, you're acquainted only with Eve and
>   with Adam?"
> Then they could hold back no longer: the girls simply
>   hooted with laughter;
> Loud laughed also the lads, and the father was holding his
>   stomach.

[36] Cf. Marvin Carlson, *Goethe and the Weimar Theater*, p. 276.

> I was embarrassed and dropped my hat on the floor, and
>   the giggling
> Went on, even through singing and playing I heard it
>   continue.
> And I went home as fast as I could in disgrace and
>   vexation,
> Hung the coat in the closet, and mussed up my hair with
>   my fingers.
> Swearing that never again would I ever set foot on their
>   threshold.
> And, indeed, I was right, for they are conceited and
>   hateful,
> And, as I hear, they are always referring to me asTamino.
>   (*Second Canto*, Verses 220-237).[37]

Toward the end of 1795, about a year and a half after Mozart's *Zauberflöte* had first been staged at Weimar, Goethe began writing his own version of *The Magic Flute: Der Zauberflöte zweiter Teil*. Within months he had completed the first five or six scenes (he finished eight) and began looking for an appropriate composer. His first choice was PaulWranitzky, music director of the Viennese court theaters, who had successfully set Wieland's *Oberon* to music. On January 24, 1796, Goethe approached the maestro with the following letter:

> The great popularity of *Die Zauberflöte* and the difficulty of writing a play that can compete with it has suggested to me the idea of taking the basis of a new work out of this very play. The public would already be favorably inclined toward it and the burden of mounting a new and complicated play would be eased for the actors and theatre directors. I think my goal of writing a second part to *Die Zauberflöte* is most likely to be successful since the characters are familiar. The actors are accustomed to the roles and the situations and relationships can be developed without strain since the audiences will already be familiar with the first play. This will give such a play much life and interest. My results will show how completely I have achieved this goal. In order for the play to be produced at once throughout Germany, I have arranged that the costumes and settings on hand for the first *Zauberflöte* can also be used for the second. If any directors wish to go further and create wholly new ones, the effect would be thereby still greater, although at the same time I would wish that the first *Zauberflöte* should be recalled, even in the settings (WA 4: XI, 13-14).[38]

---

[37] *Johann Wolfgang von Goethe. Hermann und Dorothea*, trsl. Daniel Coogan (New York: Frederick Ungar Publishing Co., 1966) p. 39. See also Paul Michael Lützeler, "Hermann und Dorothea" in *Goethes Erzählwerk: Interpretationen* (Stuttgart: Reclam, 1985), p. 256.

[38] I am quoting the English text of the letter from Marvin Carlson, *Goethe and the Weimar Theater*, pp. 86-87.

Despite Goethe's persuasive arguments, his negotiations with Wranitzky came to naught. Various factors contributed to this failure, not the least perhaps Wranitzky's understandable reluctance to compete with the immortal Mozart. But the most overt reason was this: Goethe charged too high a fee for writing the libretto. He wanted 100 ducats, whereas the Viennese maestro considered 25 quite adequate — "Die Direktion bewillige jedoch 25 Dukaten" — and subtly hinted that even Iffland and Kotzebue, popular playwrights at the time, could not command higher royalties.[39] Goethe declined but was undaunted in his effort to find a composer. In 1801 he approached his new musician friend from Berlin, Karl Friedrich Zelter, but Zelter, too, was hesitant. When, several years later, the musican's artistic appetite awakened: "Did I tell you that I've been working from time to time on your Magic Flute?..." (GZB I, 373) — it was Goethe who had lost interest. In the meantime the poet had published part of his intended sequel in *Wilman's Almanac*[40] and had, for all practical purposes, discontinued work on the project. *Der Zauberflöte zweiter Teil* remained a fragment.

In reading Goethe's extant script we quickly discover that the poet meant what he had written to Wranitzky, namely that he wished to continue the dramatic characters and designs of Schikaneder's libretto. We find all the *personae* of the original opera: Sarastro, the Queen of the Night, Tamino, Pamina, Papageno, and Papagena, even the resident bad guy, Monostatos. There is, however, one significant addition: a son is born to Tamino and Pamina, who is abducted at the moment of birth by Monostatos on order of the still vengeful Queen of the Night. The child is imprisoned in a golden casket which neither Sarastro's magic spell nor Papageno's magic flute can open, and he will die unless the casket is kept in constant motion.

The structure of the libretto follows Schikaneder's model rather closely. We find the same mix of solemnity and comedy, the same rapid alternation between spoken dialogue and singing, between solo and tutti parts, duets, quartets, choruses. Some numbers, such as the famous "Pa Pa Pa" duet reappear in Goethe's text with only minor changes (here the duet is enhanced by a chorus), other forms and designs are taken over without any alteration. One stage direction reads: "The inner curtain

---

[39] Hans-Albrecht Koch, "Goethes Fortsetzung der Schikanederschen 'Zauberflöte'," in *Jahrbuch des Freien Deutschen Hochstifts 1969*, p. 127. See also Paul Nettl, *Goethe und Mozart*, p. 18.

[40] "Der Zauberflöte zweiter Teil," in *Wilmans Taschenbuch auf das Jahr 1802*, with the following subtitle: "Der Liebe und Freundschaft gewidmet." In 1801 Goethe wrote to Zelter: "Von einem zweiten Teil der 'Zauberflöte' werden Sie die ersten Szenen in dem nächsten Wilmannischen [sic] Taschenbuch finden." (GZB I, 13).

opens. Fire and water scene as in 'The Magic Flute'" (252).[41]   Goethe's intent is clear: he wanted to write a text for music (both the completed and the incomplete parts contain copious suggestions for composers), and he wanted the text to be as close to Schikaneder's libretto as possible.

But we soon see that, from the beginning, Goethe imbued his scenes, figures, and poetic forms with his own philosophic meaning and symbolism. His settings and characters may seem familiar, but the aesthetic spirit behind them is not Viennese Baroque, but Weimar Classicism. For instance: The first appearance of the Queen of the Night is signalled by the same "thunderclap" we know from Mozart's opera, the Queen enters through the same "rock portal," etc. But in describing the queen's presence on stage, Goethe reveals very much his own theatrical style, a Classical scene of symmetry and wholeness:

> An aurora borealis, spreading from the centre, surrounds the Queen like an aureole. Comets, St. Elmo's fires and fiery orbs cross among the clouds. The whole, by means of form, colour and mysterious symmetry, should make a dreadful, yet agreeable impression (236).

Goethe not only enhanced and harmonized the stage effects and the appearance of the Queen, he added new dimensions to the *persona* and the dramatic funtion of the Queen herself. In Schikaneder's text the Queen of the Night is an ambivalent figure, half grieving mother, half vengeful queen. She both opposes and complements Sarastro, the High Priest of Isis and Osiris. Here, in Goethe's text, she is more autonomous and mysterious, an elemental being, remote and destructive. When she first appears on stage and queries: "Wer ruft mich an?" — "Who is calling me?" — we are reminded of Goethe's *Erdgeist* in *Faust*, the elemental spirit who reveals himself to the questing scholar with similar fiery effects and haughtiness: "Wer ruft mir?" (HA III, 23).

> *Die Königin* (in den Wolken):
>
> Wer ruft mich an?
> Wer wagt's, mit mir zu sprechen?
> Wer, diese Stille kühn zu unterbrechen?
> Ich höre nichts — so bin ich denn allein!
> Die Welt verstummt um mich — so soll
>   es sein.
> ....
> Woget, ihr Wolken, hin,

[41] The German quotations are from the Beutler edition, GA VI, 1091-1118. The English quotations from Eric Blom's translation of Goethe's *Der Zauberflöte zweiter Teil* which appeared in *Music and Letters*, 23 (1942), 234-254. Page references in the text are to these editions. Both versions are reprinted in the Appendix.

Decket die Erde,
Daß es noch düsterer,
Finsterer werde!
Schrecken und Schauer,
Klagen und Trauer
Leise verhalle, bang
Ende den Nachtgesang
Schweigen und Tod (1092).

Queen Of Night (in the clouds):

Who is it calls?
Who ventures to invoke me?
Who is't my solitude thus boldly broke
    me?
No answer there! Then still I am alone.
The world is silent; thus I hold mine
    own!
....
Vapours, envelop the
Earth with your cover;
Let it be drearier and
Darker than ever!
Shuddering, ailing,
Sorrow and wailing,
Distantly, softly, long,
End ye the night's dread song:
Silence and death! (235)

Even here, in the Queen's "dreadful" proclamations of silence and death, we are conscious of Goethe's attempt to harmonize both statement and effect. The rhythms, alliterations, enjambements, the "word music" of the verse, create a lyrical tonality that renders the Queen's threats euphonious and "agreeable," lifting them into a tuneful symmetry for the ear. Such poetic dimensions are entirely lacking in Schikaneder's text as well as in his dramatic conception of the Queen. Goethe created a balanced and complete character: a Queen of the Night that is both a figure of darkness and majesty, a powerful spirit of the earth.

Sarastro, too, has undergone some changes in Goethe's hands. He is still a High Priest in a monastic order, but his role and dramatic function are likewise expanded. He will give up his lofty priestly station and become, for a time, a simple pilgrim, a wanderer and helper in the real world, where he, too, will be subjected to temptations, tests, and trials — "Within these silent walls one learns to know oneself... But the august voice of nature and the speech of needy humankind become known only to the wanderer" (243). Unlike the static priestly society in Schikaneder's play, Goethe's brotherhood exists in continous exchange with the outside world. One member of the order is always in the world to aid humankind and bring worldly experience back into the sacred halls. This is clearly a Goethean concept: *vita contemplativa* interchanges with *vita activa* to keep from fruitless rigidity.

Goethe's most conscious and significant innovation, indeed the central issue of his libretto, is Genius, the newborn child of Tamino and Pamina. His struggle for life becomes, by extension, a struggle between the ever-present danger of annihilation and the principle of light. Ultimately the child lives; he escapes his "golden coffin" and "flies away." But his freedom is not accomplished through *Glockenspiel* and flute, nor through Sarastro's magic. The force liberating the child, and here again we have a very Goethean proposition, is a force greater than music, magic, or the Queen's destructiveness: *Mutterliebe* — the sacrificing love of a mother for her child:

> Einer Gattin, einer Mutter,
> Die den Sohn zu retten eilet,
> Macht das Wasser, macht das Feuer,
> In der Gruft das Ungeheuer,
> Macht der strenge Wächter Platz.
> ....
> Sieh, das Wasser, sieh, das Feuer
> Macht der Mutterliebe Platz (1116-17).

> From a consort, from a mother
> Shrink her infant's grimmest guardians,
> Spite the waters, spite the fire,
> In this cave of horror dire
> Shall our treasure not be lost.
> ....
> Fire and water yield their power
> When a mother supplicates (252-53).

At the end of Goethe's fragment, the child rises into the air — "At the moment the GUARDS thrust their spears at the GENIUS, he flies away." (254).

The similarity between Genius from Goethe's *Zauberflöte* and Euphorion, the boy figure from *Faust, Part Two*, has often been remarked upon. Euphorion, too, is one of Goethe's "figures of light," "an allegorical being," as Goethe explained, embodying the spirit of poetry. "In him is personified poetry, which is bound to neither time, place, nor person" (Eckermann December 20, 1829). Genius, the child of Tamino and Pamina, represents the same kind of spirit. As he rises into the air, part Icarus, part Orpheus, he closely resembles Euphorion, the child of Faust and Helena, who similarly rises into the air, a "naked genius unfledged ... in his hand the golden lyre, exactly like a little Phoebus" (*Faust*, 244).

Arthur Henkel has given us an intriguing interpretation of the Genius figure. In his essay "Goethes Hommage à Mozart," he suggests that Genius represents Goethe's personal homage to the genius of Mozart. The finale of Goethe's libretto, Henkel says, would have brought a "final victory of the world of light."[42] But when Goethe realized that his *Zauberflöte* was destined to remain a fragment, he symbolized in the figure of Genius his farewell to a poetic dream as well as his genuine veneration of Mozart.

Whether Goethe intended to dramatize his personal feelings about Mozart in this manner is difficult to say. Henkel's idea is charming but highly speculative. We do know, however, that an entire network of thematic, motific, symbolic, and structural links exists between Mozart's *Zauberflöte* and Goethe's *Der Zauberflöte zweiter Teil* on the one hand and several of Goethe's late works on the other.[43] It is generally agreed, for instance, that *Faust*, especially *Faust, Part Two*, received the greatest impetus as well as material input from Goethe's unfinished *Magic Flute*. Even the "Prelude in the Theater" in *Faust, Part One*, one of three prologues to *Faust* written between 1798 and 1800, contains parts that were, as Oskar Seidlin suggested,[44] originally intended for Goethe's *Der Zauberflöte zweiter Teil*:

> You know, upon our German stages
> Each man puts on just what he may;
> So spare me not upon this day
> Machinery and cartonnages.
> The great and little light of heaven
>   employ,
> The stars you may as freely squander;
> Cliff-drops and water, fire and thunder,
> Birds, animals, are in supply.
> So in this narrow house of boarded space
> Creation's fullest circle go to pace,

[42] Arthur Henkel, "Goethes 'Hommage à Mozart' — Bemerkungen zu 'Der Zauberflöte zweiter Theil,'" in *Philomathes. Studies and Essays in the Humanities in Memory of Philip Merlan*, eds. Robert B. Palmer and Robert Hamerton-Kelly (The Hague: Martinus Nijhoff, 1971), pp. 501 and 502.

[43] Walter Weiss discusses the "golden coffin" — "Kasten aus Gold" — as a motif in Goethe's late writings, e.g. *Das Märchen, Wilhelm Meisters Wanderjahre, Pandora*, etc. See "Das Weiterleben der 'Zauberflöte' bei Goethe," *Studien zur Literatur des 19. und 20. Jahrhunderts in Österreich. Festschrift für Alfred Doppler*, eds. Johann Holzner, Michael Klein, Wolfgang Wiesmüller (Innsbruck: Kowatsch, 1981), pp. 16 and 19.

[44] Oskar Seidlin, "Is the 'Prelude in the Theatre' a Prelude to *Faust*? *Essays in German and Comparative Literature* (Chapel Hill: University of North Carolina Press, 1961), pp. 60-69.

> And walk with leisured speed your spell
> From Heaven through the World to Hell
> (*Faust*, 6).

The references to water, fire, rocks, and birds all come, says Seidlin, from Goethe's *Zauberflöte* fragment, and the "Merry Person" ("Lustige Person") who speaks these lines is Goethe's own Papageno figure. In short, the "Prelude in the Theater," which introduces the entire *Faust* drama, was originally meant to introduce *Der Zauberflöte zweiter Teil*.

Bruno Walter established a similar avenue between Goethe and Mozart. The requirements of art as pronounced by the "Merry Person" in Goethe's "Prelude" to Faust,

> So do be good and act in model fashion,
> Show Fancy in her fullest panoply:
> Sense, understanding, sentiment, and
>   passion,
> And mind you, last not least, some
>   foolery (*Faust*, 3),

are not only valid for Goethe, Bruno Walter believes, they also fit the art of Mozart.[45] The mixture of childlike merriment and solemn pathos, the blend of fantasy and reason, characterize Mozart's *Zauberflöte* as well as Goethe's fragment. Musicians, poets, painters, philosophers, and scholars are attracted to both of these "Magic Flutes" because of their magical blend of feeling and moral teachings, sacred mysteries and popular gags, death and the victory of light at the end.

Ernst Bloch too reflected in his major opus, *Das Prinzip Hoffnung*, on Mozart's *Zauberflöte* in a manner that touches on both Mozart's and Goethe's versions. "There is a depth that reaches up and forward," the philosopher wrote, "where the substance of the deep — "das Abgründige" — is brought up to the light. The motion of back and forward is like the motion of a wheel that dips and gathers" — "Zurück und vorwärts sind dann wie in der Bewegung eines Rades, das zugleich eintaucht und schöpft."[46] (*Schöpfen* is used here in both its literal sense of scooping up and in its metaphoric sense of creating.)

The image that emerges from Bloch's description is that of a waterwheel which dips and rises and pours forth, continuously interacting between high and low, light and darkness, past and future. Bloch's image symbolizes the joining of all elements in a perpetual metamorphosis of the archaic into order, of dark and demonic impulses

---

[45] Bruno Walter, *Vom Mozart der Zauberflöte* (Frankfurt and New York: S. Fischer Verlag, 1956), p. 15.

[46] Ernst Bloch, *Das Prinzip Hoffnung* (Frankfurt: Suhrkamp, 1959), I, 181.

into forms of light, reason, and art. The waterwheel describes concisely and beautifully the essence and function of Mozart's and Schikaneder's *Zauberflöte* as an art form, its interchange between fairy tale and solemnity, magic and morality. By extension, Bloch 's metaphor also describes the essence and function of Goethe's fragment. Goethe recreated in his *Magic Flute* all the elements of darkness and destruction, but he balanced them through acts of altruistic love, the birth of Genius, and through the "word music" of his poetry. In contrast to Schikaneder and Mozart he did not finish his *Singspiel* (even though the fragment seems in many ways complete), yet its spirit lives on in his other "Magic Flute" writings: *Das Märchen, Novelle,* and *Faust.*

Goethe's drawing of the Queen of Night, 1796

9

Parallels of Styles and Artistic Attitudes

IN HIS ESSAY "Begegnung mit Mozart" Ernst Beutler compared several works of Goethe and Mozart by theme, spirit, and diction. Certain melodies in *Cosi fan tutte*, Beutler found, could easily fit the style and ambience of Goethe's early play *Stella*, the melancholy and the Rococo splendor of *Le Nozze di Figaro* might serve as atmospheric background to *Wilhelm Meisters Lehrjahre*, and Goethe's Classical *Iphigenie* can be related stylistically to *Idomeneo* and thematically to *La Clemenza di Tito* — "the courage to be truthful before the tyrant."[1] Karl Viëtor, another Goethean, went one step further. He not only compared literary themes and dramatic figures, he likened some of Goethe's early verses to Mozart's instrumental music. Referring to Goethe's poem "Mailied" (1771), Viëtor comments:

> These are the first verses in the German language in which life itself, the bright and joyous abundance of existence finds utterance...
>
>
>
> O earth! O sunlight!
> O bliss! O joy!
>
>
>
> Only in Mozart's symphonies can we find similar joy of life, expressed with a similar intimacy and grace.[2]

Many literary historians, musicologists, and musicians have presented similar arguments, namely that close thematic and stylistic parallels exist,

---

[1] Ernst Beutler, "Begegnung mit Mozart," in *Essays um Goethe*, pp. 248-249.

[2] Karl Viëtor, *Goethe. The Poet*, p. 8.

particularly parallels of artistic effects, between certain works by Goethe
and Mozart. At times these parallels are but reflections of themes and
styles current during the periods in which the two artists lived and
worked. In that sense they manifest their common eighteenth-century
background. At other times these artistic parallels derive from Goethe's
and Mozart's personal creativity, from similarities in ideas and forms
which they themselves contributed to European art and culture.

These contributions are numerous and their effect is in many ways
incalculable, but there are some that can be clearly identified. Both artists
helped replace — each in his artistic medium and independent from each
other — stock figures in the German-language theater with true-to-life
characters, such as Gretchen in *Faust* and Susanna in *Figaro*. Both artists
brought into their art the full range of human emotions and enhanced
thereby artistic expressivity. Yet both of them controlled these emotion-
filled expressions through clarity of diction and balance of form. Finally,
poet and composer traversed various eighteenth-century period styles,
from Rococo to Storm and Stress to Classicism to their final phases of
creativity. Surprisingly — or perhaps not so surprisingly — Mozart's
artistic growth encompassed as many contemporary styles as did
Goethe's, even though the years granted to the composer were less than
half of those given to the poet. In the following I will bring together some
representative works by Goethe and Mozart, chosen from four different
creative periods, and discuss them according to similarities in their
historical styles as well as in their personal expressions. It goes without
saying that such comparisons, i.e. creating analogues in different artistic
media, are not without methodological pitfalls, yet in this case they yield
intriguing parallels.

Rococo

The Rococo period of European art and culture, which reached its height
in about mid-eighteenth century, provided the source for Goethe's and
Mozart's earliest artistic development. When the two young artists
entered the mainstream of European art, they found before them neo-
Classical styles of the Rococo period with its bucolic imagery and
anacreontic love themes; pietism added a measure of individuality to the
rigid formalism espoused by Rococo artists, but individuality remains
largely confined to auctorial playfulness and witticisms. In general, the
trend in all the arts is away from complex structures and toward simpler
forms.

Goethe began writing in this vein as a sixteen-year old university
student at Leipzig, a self-styled "shepherd at the Pleiße river," as he
wrote in *Dichtung und Wahrheit* (HA IX, 279). His first poetic attempts
were in both the pastoral tradition, *Die Laune des Verliebten* (*The Lover's*

Mood),[3] and in the anacreontic manner — verses about love and
friendship. Twenty of these early poems were set to music by a fellow
student and amateur composer in Leipzig: *Neue Lieder in Melodien gesetzt
von Bernhard Theodor Breitkopf*.[4] They are the first in a long stream of
Goethe poems that will be set to music in the following decades. The
poem "Die Nacht" (1768), one of Goethe's personal favorites in that
collection, may serve both as an example of the poet's Rococo style and
his artistic power even as an adolescent:

> Gern verlaß ich diese Hütte,
> Meiner Liebsten Aufenthalt,
> Wandle mit verhülltem Tritte
> Durch den ausgestorbnen Wald.
> Luna bricht die Nacht der Eichen,
> Zephirs melden ihren Lauf,
> Und die Birken streun mit Neigen
> Ihr den süßen Weihrauch auf.
>
> Schauer, der das Herze fühlen,
> Der die Seele schmelzen macht,
> Flüstert durchs Gebüsch im Kühlen.
> Welche schöne, süße Nacht!
> Freude! Wollust! Kaum zu fassen!
> Und doch wollt' ich, Himmel, dir
> Tausend solcher Nächte lassen,
> Gäb' mein Mädgen Eine mir.

(Now I leave this hut, my sweetheart's dwelling,/ and walk with stealthy
steps/ through the dark and desolate woods./ The moon breaks through
the oak trees,/ the west winds are announcing her [the moon's] course,/
and the bowing birch trees scatter/ the sweetest incense in her path.
A nightly stir which sets the heart pounding,/ which melts the soul/
comes whispering through the coolness./ O what beautiful, sweet night!/
A joy, a feeling hard to   grasp!/ And yet, Heaven, I would forego a
thousand such nights,/ if my sweetheart would give me one.)[5]

The poem exhibits all the trademarks of its anacreontic genre: it is
playfully amorous, it describes a pastoral scene and atmosphere, it is
sentimental, and it comes to a witty *pointe* at the end. But the poem

---

[3] *Der junge Goethe*, ed. Max Morris, I, 254-285.

[4] *Der junge Goethe*, ed. Max Morris, I, 348-363.

[5] The German version of "Die Nacht" is taken from Max Morris, *Der junge Goethe*,
I, 351-52. The English prose version is in part from David Luke, *Goethe*, p. 5; in
part it is my own translation as Luke translated a later version of the poem, "Die
schöne Nacht."

reveals more than polish and talent. Even at that early period in his poetic life Goethe was able to give his verses a special lyrical quality, a unique blend of visual effects, word music, rhymes and rhythms, creating a dynamic imagery — "Und die Birken streun mit Neigen/ Ihr den süßen Weihrauch auf" — which goes beyond the common poetic diction or imagery of the time. Max Morris, one of the principal editors of Goethe's early writings, put it this way: "Here [in Goethe's anacreontic poetry] we have the first sample of his wonderful gift of evoking all the powers dormant in a language with his magical sense of diction" — "mit dem Geheimnis der Wortwahl."[6]

Composers too had begun to replace the older and "learned" musical styles with a lighter, more melodic diction, for instance, the *style galant*, a musical equivalent to anacreontic poetry. The new form of music "tended towards absolute strophic regularity," writes Giorgio Pestelli, "with a uniform beat and no sudden outbursts, becoming closely related to dancing..."[7] The eight-year old Wolfgang Amadeus had learned this new style literally on the knees of Johann Christian Bach in London. Many of his early serenades, symphonies, and divertimenti are written in this gallant form, often combining dance-like rhythms with a sense of measured symmetry. Typical and exquisite in this manner is the Divertimento No. 11, K. 251. The entire divertimento is distinct and elegant *style galant*, the minuets and rondos, the spirited allegro, and the "Marcia alla francese." But the movement most charming and indicative of the period style is the little "Andantino," a simple melodic rondo hovering between a song and a dance, conjuring up images of delicate pastels and porcelain figurines.

Like Goethe's poem "Die Nacht," Mozart's "Andantino" creates a light and playful atmosphere, a world of graceful artificiality. But also like Goethe's poem the composition rises above the contemporary norm, for Mozart's special gift for melodic invention and his uncanny sense for the right instrumentation (here in the horns and the oboe) manifest themselves early in his music, endowing it both with melody and the rhythms of dance characteristic of his style.

Even after the period of Storm and Stress had burst upon Germany, and subsequently all Europe, both Goethe and Mozart continued to use pastoral and anacreontic motifs and conventions. Goethe's one-act play, *Erwin und Elmire*, a *Singspiel* in the pastoral mode, was not completed until 1775, a time when he had already written *Werther*, his most influential Storm and Stress work. And it is in *Erwin und Elmire* that we

---

[6] Max Morris, *Der junge Goethe*, I, viii.

[7] Giorgio Pestelli, *The Age of Mozart and Beethoven* (Cambridge: Cambridge University Press, 1984), p. 7.

find one of the most delightful blossoms of Goethe's Rococo writing, his poem "Das Veilchen." Mozart, by fortunate coincidence, came across the poem in Joseph Anton Steffan's *Sammlung Deutscher Lieder für das Klavier* and, ten years after its initial publication, set it to music, presumably without knowing the identity of its author.[8]

> Ein Veilchen auf der Wiese stand,
> Gebückt in sich und unbekannt,
> Es war ein herzig's Veilchen.
> Da kam eine junge Schäferin
> Mit leichtem Schritt und munterm Sinn
> Daher, daher,
> Die Wiese her, und sang (HA I, 78).

(A violet stood in the meadow,/ with bowed head and unnoticed;/ it was a sweet violet./ along came a young shepherdess,/ light of step and cheerful,/ along, along,/ through the meadow, singing./)

---

[8] Joseph Anton Steffan, *Sammlung Deutscher Lieder für das Klavier* (Vienna, bey Joseph Edlen von Kurzböck, 1778-1782).

Both Goethe's text and Mozart's musical setting are anchored in the
style and spirit of Rococo art. Siegbert S. Prawer comments in his edition
of German *Lieder* on the comparability of the poetic and musical styles, as
well as on the compatibility of the two artists:

> Most of the best *Lieder* represent ... a meeting of affinities. Mozart's one
> creative encounter with Goethe (in 'Das Veilchen') is a case in point: poet
> and composer have here given us, each in his own way, the very essence of
> the pastoral Rococo at the threshold of the Age of Sensibility. The music
> follows the action and sentiment of the poem in every point — through
> rhythmical variation (beginning in 4/8 time, it quickens to 2/4 at the
> shepherdess's approach), through alternations between major and minor
> (the violet expresses its love-longing and dies in the minor key), and
> through meaningful piano interludes like that after the words *'und sang'*
> (which gives us the shepherdess's song); yet it never sacrifices one iota of
> its own inner formal logic.[9]

Goethe had written "Das Veilchen" in a playful, ironic manner.
Mozart, with unfailing artistic instinct, recreated the mood of the pastoral
as well as the playful irony by which Goethe commented on the Rococo
form. The composer adopted the same mock-pathos for the heroic little
violet which is about to be trampled underfoot by the shepherdess
striding through the meadow. He even enhanced the irony of the song by
dramatizing the text into a three-stanza entity, creating a musico-
dramatic *scena* complete with introduction, development section, and a
newly formed finale — "Das arme Veilchen! es war ein herzigs Veilchen!"
"In this song that is no song," remarked Alfred Einstein with
characteristic perceptiveness, "one genius has struck fire from another."[10]

Traces of Rococo life and art linger in Goethe's novels and in Mozart's
operas, even when the style itself had ceased to be dominant. We find
French Rococo garden architecture in *Die Wahlverwandtschaften* as a
stylized contrast to images of nature untamed, and we find, as Ernst
Beutler has mentioned, the styles and ambience of Rococo court life in
both *Wilhelm Meisters Lehrjahre* (the novel is set in the second half of the
eighteenth century) and in *Le Nozze di Figaro*. Mozart's comic opera, in
particular, is a re-enactment of both the charm and the melancholy, the
coy eroticism as well as the bucolic dreams of naturalness, so common in
the literature and music of the Rococo period. In the final scene of the
opera we hear Figaro, inmidst of intrigues and deception, intone a
pastoral theme, "Tutte è tranquillo e placido," and we hear Susanna,
disguised as the Countess in a Rococo garden setting, sing of peaceful
meadows and murmuring brooks: "Deh, vieni non tardar, oh gioia bella."

---

[9] *The Penguin Book of Lieder*, ed. and trsl. S.S. Prawer (Harmondsworth: Penguin
Books, 1964), p. 14.

[10] Alfred Einstein, *Mozart, His Character, His Work*, p. 380.

Wye Jamison Allanbrook, a Mozart scholar of unusual insight and clarity, has pointed out how much Susanna's "Deh, vieni," how much in fact the entire fourth act of *Le Nozze di Figaro*, is related musically and thematically to the pastoral mode.[11] In a moonlit Rococo garden and a comedy of deception we hear the sweetest music of love and reconciliation, music for a bucolic idyll. Yet here too we are aware that all is play within a play, that the singers are play-acting within their act (Susanna disguised as the Countess and vice versa), that the pastoral music is part genuine dream, part conscious performance. Like Goethe in his "Veilchen," Mozart created here some rare and exquisite blossoms of a waning period style; and like Goethe's bucolic setting, the scene in *Figaro* is both enchanting and ironic. Indeed, the irony in Mozart's opera deepens when we consider that the Rococo pastorals are sung by the very two figures, Figaro and Susanna, who are already poised at the threshold of a new age, the age of individualism.

Storm and Stress

Storm and Stress is a short-lived phase of eighteenth-century culture, named after the play *Sturm und Drang* (1776) by Friedrich Maximilian Klinger. The movement manifested itself primarily in German literature during the late 1760s and early 1770s, but it was neither limited to Germany nor to literature.[12] Storm and Stress came upon the German literary scene not in the bombastic and violent strides its name might suggest, but in the wake of religious sentiment and a burgeoning individualism, and on the wings of a new poetic language derived from folksong and actual life experience.

Goethe was one of the first of the young German writers to shed the pretty but artificial garb of Rococo and unbridle his feelings as well as his poetic language. His Sesenheim songs, written when he was a law student in Strasbourg, swept aside the precious constructs of anacreontic verse with a new self-awareness and a jubilant sense of love and nature. The poems are largely inspired by Friederike Brion, the young girl he met in Sesenheim (near Strasbourg), but they are also celebrations of love for love's sake — "Und doch, welch Glück, geliebt zu werden!/ Und lieben Götter, welch ein Glück!" (HA I, 29) — "And yet, what happiness to be loved!/ And to love, Gods! what happiness!"

---

[11] Wye Jamison Allanbrook, *Rhythmic Gesture in Mozart*, pp. 173-185.

[12] Cf. Barry S. Brook, "Sturm und Drang and the Romantic Period in Music," *Studies in Romanticism*, 9 (1970), 273-284.

In music, too, a new expressivity emerged, one quite similar to the new literary "sensitivity" which ushered in the Storm and Stress movement. We can hear the first sounds of musical "Empfindsamkeit" in the keyboard music of Carl Philipp Emanuel Bach, in some of his fantasies, in the rondos and adagios of his "Sonaten für Kenner und Liebhaber." It is music charged with emotion, sweet and melodic, with abrupt changes in mood and diction, music that aims at speaking "emotively without using words."[13]

In Mozart's music the new style ranges from lyrical, dance-like structures to the subdued energy of Symphony 25, K. 183. The "Andante sostenuto" of Mozart's Sonata for Piano and Violin, K. 296 (partially printed on the next page), is an example of "empfindsamer Stil," but without abrupt shifts in tone and diction. The simple lyricism of its melody conveys the tenderest emotion and sounds as if one of Goethe's Sesenheim love poems had been rendered into music. The "Adagio" from Mozart's Violin Concerto No. 3, K. 216, conveys a similar personal expression. The muted violins, the plaintive voice of the solo instrument, the poignant, tentative melody, all these elements create a listening experience that moved Alfred Einstein to comment with unabashed emotion: "Suddenly there is new depth and richness to Mozart's language: instead of an Andante there is an Adagio that seems to have fallen from heaven."[14]

The new depth that Einstein speaks of, the heightened expressivity indicated by an "Adagio" instead of an "Andante," is a new directness and intensity of feeling, a communication of self in the form of musical sound. The lonely voice of the solo violin speaks with the warmth and sadness of a young lover. Only in Goethe's poetry of the early 1770s — to turn Viëtor's earlier statement around — can we find similar expressions of youthful emotions rendering both the joys and sorrows of a loving heart:

> Ein zärtlich-jugendlicher Kummer
> Führt mich ins öde Feld; es liegt
> In einem stillen Morgenschlummer
> Die Mutter Erde. Rauschend wiegt
> Ein kalter Wind die starren Äste
> (HA I, 32).

(A tender youthful grief/ sends me into barren nature;/ Mother Earth is slumbering still. The cold wind/ rustles through the bare trees...)

[13] Eugene Helm, "Carl Philipp Emanuel Bach" in *The New Grove: Bach Family*, ed. Christoph Wolff *et al.* (New York: W.W. Norton, 1983), p. 274. See also: Giorgio Pestelli, *The Age of Mozart and Beethoven*, p. 25.

[14] Alfred Einstein, *Mozart, His Character, His Work*, p. 280.

The melancholic lyricism of Mozart's "Adagio," written when the composer was nineteen, corresponds closely to the thoughts and sentiments of Werther, Goethe's youthful hero, who suffers all the trials and tribulations, all the contradictions of young love: ecstasy and violent depression, self-adulation and neurotic death-wish. *The Sufferings of Young Werther* (1774) not only presents a new, all-embracing individualism, but a new form of aestheticism as well. Art is no longer seen as a form of skill and craftsmanship; it is now extolled as "the whole of life,"[15] as a total, unified experience of the artist and his nature. It is this totality of being which is palpably present in Goethe's Storm and Stress works, in his poetry, his dramatic experiments (for example, in the early scenes of *Faust*), as well as in his early novel.

The sense of wholeness, a unity of sound and feeling, is present too in the enthusiastic, energetic expressions of Mozart's Divertimento in D

[15] Giorgio Pestelli, *The Age of Mozart and Beethoven*, p. 102.

Major, K. 136, in his jubilant Symphony No. 29, K. 201, whose last movement so resembles Goethe's " Mailied" in its spring-like exuberance, and in Symphony No. 25, K. 183, whose minor key tonalities belong to those stylistic elements that represent Storm and Stress music most directly. Here is how the musicologist Barry S. Brook defines this brief period in musical history:

> The characteristics of the Sturm und Drang in music which, taken together, differentiate it from other music of the decade, may be summed up as follows: stress on the minor mode, driving, syncopated rhythms, melodic motives built on wide leaps, harmonies full of tension, pointed dissonances, extended modulations, greater breadth of dynamics and accentuation, and a fascination with contrapuntal devices, canons, fugatos, etc.[16]

It was Joseph Haydn who, by general consensus, wrote the most extensive and significant Storm and Stress music, but we can find this mode of expression in Mozart as well. One of the composer's earliest and most conspicuous examples is the overture in D Minor of the oratorio *La Betulia Liberata*, K. 118. Brook's description of it is not only an interesting piece of musical analysis, but it can serve to define Storm and Stress in music:

> The overture is scored for oboes, bassoons, trumpets, four horns and strings, a powerful orchestra for Mozart in this period. The date is 1771, which makes it Mozart's first instrumental Sturm und Drang piece. All of the standard hallmarks are present: imitation (in the Andante and Presto), syncopation (in the Presto), driving climaxes (in the Allegro and Presto). The three movements, Allegro-Andante-Presto, are all in D minor and are connected to one another (by an augmented sixth and a dominant seventh chord) so that there are no pauses. The Allegro and Presto share the same opening motive. In the four minutes it takes to perform this piece one feels the impact of a young volcano.[17]

Goethe's most conspicuous Storm and Stress poetry, his wildest "syncopations" and metrical free forms, can be found in his early hymns, poems following the Sesenheim lyrics, as, for instance, "Prometheus," "An Schwager Kronos," and "Wandrers Sturmlied."

Wandrers Sturmlied

Wen du nicht verlässest, Genius,
Nicht der Regen, nicht der Sturm
Haucht ihm Schauer übers Herz.
Wen du nicht verlässest, Genius,

---

[16] Barry S. Brook, "Sturm und Drang and the Romantic Period in Music," p. 278.

[17] Brook, p. 281. *La Betulia Liberata*, Mozart's only oratorium, is available on the Musical Heritage Society label MHS Nos. 3086/87/88.

wird der Regenwolke,
Wird dem Schloßensturm
Entgegensingen
Wie die Lerche
Du dadroben (HA I, 33).

Wanderer's Storm-Song

Spirit, he whom you do not forsake,
Rain does not, nor tempest,
Breathe across his heart the horrors.
Spirit, he whom you do not forsake,
Will to the raincloud,
Will to the hailstorm
Sing out
Like the lark,
You lark aloft there.[18]

The poem combines traditional structures and motifs (some derived from Pindaric odes) with enthusiastic self-proclamations, mixing Greek myths with the wanderer motif, a distinct Goethean self-representation. But most important, in its slightly fragmented syntax the poem releases new poetic energies, an emotional impact which is very close to the driving "Presto," the modulations and structural leaps we can observe in the music of the adolescent Mozart. Goethe will harness this youthful poetic ecstasy (which he called "Halbunsinn" — "half-nonsense") and mold it into Classical diction after he arrives in Weimar. But the emotional power from which it springs will remain a source of continuing vitality giving his writing a unique depth and strength of feeling, even in his old age.

Mozart's Storm and Stress, the combination of individual expression and structural tension that characterizes that style, remained, as in Goethe's case, a permanent element of his art. We hear it in later pieces, in the passionate rhythms of his A Minor Piano Sonata, K. 310, in the tense minor modes of the *Don Giovanni* overture, in the late symphonies. And while Mozart is not known for his literary descriptions of period styles, it is he who, *nolens volens*, explains most succinctly the lyrical expressivity that characterizes the Storm and Stress mood and style.

> Let me now turn to Belmonte's aria in A major, 'O wie ängstlich, o wie feurig.' Would you like to know how I have expressed it — and even indicated his throbbing heart? By the two violins playing octaves ... You see the trembling — the faltering — you see how his throbbing breast begins to swell; this I have expressed by a *crescendo*. You hear the

---

[18] *Goethe. Selected Poems*, ed. Christopher Middleton, p. 17.

whispering and the sighing — which I have indicated by the first violins with mutes and a flute playing in unison (LM Sep. 26, 1781).

Nothing can convey the difference between Rococo and Storm and Stress more graphically than this statement and, of course, Mozart's actual music for Belmonte. In his earlier, elegantly melodious Rococo piece *Il Re Pastore* (*The Shepherd King*, K. 208),[19] Mozart's music for the male lead (the shepherd Aminta) was written for a castrato — and, indeed, the role was sung by the castrato Tommaso Consoli when the pastoral was first performed in Salzburg in 1775. In *Die Entführung*, written seven years later, the part of the Romantic lead (Belmonte) was not sung by a castrato but by a natural tenor with a musical accompaniment expressing the hero's innermost feelings, even the palpitations of his loving heart. The pretty harmonies and artificial voices of the Rococo had given way to a style that rendered the natural rhythms and voices of life.

Classicism

"The creation of a classical style," writes Charles Rosen, "was not so much the achievement of an ideal as the reconciliation of conflicting ideals — the striking of an optimum balance between them."[20] Dramatic forms as well as the rendering of sentiments, Rosen continues, had already found musical expression in the high Baroque (and, we might add, in the Storm and Stress), but what was still lacking was a certain elegance of style. "Not until Haydn and Mozart, separately and together, created a style in which a dramatic effect seemed at once surprising and logically motivated, in which the expressive and the elegant could join hands, did the classical style come into being."

In December 1782, Mozart wrote to his father about three of his piano concertos, K. 413, 414, and 415, works which had obvious audience appeal and gave pleasure to the composer as well:

> These concertos are a happy medium between what is too easy and too difficult; they are very brilliant, pleasing to the ear, and natural, without being vapid. There are passages here and there from which connoisseurs alone can derive satisfaction; but these passages are written in such a way that the less learned cannot fail to be pleased, though without knowing why. (LM Dec. 28, 1782).

Mozart was only partially referring to a balance between technical difficulties and beautiful sound. Later in the same letter he expressed

---

[19] *Il Re Pastore*, Arabesque Recordings 8050-2L.

[20] Charles Rosen, *The Classical Style*, p. 43 and 44.

himself on the subject of mediation and proportion in a more fundamental, philosophical way:

> The golden mean of truth in all things — "das mittelding — das wahre in allen sachen" — is no longer either known or appreciated. In order to win applause one must write stuff which is so inane that a coachman could sing it, or so unintelligible that it pleases precisely because no sensible person can understand it.

Mediation and reconciliation in expression, stylistic balance as a form of truth — this statement would have delighted the poet in Weimar had he known Mozart's letter. Mozart agrees here in essence with one of Goethe's most basic tenets, namely that all poetical works should aim at a "conciliating balance and resolution" — "diese aussöhnende Abrundung, welche eigentlich ... von allen poetischen Werken gefordert wird."[21] Indeed, three decades later, when he felt himself surrounded by what he considered an excessive and even pathological subjectivism by his Romantic colleagues, Goethe might have found Mozart's dictum of the "golden mean of truth" highly reassuring.

The Goethe scholar Stuart Atkins approaches a definition of Classicism from a literary, specifically Goethean, perspective. A true work of art, Atkins paraphrases Goethe, is dependent on both import and form (import defined here as content, meaning, feeling, "Gehalt"), and it is the "congruence of import and form" that "distinguishes Goethe's Classicism from earlier academic Classicism and from later art-for-art's-sake formalism."[22] Goethe did not think of himself consciously as a "Classical" writer, but he did distinguish his middle period of creativity (roughly from 1775 to 1810) from his preceding phase of Storm and Stress and from his later period. And he created his most manifest Classicism during the middle period, when he most effectively integrated form and content, reconciled intellectual and artistic conflicts, and experienced art as a process toward self-understanding rather than self-expression. Goethe's most significant works of the middle period — *Tasso, Iphigenie, Hermann und Dorothea, Römische Elegien, Die Wahlverwandtschaften* — are works characterized by precision in language and shaped by stylistic restraint, they are balanced, proportioned, limited, and designed to be conciliatory. A good example of this artistic style and process is Goethe's poem " An den Mond," a work originally conceived in his early Weimar years (1777), then reworked after his return from Italy (1789). I am quoting the later version:

---

[21] "Nachlese zu Aristoteles' Poetik," (HA XII, 343).

[22] Stuart Atkins, "On Goethe's Classicism," in *Goethe Proceedings*, eds. Clifford A. Bernd *et al.* (Camden House: Columbia, S.C., 1984), pp. 10-11, 15, 20.

An den Mond

Füllest wieder Busch und Tal
Still mit Nebelglanz,
Lösest endlich auch einmal
Meine Seele ganz;

Breitest über mein Gefild
Lindernd deinen Blick,
Wie des Freundes Auge mild
Über mein Geschick.

(Silently, once more, you fill the bushes and the valley/ with misty
radiance,/ and at last, too, you bring/ complete peace to my soul;//

Soothingly you spread your bright gaze/ over the fields around me,/ like
my beloved watching my destiny/ with gentle eyes.//)

It is a poem of completely regular design. The meter is trochaic with
four and three stresses alternating from line to line; the rhythm is smooth
and flowing, rounded off by an 'abab' rhyme scheme. Finely tuned
alliterations add word music to the even flow of the rhythmic cadences.
Yet underneath this tranquil surface lie the tense and volatile emotions of
a poetic *persona* wandering in the night:

Jeden Nachklang fühlt mein Herz
Froh- und trüber Zeit,
Wandle zwischen Freud' und Schmerz
In der Einsamkeit.

Fließe, fließe, lieber Fluß!
Nimmer werd' ich froh,
So verrauschte Scherz und Kuß,
Und die Treue so.

Ich besaß es doch einmal,
Was so köstlich ist!
Daß man doch zu seiner Qual
Nimmer es vergißt!

(All the gladness and sorrows of the past/ re-echo in my heart,/ and I
walk between joy and pain,/ in solitude.//

Run on, run on, dear river!/ Gladness will never come back to me!/ This
was how they streamed away-/ laughter, and kisses, and fidelity.//

Yet once I possessed/ what is so precious!/ Ah, the torment/ of never
being able to forget it!//)

The wanderer stops at a river, gazing at the waters, but the flow of the stream immediately evokes memories of the past, of love and happier days, memories which rise with the swiftness of the current and turn quickly to agonized reflection. The calm, moonlit landscape is transformed into a scene of distress and potential destruction, and the word music of the poem changes from a sweet and flowing melody — "Fließe, fließe, lieber Fluß" — to the sounds of surging flood waters threatening the budding flowers, the harbingers of spring:

> Rausche, Fluß, das Tal entlang,
> Ohne Rast und Ruh,
> Rausche, flüstre meinem Sang
> Melodien zu,
>
> Wenn du in der Winternacht
> Wütend überschwillst,
> Oder um die Frühlingspracht
> Junger Knospen quillst.

(Rush, oh river, down the valley,/ ceaselessly, restlessly;/ murmur and whisper melodies/ for my song,//
When on winter nights/ you rage and overflow,/ or when you surge round the spring splendour/ of young buds./)

As we observe the landscape transform itself, changing a scene of peace and quiet to winter threat and icy waters, we are actually witnessing the poetic process at work. We observe the power of imagination re-creating images through a release of suppressed emotions. But before memory and fantasy rage out of control, the poet steps back abruptly and restores peace and quiet — in the landscape as well as in the soul of the poetic *persona*:

> Selig, wer sich vor der Welt
> Ohne Haß verschließt,
> Einen Freund am Busen hält
> und mit dem genießt,
>
> Was, von Menschen nicht gewußt,
> Oder nicht bedacht,
> Durch das Labyrinth der Brust
> Wandelt in der Nacht (HA I, 129-130).

(Happy are we if without resentment/ we withdraw from the world/ and hold a friend to our breast/ and with him enjoy//

that which, unknown or ignored/ by mankind,/ wanders through the heart's labyrinth/ in darkness./)[23]

The poem ends with an image that points back to its beginning — "Wandelt in der Nacht" — indicating perhaps that the interplay between memory, passion, and form, the poetic process, will soon repeat itself, creating yet another cycle of memories, more agony, more poetry.

Controlled artistic language, controlled diction and structure, control of emotions, were elements as important to Mozart as they were to Goethe. Indeed, they are intrinsic to Mozart's art, and it is from this vantage point that Leonard Bernstein described and defined Mozart's Symphony No. 40, K. 550, as a "work of utmost passion utterly controlled."[24] Mozart achieved an ultimate balance of expression in this symphony, says the musician, by an ingenious interplay between chromaticism (which Bernstein interprets as a signifier of passion in music) and diatonicism (harmonic structures). Bernstein illustrates his thesis with the following simplified scores of the first measures of Mozart's G Minor symphony. (See following page.)

Figure 1 depicts the opening theme in the first movement, figures 2 and 3 show the initial measures of the second theme, indicating a melodic line descending by half-steps. Both themes contain chromatic figures (in the right hand) which are harmonically contained and controlled by the at times inverted tonic-dominant structures (in the left hand). The musical effect of this interplay of chromatic and diatonic structures, the "diatonic containment of chromaticism," as Bernstein calls it, is at once orderly and emotional, pleasing to the ear, yet charged with disharmonic nuances creating drama and tension, ultimately conveying that sense of conciliatory resolution, "diese aussöhnende Abrundung," that Goethe required of all great art.

Both artists' Classical effects are, of course, more complex than the analysis of one poem or the simplified illustrations of a few measures of music can indicate. Goethe's outward simplicity of form and poetic beauty rest on complicated aesthetic processes, involving congruence of image, sound, rhythm, the correspondence of psychic motion and outward restraint (as, for instance, in *Iphigenie*). Mozart's Classical sound and structure (which begins with *Die Entführung aus dem Serail*) derive from many more stylistic devices than are mentioned here, for instance, deletions and accentuations, inversions and transpositions, figures of counterpoint and conjoinings, etc. Together these elements of style create Mozart's characteristic Classical tone. But for all the internal, technical,

[23] This prose translation is for the most part from David Luke, *Goethe*, pp. 52-53.

[24] Leonard Bernstein, *The Unanswered Question*, pp. 39-49.

Figure 1

Figure 2

Figure 3

and emotional complexities, both artists succeeded in giving their creations in this, their most extended period of style, a face of unusual clarity as well as a sense of proportion and completeness, creating living art that is well defined, objective, and elegant.

Late Styles

The historic high point of Goethe's and Mozart's Classicism is the year 1787, when *Iphigenie* appeared and *Don Giovanni* was first performed in Prague. It is also the year in which Friedrich Schiller published the verse version of his drama *Don Carlos* and Immanuel Kant's second critique,

Kritik der praktischen Vernunft, went into print. 1787 is a kind of *annus mirabilis* of German-Austrian intellectual and cultural history.

But neither Goethe nor Mozart remained strict Classicists to the end of their lives. While they never completely abandoned their Classical stance, they did engage in their later years in a variety of styles and formal experiments, reaching back at times to the counterpoint and dramatic structures of the Baroque, at other times incorporating elements of Romanticism and Mysticism in their works, and finally developing a style of their own, a kind of *Altersstil* characterized by utter simplicity and concentration of form.

Much of Goethe's writing during his late period (after 1810) tends to be symbolic, allegorical, mystical, and often experimental. Some of his works, such as *Wilhelm Meisters Wanderjahre* (1829) and *Faust, Part Two* (1832), incorporate a wealth of disparate forms, figures, and attitudes in one single opus. Other writings are stylistically uniform and cogent within themselves, but very different from each other in expression and purpose. In his *West-östlicher Divan* (1814/19), for example, Goethe adopted the poetic refinements of a distant culture (medieval Persia) with great empathy and lyrical sensitivity, whereas in *Des Epimenides Erwachen* (1815) he re-created a German Baroque opera text as a *Festspiel* in honor of King Frederic William III of Prussia with little inspiration and little success. But for all the profusion of styles in Goethe's later years, two fundamental tenets of his art and creativity continued unchanged and undiminished: exceptional lyrical power and an attitude of conciliation.

When Duke Carl August of Weimar, Goethe's friend and patron for more than fifty years, died in June of 1828, the poet excused himself from the funeral and fled, as was his wont, to the castle of Dornburg (on the Saale river), his favorite refuge in times of grief and crises. "The view is marvelous and cheerful," he wrote to Zelter shortly after his arrival. "The flowers are in bloom in the well-tended garden; grapes are abundant on the espalier and below my window I see a vineyard which was planted by the Duke just three years ago on a barren slope" (GZB III, 47-48). Goethe had brought his *Faust* manuscript, botanical studies, and his usual wide range of reading: Plautus, Dante, Shakespeare, Byron; histories of Israel and of the discovery of America. He then focused on some meteorological studies, and turned once again to his favorite occupation: writing poetry.

The poems Goethe wrote during this visit to Dornburg castle (his last) are not his final poetic writings, but they are part of his final creative effort to transcribe in words and images his inner thoughts, visions, and emotions. What strikes the reader in these late verses are the poet's almost youthful sentiments, his undiminished verbal power and concentration, a concreteness of description which borders on the mystical: "Früh, wenn Tal, Gebirg und Garten/ Nebelschleiern sich enthüllen/ ..." — "To veils of mist in morning light/ Disclosed are garden, valley, hill ...."[25] In "Dem aufgehenden Vollmonde" we feel ourselves transported back to the poet's days at Sesenheim, for as in times past, he speaks of love, both the need to love and the need to be loved, and as in times past, he confides his private thoughts and sentiments to the moon, his confidante in many a nightly dialogue:

Dem aufgehenden Vollmonde

Dornburg, den 25. August 1828

Willst du mich sogleich verlassen?
Warst im Augenblick so nah!
Dich umfinstern Wolkenmassen,
Und nun bist du gar nicht da.

Doch du fühlst, wie ich betrübt bin,
Blickt dein Rand herauf als Stern!
Zeugest mir, daß ich geliebt bin,
Sei das Liebchen noch so fern.

So hinan denn! hell und heller,
Reiner Bahn, in voller Pracht!
Schlägt mein Herz auch schmerzlich
      schneller,
Überselig ist die Nacht (HA I, 391).

To the Rising Full Moon
(Will you leave me already?/ You were so near to me a moment ago!/ Cloud-masses overshadow you/ and now you are gone.//
And yet you feel how sad I am,/ your gleaming edge peeps over like a star!/ You bear me witness that I am loved,/ however far away my darling may be.//
Move onward then, radiant and ever more radiant,/ on your pure course, in your full splendour!/ Though my heart beats faster and hurts,/ there are no words for the blessedness of this night.)[26]

It is difficult to think of these verses as the product of a near-octogenarian (Goethe turned seventy-nine in August 1828). They combine the emotional power and dynamics of a young lover with the resoluteness of the aged philosopher — "So hinan denn! hell und heller..." — "Onward then! [be] more and more radiant...". The poem

---

[25] *Goethe. Selected Poems*, ed. Chr. Middleton, p. 263.

[26] David Luke, *Goethe*, p. 332.

concludes with one of the most stunning lines in all of Goethe's works, an image combining thought and feeling in a rapturous embrace of the night, of life, of self, of death — "Überselig ist die Nacht" — "More than blessed is the night."

The "Dornburger Gedichte" are part of Goethe's poetic summation of life, an affirmative recognition of life in the face of increasing age, declining health, and the loss of friends. "Wie es auch sei, das Leben, es ist gut" — "However it may be, life is blessed," concludes another of these poems ("Der Bräutigam") even more pointedly. After a long and rich life, one he often condemned for its burdens and agonies, Goethe found the strength and objectivity to write these simple words of affirmation, not once, but twice, for they also appear in the "Song of Lynceus," (written about 1828), a poetic high point of *Faust, Part Two*:

Tiefe Nacht

Lynkeus der Türmer auf der Schloßwarte,
   singend

Zum Sehen geboren,
Zum Schauen bestellt,
Dem Turme geschworen,
Gefällt mir die Welt.
Ich blick' in die Ferne,
Ich seh' in der Näh'
Den Mond und die Sterne,
Den Wald und das Reh.
So seh' ich in allen
Die ewige Zier,
Und wie mir's gefallen,
Gefall' ich auch mir.
Ihr glücklichen Augen,
Was je ihr gesehn,
Es sei wie es wolle,
Es war doch so schön! (HA III, 340)

Deep Night

Lynceus, the keeper on the watch tower of the
   palace, singing.

To seeing born,
To scanning called,
To the watchtower sworn,
I relish the world.
Sighting the far,
Espying the near,
Moon-disc and star,

Forest and deer.
In all I behold
Ever-comely design,
As its virtues unfold
I take pleasure in mine.
You fortunate eyes,
All you ever did see,
Whatever its guise,
Was so lovely to me! (*Faust*, 286f.)

We must keep in mind, however, that these beautiful, affirmative words are spoken while a scene of destruction, the fiery death of three innocent people, is in the making. Goethe's poetic testament is not unambiguous. Still, against all destruction and despair, against all Faustian irony and guilt, the poet erected a counter-structure: a song in praise of life and the grand design. It is a song simple, concrete, and essential, a poem of such transparency that it allows us to see the deeper, idealizing visions of the poet at the end of his life.

Mozart's late styles are as varied as Goethe's, even though the composer's last phase was considerably shorter than the poet's — three years instead of twenty. Still, between 1789 and the end of 1791, the composer created an astonishing array of musical genres and expressions, works as disparate as a German *Ländler* and a requiem mass, or a Masonic choral piece and the ditty "Caro mio, Schluck und Druck." But within this profusion of themes and styles, and quite analogous to Goethe, a distinctive Mozartian late style emerges, a musical expression of formal simplicity and emotional tranquility.

Much has been written in this connection about Mozart's Piano Concerto in B-flat Major, K. 595, his last piano concerto, one for which the composer barely found an audience. Musicologists describe it as autumnal and valedictory, as a melancholic private statement, a work of Franciscan mildness. Alfred Einstein speaks of the composer's attainment of a "second naiveté" in this piece, relating it in its meaning to Goethe's famous dictum from *Tasso*: "Und wenn der Mensch in seiner Qual verstummt/ Gab mir ein Gott, zu sagen, wie ich leide" (HA V, 166).
——"And when all fall silent in their human agony,/ a God gave me the ability to tell my suffering." Einstein wrote: "But the most moving thing about it [the B-flat Major Concerto] is that in it Mozart received the divine gift of being able *Zu sagen was er leide* (to tell the fullness of his suffering)."[27]

---

[27] Alfred Einstein, *Mozart, His Character, His Life*, p. 315.

Mozart's last piano concerto stands out among his final creations as a personal work, one of quiet resignation but not of pessimism. In spite of the unbearable conditions of his final years, this work reaches beyond expressions of despair (still present in the G Minor Quintet) and transcends all irony and existential doubt (still present in *Cosi fan tutte*). The concerto seems open and accessible, yet it is unfathomable in its mystery and transparent beauty. It is not the composer's last artistic statement, but it is part of his final communication as an artist and as an individual. It is a work both positive and somber, cheerful in its third ("Allegro") movement, but it contains even there, as Eric Blom says, "that mysterious Mozartian strain of sadness."[28]

Goethe was eighty years old when he wrote the "Dornburger Gedichte," a poetic summing up tinted by the consciousness of his ripe age. Mozart was all of thiry-five when he composed the B-flat Major concerto, far too early for a summing up, but life had worn down his fragile body, and the composer knew it. The "Requiem," and even more the story surrounding it, are indications that Mozart knew his time had come. His last piano concerto expresses that knowledge, the poignancy of it, and the relief.

[28] Eric Blom, *Mozart* (London: J.M. Dent & Sons, 1974), p. 230.

10

Reconciliations

HUGO VON HOFMANNSTHAL, THE GREAT AUSTRIAN POET, wrote in his fictional *Letter from Lord Chandos to Francis Bacon* that the modern times, Hofmannsthal's own times, were no longer conducive to creating what the Classical writers, formalists like Seneca and Cicero, had been able to create: a "harmony of limited and ordered concepts" — "Harmonie begrenzter und geordneter Begriffe."[1] Had Hofmannsthal written from his own perspective rather than from a sixteenth-century point of view, he might well have turned to Goethe and Mozart as two artists who could serve as models for his dictum. For Goethe and Mozart espoused an aesthetic universe that was limited, proportionate, and ordered. In *Iphigenie, Hermann und Dorothea, Faust,* in *Don Giovanni, Cosi fan tutte, Die Zauberflöte,* both artists exhibit a full scale of human emotions and a dazzling range of artistic forms, yet the most common and enduring characteristic of their creativity is a unified style, a balanced structure, harmony through form.

The heart of Mozart's music consists of melody, clear syntax, and the rhythmic patterns of the dance.[2] It is music that affects us as harmonious because it is conciliatory in its structure, and it affects us as humane because it is vibrant with the motion of dance which gives it gracefulness

---

[1] Hugo von Hofmannsthal, "Ein Brief," *Ausgewählte Werke,* ed. Rudolf Hirsch (Frankfurt: S. Fischer, 1957) II, 343.

[2] Wye Jamison Allanbrook, *Rhythmic Gesture in Mozart,* especially emphasizes the importance of dance rhythms in Mozart's music.

and human relatedness. Mozart was a mediator *par excellence*. He mediated within his own craft — "between what is too easy and too difficult" (LM Dec. 28, 1782) — between Bach and Beethoven, between the musical languages of Italy and Germany. He was well familiar with human suffering, but he transcended personal misery and frailty in the "golden solemnity" of his B-flat Major Piano Concerto, in the A Major Clarinet Concerto, in *Die Zauberflöte*. Indeed, some of the tenderest music in his stage works is given to moments of forgiveness and reconciliation. *Le Nozze di Figaro* contains one such glorious moment at the end of the opera:

Count Almaviva is on his knees before Countess Rosina, begging forgiveness for his amorous transgressions. A traditional conclusion of an *opera buffa*? Perhaps as far as Beaumarchais' original play is concerned, perhaps even in Da Ponte's libretto; but not in Mozart's music. In this scene it is not the playwright or the librettist who tells the story, but the composer. And Mozart changes suddenly, within a few measures, from a giddy masquerade in a moonlit Rococo garden to a moment of serious contemplation, a moment of genuine affection between the Countess and the Count. In the midst of the non-committal merriment of *opera buffa* Mozart overwhelms us with a hymn-like plea, almost a prayer, by the Count, "Contessa, perdono," whose hushed resonance not only moves the Countess to grace and forgiveness, but affects our own deepest emotions.

Like Shakespeare, with whose dramatic art Mozart's music has often been compared, Mozart presents in his major works the total scale of human feelings, and like Shakespeare in his plays, Mozart moves freely and swiftly from one part of the human scale to another, from laughter to tears and back again to laughter. In *Le Nozze di Figaro* the slenderest musical motif transforms comedy into serious drama, expanding the scale just enough to accomodate an act of love and forgivenesss. Then the rule of comedy reasserts itself and the play hastens to a merry end. Joseph Kerman, in a brilliant discussion of this scene, makes the following assessment:

> Cruelty and shame have their place in Mozart's picture of human fallibility; particularly in this context, his drama reveals a view of life that is realistic, unsentimental, optimistic, and humane. Probably no one has left a performance of *Figaro* without reflecting that the Count will soon be philandering again. But just as surely there will be another reconciliation, another renewal as genuine on both sides, as contrite and as beautiful.[3]

In *Le Nozze di Figaro* and elsewhere Mozart's artistic attitude is directed toward reconciliation, toward artistic equilibrium and what he himself called "das mittel-ding, das wahre in allen sachen." (LM Dec. 28,

---

[3] Joseph Kerman, *Opera as Drama*, pp. 107-08.

1782). "He observes moderation," mused Karl Barth, theologian and Mozart lover, "Mozart makes music, knowing everything from a mysterious center, and thus he knows and keeps the boundaries on the right and on the left, upward and downward."[4] And Alfred Einstein, on whose musicological insights I have drawn so often, has something of note to say in this context as well: "Mozart seems never to want to exceed the bounds of convention. He wanted to *fulfil* the laws, not violate them."[5]

Goethe was one of the first to fully comprehend these elements in Mozart's art. The poet heard more than harmonious sound when listening to Mozart. He perceived a fully integrated art form, an essentially non-violent and non-tragic view of life. It is a disposition that Goethe himself aspired to. Late in his life he wrote to Zelter:

> As far as tragedy is concerned I regard it as a ticklish point. I myself am not a writer of tragedies because my nature is conciliatory — "da meine Natur konziliant ist." — I am therefore not really interested in the purely tragic situation which must be in essence irreconcilable. And I find in this rather flat world the irreconcilable as a total absurdity (GZB III, 502).

We know that Goethe concealed within himself a powerful potential for nihilism and tragedy. *Werther* is proof of that potential, and so are *Die Wahlverwandtschaften* and *Faust*. But all his life the poet battled to overcome his destructive inclinations, and he succeeded. He emerged as the poet of transformation, not of conflict; his growth was toward wholeness, not disintegration. He resolutely refused to recognize evil, "das Böse," as an archetypal phenomenon of the human condition,[6] and in *Faust* he turned the principle of negation into a constructive force to accomplish good. Karl Jaspers found Goethe's sense of reconciliation so strong and pervasive that, deeply shaken by the horrors of the Hitler regime, he even questioned its validity in times of moral darkness:

> There is an antagonism against what we might call Goethe's fundamental concept of reconciliation — "die *harmonische Grundauffassung* Goethes" — his pagan affirmation of life. The accusation against the suffering of the world, against the domination of evil, requires the scream of horror and can no longer tolerate a loving consensus with the world. We have gone

---

[4] Karl Barth, "My Faith in Mozart," in *Religion and Culture: Essays in Honor of Paul Tillich*, ed. Walter Leibrecht (New York: Harper and Bros., 1959), p. 76.

[5] Alfred Einstein, *Greatness in Music*, p. 153.

[6] See Eudo C. Mason, "Goethe's Sense of Evil," *Publications of the English Goethe Society*, N.S. 34 (1964), p. 6.

through times where we could no longer read Goethe, but reached for Shakespeare, the Bible, Aeschylos, if we could read at all.[7]

But two years later, Jaspers revised his judgment of Goethe's conciliatory stance. In a speech entitled "Goethe's Humanity," the philosopher reconsidered. The poet, he said, was not unfamiliar with the sick, the horrid, and the tragic, but he did not allow those elements to have control over him. He held on to his conciliatory humanism *because* he knew of the existence of evil: "It seems that because he harbored within himself everything a human being can be, Goethe could put it into language. It is as if he knew everything." — "Weil — so scheint es — alles, was ein Mensch sein kann, als Möglichkeit in ihm lag, konnte Goethe ihm Sprache verleihen. Es ist, als ob er alles wisse."[8]

Mediation and reconciliation: they are the basis and common ground of Goethe's and Mozart's Classical language, and they are the nourishing ground for their fundamental humanism. Their language and humanism, their forms of reconciliation, radiate with undiminished strength into our own unharmonious, technological age. We may hear Goethe's and Mozart's voices separately, we may hear one and not the other, but in principle they speak as one, for they are brothers in art and spirit, the two great harmonizers and conciliators. Goethe had an inkling of such an affinity with Mozart and he, the famous poet laureate, bowed before the younger artist and revered him as a higher being, a "miracle that cannot be explained" — "ein Wunder, das weiter nicht zu erklären ist."

[7] Karl Jaspers, *Unsere Zukunft und Goethe* (Zurich: Artemis Verlag, 1948), pp. 21-22. Jaspers gave this speech in 1947 in Frankfurt on the occasion of his being awarded the Goethe Prize.

[8] Karl Jaspers, "Goethes Menschlichkeit," *Basler Universitätsreden* (Basel: Helbing und Lichtenhahn, 1949), Heft 26, p. 28.

Appendix

The following text of Goethe's *Der Zauberflöte zweiter Teil* is a reprint from the *Goethe Gedenkausgabe der Werke, Briefe und Gespräche*, ed. Ernst Beutler (Zurich: Artemis Verlag, 1954) VI, 1091-1118. The English translation is by the Mozart scholar Eric Blom. It appeared in *Music and Letters*, vol 23 (1942) with the following annotation which I quote in full:

> Readers of Mozart's biographies are aware of the fact that Goethe, a great admirer of that master though scarcely more musical than poets usually are, was moved to attempt a sequel to 'The Magic Flute'. Few, however, have read the piece, which is not very easily accessible, and in England is almost totally unknown: hence this attempt at a translation. That the sequel remained unfinished was perhaps due to the fact that Mozart was dead and Goethe, who once declared that no other composer could have adequately dealt with his 'Faust', could not really believe that it would ever be set to music. Possibly, too, he realized that his sketch was not likely to turn into a masterpiece, though it was easy for him to outdo Schikaneder. The reader who, quite rightly, thinks my verse undistinguished may be assured that it is frequently so in the original, to which I am faithful at least to that extent. I am almost wholly so, too, to Goethe's varied metres, which here, as in 'Faust', not only make an admirably flexible word-music, but were well calculated to give a musician endless rhythmic opportunities. My only liberties have been an occasional substitution of monosyllabic for disyllabic rhymes, a displacement or omission of rhymes here and there, and now and again an interchange of the sense of some lines merely for grammatical reasons. The symbolism of the libretto, if any, I have not attempted to elucidate – or indeed even to understand. We have no means of knowing whether it would have become clearer if Goethe had completed the piece; we do not even know whether the present ending was intended to be conclusive or whether something more was meant to come after. It certainly would not make a good operatic close as it stands, and it will be noticed that elsewhere good care is taken to provide concerted numbers admirably planned for musical treatment. On the whole it seems likely that a grand concerted finale, if not more, was still to come.

Der Zauberflöte zweiter Teil: Fragment

Tag, Wald, Felsengrotte, zu einem ernsthaften Portal zugehauen.
Aus dem Walde kommen Monostatos, Mohren

MONOSTATOS.

> Erhebet und preiset,
> Gefährten, unser Glück!
> Wir kommen im Triumphe
> Zur Göttin zurück.

CHOR.

> Es ist uns gelungen,
> Es half uns das Glück!
> Wir kommen im Triumphe
> Zur Göttin zurück.

MONOSTATOS.

> Wir wirkten verstohlen,
> Wir schlichen hinan;
> Doch, was sie uns befohlen,
> Halb ist es getan.

CHOR.

> Wir wirkten verstohlen,
> Wir schlichen hinan;
> Doch, was sie uns befohlen,
> Bald ist es getan.

MONOSTATOS.

> O Göttin! die du in den Grüften
> Verschlossen mit dir selber wohnest,
> Bald in den höchsten Himmelslüften,
> Zum Trutz der stolzen Lichter, thronest,
> O höre deinen Freund! höre deinen künftigen Gatten!
> Was hindert dich, allgegenwärtige Macht,
> Was hält dich ab, o Königin der Nacht,
> In diesem Augenblick uns hier zu überschatten!

The Magic Flute, Part II

By Johann Wolfgang von Goethe
Translated by Eric Blom

Daylight. A forest with a rocky cave hewn into a severe portal.
Enter, from the depth of the forest, Monostatos and Blackamoors.

Mon.	Exult ye and praise ye! Her gratitude we earn; In triumph we, and hope, to Our goddess return.
Chorus.	We set out, succeeding, Good fortune to learn; In triumph we, and hope, to Our goddess return.
Mon.	We lurked and we hid us, Detection to shun; And that which she did bid us, Is partially done.
Chorus.	We lurked and we hid us, Detection to shun; And that which she did bid us, Ere long will be done.
Mon.	O goddess! thou, who in these hollows Secluded and remotely living, Shalt rise where never mortal follows, Defying light, thine own light giving; O hear thy trusty friend, hear thy predestined lover! What holds thee, in thy ever-present might, What hinders thee, O dreaded Queen of Night, Thy shadowy majesty to us to uncover?

Donnerschlag. Monostatos und die Mohren stürzen zu Boden. Finsternis. Aus dem Portal entwickeln sich Wolken und verschlingen es zuletzt
DIE KÖNIGIN *in den Wolken.*

> Wer ruft mich an?
> Wer wagt's, mit mir zu sprechen?
> Wer, diese Stille kühn zu unterbrechen?
> Ich höre nichts – so bin ich denn allein!
> Die Welt verstummt um mich – so soll es sein.

Die Wolken dehnen sich über das Theater aus und ziehen über Monostatos und die Mohren hin, die man jedoch noch sehen kann

> Woget, ihr Wolken, hin,
> Decket die Erde,
> Daß es noch düsterer,
> Finsterer werde!
> Schrecken und Schauer,
> Klagen und Trauer
> Leise verhalle, bang
> Ende den Nachtgesang
> Schweigen und Tod.

MONOSTATOS und CHOR *in voriger Stellung, ganz leise*

> Vor deinem Throne hier
> Liegen und dienen–

KÖNIGIN.

> Seid ihr Getreuen mir
> Wieder erschienen?

MONOSTATOS.

> Ja, dein Getreuer,
> Geliebter, er ist's.

KÖNIGIN.

> Bin ich gerochen?

CHOR.

> Göttin, du bist's!

KÖNIGIN.

> Schlängelt, ihr Blitze,
> Mit wütendem Eilen,
> Rastlos, die lastenden
> Nächte zu teilen!
> Strömet, Kometen,
> Am Himmel hernieder!

Thunderclap. Monostatos and the Blackamoors throw themselves upon the ground. Darkness. The portal emits clouds, which end by enveloping it.

Queen of Night (*in the clouds*).

      Who is it calls?
      Who ventures to invoke me?
      Who is't my solitude thus boldly broke me?
      No answer there! Then still I am alone.
      The world is silent; thus I hold mine own!

The clouds spread over the scene and pass over Monostatos and the Blackamoors, who however still remain visible.

      Vapours, envelop the
      Earth with your cover;
      Let it be drearier and
      Darker than ever!
      Shuddering, ailing,
      Sorrow and wailing,
      Distantly, softly, long,
      End ye the night's dread song:
      Silence and death!

Mon. & Cho. (*in the same attitude, very softly*).

      Prostrate before thy throne,
      Fain to attend thee...

Que.   Are ye returned again,
      Succour to lend me?

Mon.   See, thy beloved,
      Thy servant, 'tis he.

Que.   Am I avenged?

Chor.   Yea, thou shalt be!

Que.   Flash, then, O lightning,
      Effulgent, unceasing,
      Night's laden silence
      Disturbing and teasing!
      Planets and comets,
      Descend from the heaven!

Wandelnde Flammen,
Begegnet euch wieder,
Leuchtet der hohen
Befriedigten Wut!

MONOSTATOS und CHOR.

Siehe! Kometen,
Sie steigen hernieder,
Wandelnde Flammen
Begegnen sich wieder,
Und von den Polen
Erhebt sich die Glut.

Indem ein Nordlicht sich aus der Mitte verbreitet, steht die Königin wie in einer Glorie. In den Wolken kreuzen sich Kometen, Elmsfeuer und Lichtballen. Das Ganze muß durch Form und Farbe und geheime Symmetrie einen zwar grausenhaften, doch angenehmen Effekt machen

MONOSTATOS.

In solcher feierlicher Pracht
Wirst du nun bald der ganzen Welt erscheinen;
Ins Reich der Sonne wirket deine Macht.
Pamina und Tamino weinen;
Ihr höchstes Glück ruht in des Grabes Nacht.

KÖNIGIN.

Ihr neugeborner Sohn, ist er in meinen Händen?

MONOSTATOS.

Noch nicht; doch werden wir's vollenden,
Ich les es in der Sterne wilder Schlacht.

KÖNIGIN.

Noch nicht in meiner Hand? was habt ihr denn getan?

MONOSTATOS.

O Göttin, sieh uns gnädig an!
In Jammer haben wir das Königshaus verlassen.
Nun kannst du sie mit Freude hassen.
Vernimm! – Der schönste Tag bestieg schon seinen Thron,
Die süße Hoffnung nahte schon,
Versprach, der Gattentreue Lohn,
Den langerflehten, ersten Sohn.
Die Mädchen wanden schon die blumenreichsten Kränze,
Sie freuten sich auf Opferzug und Tänze,

Flames, reuniting,
By counter-flames riven,
Shine on the noble,
The satisfied rage!

Mon. & Cho.   See how the comets
And planets from heaven
mingle with flames that,
By other flames riven,
Rise to the firmament,
Stage upon stage!

An aurora borealis, spreading from the centre, surrounds the Queen like an aureole. Comets, St. Elmo's fires and fiery orbs cross among the clouds. The whole, by means of form, colour and mysterious symmetry, should make a dreadful, yet agreeable impression.

Mon.   Amid a like resplendent sight
Ere long shalt thou before the world be borne;
The suns's own realm shall yield unto thy might.
              Pamina and Tamino mourn;
Their dearest hope descends into the night.

Que.   Their new-born son, is he then in my hand?

Mon.   Not yet, but soon our quest will end.
I read it in this starry, cosmic fight.

Que.   He is not in my grasp? What, varlet, then is done?

Mon.   O goddess, look in mercy on!
The royal house, of joy hath hideous grief bereft it,
With pleasure mix thy hatred, since we left it.
'Twas thus: the fairest day, the day of days came nigh,
The sweetest promises ran high,
Fulfilment of a hope long stored,
A son for wedded love's reward.
The maidens early wound their flower-laden chains,
They looked for song and dance to pay their pains,

Und neue Kleider freuten sie noch mehr.
Indes die Fraun mit klugem Eifer wachten,
Und mütterlich die Königin bedachten–
Unsichtbar schlichen wir durch den Palast umher–
Da rief's: ein Sohn! ein Sohn! Wir öffnen ungesäunmt
Den goldnen Sarg, den du uns übergeben:
Die Finsternis entströmt, umhüllet alles Leben,
Ein jeder tappt und schwankt und träumt.
Die Mutter hat des Anblicks nicht genossen,
Der Vater sah noch nicht das holde Kind,
Mit Feuerhand ergreif ich es geschwind,
In jenen goldnen Sarg wird es sogleich verschlossen–
Und immer finstrer wird die Nacht,
In der wir ganz allein mit Tigeraugen sehen;
Doch ach! da muß, ich weiß nicht welche Macht
Mit strenger Kraft uns widerstehen.
Der goldne Sarg wird schwer–

CHOR.   Wird schwerer uns in Händen.

MONOSTATOS.   Wird schwerer, immer mehr und mehr!
Wir können nicht das Werk vollenden.

CHOR.   Er zieht uns an den Boden hin.

MONOSTATOS.   Dort bleibt er fest und läßt sich nicht bewegen.
Gewiß! es wirkt Sarastros Zaubersegen.

CHOR.   Wir fürchten selbst den Bann und fliehn.

KÖNIGIN.   Ihr Feigen, das sind eure Taten?
Mein Zorn–

CHOR.   Halt ein den Zorn, o Königin!

MONOSTATOS.   Mit unverwandtem, klugem Sinn
Drück ich dein Siegel schnell, das niemand lösen kann,
Aufs goldne Grab und sperre so den Knaben
Auf ewig ein.
So mögen sie den starren Liebling haben!
Da mag er ihre Sorge sein!
Dort steht die tote Last, der Tag erscheinet bange,
Wir ziehen fort mit drohendem Gesange.

New dresses they with still more joy expected.
But while the women tended well their queen,
With motherly care, her ev'ry need foreseen,
We through the palace crept in darkness, undetected.
"A son," a glad voice called. Thus opened we at once
The golden coffin thou didst give,
Whence darkness, streaming forth, enveloped all that live,
Who staggered, fell into a trance;
Before the mother feasted yet her eyes,
Before the father knew as yet his heir,
Like lightning did my fingers seize him there
And locked him in the coffin in a trice.
Then dense obscurity began to lour,
In which alone our feline eyes can see;
Yet, woe is me! I know not by what pow'r
That all at once resisted me,
The gold sarcophagus, like lead ...

Cho.	Like lead it hung upon us.
Mon.	We could not do our task, instead
	It ever heavier grew upon us.
Cho.	It dragged us down upon the ground.
Mon.	And there it stood, no effort, none advanced it.
	Be sure Sarastro's wizardry entranced it.
Cho.	With dread the sorcery filled us, and we fled.
Que.	Ye cravens! Thus your task you did?
	Revenge ...
Cho.	Denounce us not, O queen!
Mon.	Desist, for soon I remedied

The ill. Thy seal, as strong as ever it hath been,
I quickly set upon the tomb, entrapping
The child for aye.
So may they have him: there is no unwrapping
Of that stark form for ever and a day.
There rests the rigid corse; then broke the evil day,
And we with threat'ning song went on our way.

CHOR.   Sähe die Mutter je,
                                Säh sie den Sohn,
                                Risse die Parze gleich
                                Schnell ihn davon.
                                Sähe der Vater je,
                                Säh er den Sohn,
                                Risse die Parze gleich
                                Schnell ihn davon.

MONOSTATOS.   Zwar weiß ich, als wir uns entfernt,
                   Ist federleicht der Sarkophag geworden.
                   Sie bringen ihn dem brüderlichen Orden,
                   Der, still in sich gekehrt, die Weisheit lehrt und lernt.
                   Nun muß mit List und Kraft dein Knecht aufs neue wirken!
                   Selbst in den heiligen Bezirken
                   Hat noch dein Haß, dein Fluch hat seine Kraft.
                   Wird sie der Anblick ihres Kinds entzücken,
                   So sei es gleich auf ewig weggerafft.

KÖNIGIN, MONOSTATOS und CHOR.
                                Sehen die Eltern je,
                                Sehn sie sich an,
                                Fasse die Seele gleich
                                Schauder und Wahn!

                                Sehen die Eltern je,
                                Sehn sie den Sohn,
                                Reiße die Parze gleich
                                Schnell ihn davon!

Das Theater geht in ein Chaos über, daraus entwickelt sich

*Ein königlicher Saal. Frauen tragen auf einem goldnen Gestelle, von welchem
ein prächtiger Teppich herabhängt, einen goldnen Sarkophag. Andre tragen
einen reichen Baldachin darüber. Chor*

CHOR DER FRAUEN.   In stiller Sorge wallen wir
                                Und trauern bei der Lust;

Cho.	Let but the mother set Eyes on her son, By the Weird Sisters to Death he'll be done.
	Let but the father set Eyes on his son, By the Weird Sisters to Death he'll be done.
Mon.	Yet know I that we were no sooner hence, Than once again the coffin, growing lighter, Was carried where, adorned with stole and mitre, The sacred brotherhood its wisdom doth dispense. Now must with strength and ruse thy slave again endeavor! For even in those hallowed realms shall never Thy hatred and thy curse be without force. Let but the spouses meet, their minds shall be benighted; Let them be by their offspring's sight delighted, That instant shall it turn into a corse.
Que., Mon. & Cho.	Let but the spouses meet, Keeping their troth, Horror and madness shall Light on them both. Let but the parents set Eyes on their son, By the Weird Sisters to Death he'll be done.

The stage dissolves into chaos, which turns into

                A Royal Apartment.

Women carry a golden framework hung with a sumptuous carpet, on which is placed a golden sarcophagus. Others hold a rich canopy over it.

Chorus of Women.	In silent care we wander on, We mourn and never rest;

Ein Kind ist da, ein Sohn ist hier,
Und Kummer drückt die Brust.

EINE DAME.

So wandelt fort und stehet niemals stille,
Das ist der weisen Männer Wille,
Vertraut auf sie, gehorchet blind;
Solang ihr wandelt, lebt das Kind.

CHOR.

Ach armes eingeschloßnes Kind,
Wie wird es dir ergehen!
Dich darf die gute Mutter nicht,
Der Vater dich nicht sehen.

EINE DAME.

Und schmerzlich sind die Gatten selbst geschieden,
Nicht Herz an Herz ist ihnen Trost gegönnt;
Sarastro nur verschafft dem Hause Frieden.

CHOR.

O schlafe sanft, o schlafe süß,
Du längst erwünschter Sohn!
Aus diesem frühen Grabe steigst
Du auf des Vaters Thron.

EINE DAME.

Der König kommt, laßt uns von dannen wallen.
Im öden Raum läßt er die Klage schallen,
Schon ahnet er die Öde seines Throns:
Er sehe nicht den Sarg des teuren Sohns.

Sie ziehen vorüber

TAMINO.

Wenn dem Vater aus der Wiege
Zart und frisch der Knabe lächelt,
Und die vielgeliebten Züge
Holde Morgenluft umfächelt,
Ja! dem Schicksal diese Gabe
Dankt er mehr als alle Habe:
Ach es lebt, es wird geliebt,
Bis es Liebe wieder gibt.

DIE FRAUEN *in der Ferne*

Ach es lebt, es wird geliebt,
Bis es Liebe wieder gibt.

A child was born, a son is here,
Yet sorrow weighs our breast.

A LADY.
So wander onward, never standing still,
It is the holy brethren's will;
Believe them, blind obedience give,
For while ye move, the child shall live.

Cho.
Ah, poor, unhapy prisoner,
What shall become of thee?
For thee thy mother never may,
Nor yet thy father, see.

Lady.
How painfully the spouses too did part,
Not heart to heart may they console each other.
Here goes the father weeping, there the mother;
   Sarastro can alone repair their smart.

Cho.
   Oh slumber soft, oh slumber sweet,
Thou scion of the great!
From this, thy early tomb shalt thou
Arise and reign in state.

LADY.
   Here is the king; come then, let him alone
Lament his loss, bewail his empty throne;
Let none be witness to his dreadful pain,
Let him not see his infant's tomb again.

Exeunt; enter Tamino.

TAM.
   When from out his cradle sweetly,
Tenderly the infant smileth;
When his well-belovéd features
Fresh the morning's air beguileth;
To the gods the parents render
Thanks for what they hold most tender,
Cherish him while he doth live,
Till he love for love can give.

WOMEN *(in the distance).*
Cherish him while he doth live,
Till he love for love can give.

TAMINO.   Dämmernd nahte schon der Tag
                              In Aurorens Purpurschöne–
                              Ach! ein grauser Donnerschlag
                              Hüllt in Nacht die Freudenszene.
                              Und was mir das Schicksal gab,
                              Deckt so früh ein goldnes Grab.

DIE FRAUEN *in der Ferne*

                              Ach was uns das Schicksal gab,
                              Deckt so früh ein goldnes Grab.

TAMINO.   Ich höre sie, die meinen Liebling tragen.
                              O kommt heran! Laßt uns zusammen klagen!
                              O sagt! wie trägt Pamina das Geschick?

EINE DAME.   Es fehlen ihr der Götter schönste Gaben,
                              Sie seufzt nach dir, sie jammert um den Knaben.

TAMINO.   O sagt mir, lebt noch mein verschloßnes Glück?
                              Bewegt sich's noch an seinem Zauberplatze?
                              O gebt mir Hoffnung zu dem Schatze!
                              O gebt mir bald ihn selbst zurück!

DAMEN.   Wenn mit betrübten Sinnen
                              Wir wallen und wir lauschen,
                              So hören wir da drinnen
                              Gar wunderlich es rauschen.
                              Wir fühlen was sich regen,
                              Wir sehn den Sarg sich bewegen,
                              Wir horchen und wir schweigen
                              Auf diese guten Zeichen.
                              Und nachts, wenn jeder Ton verhallt,
                              So hören wir ein Kind, das lallt.

TAMINO.   Ihr Götter! schützet es auf wunderbare Weise!
                              Erquickt's mit eurem Trank! Nährt es mit eurer
                                   Speise!
                              Und ihr beweist mir eure Treue.
                              Bewegt euch immer fort und fort!
                              Bald rettet uns mit heilger Weihe
                              Sarastros lösend Götterwort.

TAM.

> Fair and happy dawned the morn,
> Purpled in Aurora's splendour,
> When the day, by thunder torn,
> Did unto the night surrender.
> Him, with whom love's fortune dowered us,
> A gilt sepulchre devoured us.

WOM. *(in the distance)*

> Him, with whom good fortune dowered you,
> A gilt sepulchre devoured you.

TAM.

> Ye women who my infant tend, come hither,
> Come, let us lamentations raise together!
> Oh say, how did Pamina bear her pain?

A LADY.

> She pines and languishes for her lost joys,
> Laments thy fate, bewails the hapless boy's.

TAM.

> How fares my child? To hear it I am fain.
> Is he still stirring in his gilded tomb?
> Oh say if for some hope there is yet room!
> When shall I have him to myself again?

WOM.

> In doing our sad task,
> Bearing the golden bier,
> We listen and we ask:
> What is it that we hear?
> We feel a wondrous stirring,
> We see the coffin move,
> We harken to a whirring,
> As from wings of love.
> At night, as though it were a token,
> We hear the child, its silence broken.

TAM.

> Ye gods, protect my son, to my dear son be good!
> Let him not suffer thirst! Sustain him with your food!
> And ye, his guardians, with devotion
> Move on and on, and never rest.
> Sarastro's wisdom shall inspire him,
> Till he be saved, till we be blest!

	Lauschet auf die kleinste Regung,
	Meldet jegliche Bewegung
	Dem besorgten Vater ja.
TAMINO und CHOR.	Und befreiet und gerettet,
	An der Mutter Brust gebettet,
	Lieg er bald ein Engel da.

Wald und Fels, im Hintergrund eine Hütte, an der einen Seite derselben ein goldner Wasserfall, an der andern ein Vogelherd. Papageno, Papagena sitzen auf beiden Seiten des Theaters voneinander abgewendet

SIE *steht auf und geht zu ihm.* Was hast du denn, mein liebes Männchen?

ER *sitzend.* Ich bin verdrießlich, laß mich gehn!

SIE. Bin ich denn nicht dein liebes Hennchen?
  Magst du denn mich nicht länger sehn?

ER. Ich bin verdrießlich! bin verdrießlich!

SIE. Er ist verdrießlich! ist verdrießlich.

BEIDE. Die ganze Welt ist nicht mehr schön.

Sie setzt sich auf ihre Seite

ER *steht auf und geht zu ihr.* Was hast du denn, mein liebes Weibchen?

SIE. Ich bin verdrießlich, laß mich gehn!

ER. Bist du denn nicht mein süßes Täubchen?
  Will unsre Liebe schon vergehn?

SIE. Ich bin verdrießlich! bin verdrießlich!

ER *sich entfernend.* Ich bin verdrießlich! bin verdrießlich!

BEIDE. Was ist uns beiden nur geschehen?

ER. Mein Kind! Mein Kind! laß uns nur ein bißchen zur Vernunft kommen. Sind wir nicht recht undankbar gegen unsere Wohltäter, daß wir uns so unartig gebärden?

SIE. Ja wohl! ich sag es auch, und doch ist es nicht anders.

ER. Warum sind wir denn nicht vergnügt?

SIE. Weil wir nicht lustig sind.

Not the smallest message hiding,
To his father bring the tiding:
Thus your duty ye perform!

TAM. & CHO.   Till upon his mother's breast,
Free from bondage and at rest,
See we his angelic form.

Rocky woodland with a hut in the background, a golden waterfall on one side of it and a bird sanctuary on the other.

Papageno and Papagena sit on either side of the stage, turning their backs on each other.

SHE *(rising and approaching him)*. What ails thee now, my dearest rooster?

HE *(still seated)*. I am disgruntled; let me go!

SHE. Am I not thy beloved chicken?
Why of a sudden treat me so?

HE. I am disgruntled, discontented!

SHE. He is disgruntled, discontented!

BOTH. No pleasure has the world to show.

        Papagena resumes her seat.

HE *(rising and approaching her)*. What is that you lack, my cosset?

SHE. I am despondent; let me go!

HE. Am I thy turtledove no longer?
Is love and bliss to vanish so?

SHE. I am despondent, discontented!

HE *(drawing apart)*. I am despondent, discontented!

BOTH. What is amiss, I'd like to know?

HE. My dear! My sweet! Let us look at things reasonably. Are we not all too ungrateful to our benefactors to take on so naughtily?

SHE. It's true, I admit; yet there it is.

HE. But why are we not merry?

SHE. Because we are out of humour.

ER. Hat uns nicht der Prinz zum Hochzeitsgeschenk die kostbare Flöte gegeben, mit der wir alle Tiere herbeilocken, hernach die schmackhaften aussuchen und uns die beste Mahlzeit bereiten?

SIE. Hast du mir nicht gleich am zweiten Hochzeittag das herrliche Glockenspiel geschenkt? Ich darf nur darauf schlagen, sogleich stürzen sich alle Vögel ins Netz. Die Tauben fliegen uns gebraten ins Maul.

ER. Die Hasen laufen gespickt auf unserm Tisch! und Sarastro hat uns die ergiebige Weinquelle an unsere Hütte herangezaubert – und doch sind wir nicht vergnügt.

SIE *seufzend*. Ja! es ist kein Wunder.

ER *seufzend*. Freilich! kein Wunder.

SIE. Es fehlt uns–

ER. Leider, es fehlen uns–

SIE *weinend*. Wir sind doch recht unglücklich!

ER *weinend*. Ja wohl, recht unglücklich!

SIE *immer mit zunehmendem Weinen und Schluchzen*. Die schönen,

ER *gleichfalls*. Artigen,

SIE. Kleinen,

ER. Scharmanten,

SIE. Pa–

ER. Pa–

SIE. Papa–

ER. Papa–

SIE. Ach der Schmerz wird mich noch umbringen!

ER. Ich mag gar nicht mehr leben!

SIE. Mich deuchte, sie wären schon da.

ER. Sie hüpften schon herum.

SIE. Wie war das so artig!

ER. Erst einen kleinen Papageno.

SIE. Dann wieder eine kleine Papagena.

ER. Papageno.

SIE. Papagena.

ER. Wo sind sie nun geblieben?

SIE. Sie sind eben nicht gekommen.

HE. Come, did not the prince give us his precious flute for a wedding gift, to entice all the animals, from which we may choose the tastiest and cook ourselves the choicest morsels?

SHE. And did you not present me with your magic bells the very day after our marriage? I need but play them, and all the birds swarm into the net. The pigeons fly into our mouths ready roasted.

HE. Hares run to our table larded! And Sarastro's magic has called forth a spring of wine at our very door. And yet we are not happy.

SHE *(with a sigh)*. Ah, no wonder!

HE *(sighing)*. True, it's no wonder!

SHE. So long as we miss ...

HE. Alas! yes, we miss ...

SHE *(weeping)*. How unhappy we are!

HE *(likewise)*. Ah yes, very unhappy!

SHE *(weeping and sobbing more and more)*. Some pretty ...

HE *(likewise)*. Sweet ...

SHE. Little ...

HE. Charming ...

SHE. Pa ...

HE. Pa ...

SHE. Papa ...

HE. Papa ...

SHE. Oh, I shall die with grief!

HE. I am tired of life!

SHE. It seemed as if they were here already.

HE. They were already hopping about.

SHE. How pretty it was.

HE. First a little Papageno.

SHE. Next a little Papagena.

HE. Papageno.

SHE. Papagena.

HE. And now where are they?

SHE. Well, they never came.

ER. Das ist ein rechtes Unglück! Hätte ich mich nur beizeiten gehangen!

SIE. Wär ich nur eine alte Frau geblieben!

BEIDE. Ach wir Armen!

CHOR *hinter der Szene.* Ihr guten Geschöpfe,
Was trauert ihr so?
Ihr lustigen Vögel,
Seid munter und froh!

ER. Aha!

SIE. Aha!

BEIDE. Es klingen die Felsen,
Sie singen einmal.
So klangen,
So sangen
Der Wald sonst und der Saal.

CHOR. Besorgt das Gewerbe,
Genießet in Ruh,
Euch schenken die Götter – *Pause.*

ER. Die Pa?

CHOR *als Echo.* Die Pa, Pa, Pa.

SIE. Die Pa? Pa? Pa?

CHOR *als Echo.* Pa, Pa, Pa, Pa.

ER. Die Papagenos? *Pause.*

SIE. Die Papagenas? *Pause.*

CHOR. Euch geben die Götter
Die Kinder dazu.

ER. Komm, laß uns geschäftig sein,
Da vergehn die Grillen.
Erstlich noch ein Gläschen Wein–

Sie gehn nach der Quelle und trinken

BEIDE. Nun laß uns geschäftig sein!
Schon vergehn die Grillen.

Er nimmt die Flöte und sieht sich um, als wenn er nach dem Wilde sähe. Sie setzt
sich in die kleine Laube an den Vogelherd und nimmt das Glockenspiel vor sich.
– Er bläst

HE. Oh, what a misfortune! I wish I had hanged myself after all.

SHE. If only I had remained an old woman!

BOTH. Poor things that we are!

CHORUS *(off stage)*.   Ye fortunate creatures,
Why are ye so sad?
Ye lovebirds, take heart and
Be merry and glad!

HE.   Aha!

SHE.   Aha!

BOTH.   The rocks are resounding,
They sing us a song,
It's singing
And ringing
The woodland glades along.

CHO.   But labour by day and
At night take your rest;
The gods then will give you …

HE.   Some Pa … ?

CHO. *(as echo)*.   Some Pa … Pa … Pa …

SHE.   Some Pa … ? Pa … ? Pa … ?

CHO.   Pa … Pa … Pa … Pa …

HE.   Some Papagenos? *(Pause.)*

SHE.   Some Papagenas? *(Pause.)*

CHO.   The gods then will see that
By children you're blest.

HE.   Come now, busy as a bee,
We shall chase our troubles.
First of all a sip of wine …

They go to the waterfall and drink.

BOTH.   We a golden future see
While the winecup bubbles.

*Papageno takes the flute and gazes around, as though looking for game.
Papagena sits down in a small arbour near the bird sanctuary and sets the
chime-bells before her. He plays.*

SIE *singt.*	Laß, o großer Geist des Lichts, Unsre Jagd gelingen! *Sie spielt.*
BEIDE *singen.*	Laß der Vögel bunte Schar Nach dem Herde dringen! Er *bläst.*
SIE *singt.*	Sieh! die Löwen machen schon Frisch sich auf die Reise. *Sie spielt.*
ER *singt.*	Gar zu mächtig sind sir mir. Sie sind zähe Speise. *Er bläst.*
SIE *singt.*	Hör, die Vöglein flattern schon, Flattern auf den Ästen. *Sie spielt.*
ER *singt.*	Spiele fort! Das kleine Volk Schmeckt am allerbesten. Auf dem Felde hüpfen schon Schöne fette Hühnchen. *Er bläst.*
SIE *spielt und singt.*	Blase fort! Da kommen schon Hasen und Kaninchen.

Es erscheinen auf dem Felsen Hasen und Kaninchen. Indessen sind auch die Löwen, Bären und Affen angekommen und treten dem Papageno in Weg. – Sie spielt

ER *singt.*	Wär ich nur die Bären los! Die verwünschten Affen! Jene sind so breit und dumm, Das sind schmale Laffen.

Auf den Bäumen lassen sich Papageien sehen

SIE *spielt und singt.*	Auch die Papageienschar Kommt von weiten Reisen. Glänzend farbig sind sie zwar, Aber schlecht zu speisen.

ER hat indessen den Hasen nachgestellt und einen erwischt und bringt ihn an den Löffeln hervor

Sieh, den Hasen hascht ich mir
Aus der großen Menge.

SHE *(singing)*.	Let, O Spirit of the Light,
	Prosper our endeavor. *(Plays.)*
BOTH *(singing)*.	At our hearth let all the birds
	Congregate for ever. *(Papageno plays.)*
SHE *(singing)*.	See, the lions there prepare
	This way quick to turn them. *(Plays.)*
HE *(singing)*.	All too strong are they and tough;
	As a food I spurn them. *(Plays.)*
SHE *(singing)*.	Listen to the birds, they come
	Flutt'ring here and hasty. *(Plays.)*
HE *(singing)*.	Tinkle on! The smallest are
	Tenderest, and tasty.
	See, my music forces all
	To forsake their habits. *(Plays.)*
SHE *(playing and singing)*.	Blow thy flute! Entice the grouse,
	Pullets, hares and rabbits.

Hares and rabbits appear on the rocks. Meanwhile lions, bears and monkeys have also arrived and get into Papageno's way. Papagena plays on.

HE *(singing)*.	Rid me of the clumsy bears,
	The accursèd monkeys!
	Dull are these; the latter are
	Obstinate as donkeys.

Parrots are seen on the trees.

SHE *(playing and singing)*.	See the gaudy popinjays
	From far countries meeting.
	Beautiful of colour they,
	But pernicious eating.

HE *(having in the meantime pursued and captured a hare, and holding it out by the ears)*.

> Look, a handsome hare I caught
> From the throng of creatures.

SIE *hat indessen das Garn zugeschlagen, in welchem man Vögel flattern sieht*
Sieh, die fetten Vögel hier
Garstig im Gedränge.

Sie nimmt einen Vogel heraus und bringt ihn an den Flügeln hervor.

BEIDE.   Wohl, mein Kind, wir leben so
Einer von dem andern.
Laß uns heiter, laß uns froh
Nach der Hütte wandern.

CHOR *unsichtbar.*   Ihr lustigen Vögel,
Seid munter und froh!
Verdoppelt die Schritte!
Schon seid ihr erhört:
Euch ist in der Hütte
Das Beste beschert.

Bei der Wiederholung fallen ER *und* SIE *mit ein*

Verdopple die Schritte!
Schon sind wir erhört:
Uns ist in der Hütte
Das Beste beschert.

Tempel. Versammlung der Priester

CHOR.   Schauen kann der Mann und wählen!
Doch was hilft ihm oft die Wahl?
Kluge schwanken, Weise fehlen,
Doppelt ist dann ihre Qual.
Recht zu handeln,
Grad zu wandeln,
Sei des edlen Mannes Wahl.
Soll er leiden,
Nichts entscheiden,
Spreche Zufall auch einmal.

*Sarastro tritt vor dem Schlusse des Gesanges unter sie. Sobald der Gesang
verklungen hat, kommt der Sprecher herein und tritt zu Sarastro*

SHE *(having by this time closed the net, in which birds are seen fluttering).*
     See, our net holds crowds of fat
     Birds of various features.

   She takes out a bird and carries it by its wings.

BOTH.   Thus we live, for such is life,
     One upon another.
     Happy are we, man and wife;
     Father soon, and mother!

CHORUS *(invisible).*   Ye lovebirds, take heart, then,
     Be merry and glad!
     Redouble your footsteps!
     Your prayer is heard;
     Now enter your dwelling:
     Your bliss is prepared.

Papageno and Papagena join in the repetition:
     Redouble our footsteps!
     Our prayer is heard;
     We enter our dwelling:
     Our bliss is prepared.

       Temple.
      Assembly of Priests.

CHORUS.   Man may choose and man may reason,
     Yet what boots him oft the choice?
     Virtue's self may yield to treason,
     Goodness heed the tempter's voice.
       Evil foiling,
       Noble toiling
     Be the upright man's delight.
       Only if he
       Weak to judge be,
     Then may chance for once decide.

Sarastro joins them before the chorus is finished. As soon as that is done, the speaker enters and goes to Sarastro's side.

DER SPRECHER. Vor der nördlichen Pforte unserer heiligen Wohnung stehet unser Bruder, der die Pilgrimschaft unseres Jahres zurückgelegt hat, und wünscht, wieder eingelassen zu werden. Er übersendet hier das gewisse Zeichen, an dem du erkennen kannst, daß er noch wert ist, in unsere Mitte wieder aufgenommen zu werden.

Er überreicht Sarastro einen runden Kristall an einem Bande

SARASTRO. Dieser geheimnisvolle Stein ist noch hell und klar. Er würde trüb erscheinen, wenn unser Bruder gefehlt hätte. Führe den Wiederkehrenden heran!

Der Sprecher geht ab

SARASTRO. In diesen stillen Mauern lernt der Mensch sich selbst und sein Innerstes erforschen. Er bereitet sich vor, die Stimme der Götter zu vernehmen; aber die erhabene Sprache der Natur, die Töne der bedürftigen Menschheit lernt nur der Wandrer kennen, der auf den weiten Gefilden der Erde umherschweift. In diesem Sinne verbindet uns das Gesetz, jährlich einen von uns als Pilger hinaus in die rauhe Welt zu schicken. Das Los entscheidet, und der Fromme gehorcht. Auch ich, nachdem ich mein Diadem dem würdigen Tamino übergeben habe, nachdem er mit junger Kraft und frühzeitiger Weisheit an meiner Stelle regiert, bin heute zum erstenmal auch in dem Falle, so wie jeder von euch in das heilige Gefäß zu greifen und mich dem Ausspruche des Schicksals zu unterwerfen.

Der Sprecher mit dem Pilger tritt ein

PILGER. Heil dir, Vater! Heil euch, Brüder!

ALLE. Heil dir!

SARASTRO. Der Kristall zeigt mir an, daß du reines Herzens zurücke kehrst, daß keine Schuld auf dir ruht. Nun aber teile deinen Brüdern mit, was du gelernt, was du erfahren hast, und vermehre die Weisheit, indem du sie bestätigst. Vor allem aber warte noch ab, wem du deine Kleider, wem du dieses Zeichen übergeben sollst, wen der Wille der Götter für diesmal aus der glücklichen Gesellschaft entfernen wird.

SPE. At the northern portal of our sacred dwelling stands the brother who has accomplished the year's pilgrimage on our behalf. He asks to be re-admitted, and he sends thee the token whereby thou mayest judge that he has remained worthy to be taken into our midst.

He hands Sarastro a round crystal hung on a ribbon.

SAR. The mysterious stone has remained bright and clear. It would appear clouded if our brother had erred. Admit him!

Exit the Speaker.

SAR. Within these silent walls man learns to know himself and his inmost being. He prepares to listen to the voice of the gods; but the august voice of nature and the speech of needy humankind become known only to the wanderer who strays over the vast expanses of the earth. Thus our law wills it that each year one of us should be sent out into the rough world as a pilgrim. I too, having surrendered my crown to the worthy Tamino, to reign in my stead with youthful force and timely wisdom, for the first time become subject to the duty to dip into the holy receptacle and, like all of you, to submit to the dictates of destiny.

The Speaker returns with the Pilgrim.

PIL. Hail to thee, father! Hail to ye, brethren!

ALL. Hail to thee!

SAR. The crystal shows that thou hast returned with a pure heart and guiltless. Go now and tell thy brethren what thou hast learnt, what thou hast experienced, and so augment wisdom by confirming it. But first wait to discover to whom thou shalt surrender thy garment, to whom thou shalt hand on this token, and who, by the will of the gods, shall this day be removed from our happy brotherhood.

Er gibt dem Pilger die Kugel zurück. Zwei Priester bringen einen tragbaren Altar, auf welchem ein flaches goldnes Gefäß steht. Der Altar muß so hoch sein, daß man nicht in das Gefäß hineinsehen kann, sondern in die Höhe reichen muß, um hineinzugreifen

Chorgesang

SARASTRO *der seine Rolle auseinanderwickelt.* Mich traf das Los, und ich zaudere keinen Augenblick, mich seinem Gebote zu unterwerfen. Ja, die Ahnung ist erfüllt. Mich entfernen die Götter aus eurer Mitte, um euch und mich zu prüfen. Im wichtigen Augenblicke werde ich abgerufen, da die Kräfte feindseliger Mächte wirksamer werden. Durch meine Trennung von euch wird die Schale des Guten leichter. Haltet fest zusammen, dauert aus, lenkt nicht vom rechten Wege, und wir werden uns fröhlich wiedersehen.

> Die Krone gab ich meinem lieben,
> Ich gab sie schon dem werten Mann.
> Die Herrschaft ist mir noch geblieben,
> Daß ich euch allen dienen kann.
> Doch wird auch das mir nun entrissen;
> Ich werd euch heute lassen müssen,
> Und von dem heilig lieben Ort–
> Ich gehe schon.
> Leb wohl, mein Sohn!
> Lebt wohl, ihr Söhne!
> Bewahrt der Weisheit hohe Schöne.
> Ich gehe schon
> Vom heilig lieben Ort
> Als Pilger aus der Halle fort.

Während dieser Arie gibt Sarastro sein Oberkleid und die hohenpriesterlichen Abzeichen hinweg, die nebst dem goldnen Gefäße weggetragen werden. Er empfängt dagegen die Pilgerkleider, das Band mit der Kristallkugel wird ihm ungehangen, und er nimmt den Stab in die Hand. Hierzu wird der Komponist zwischen den verschiedenen Teilen der Arie, jedoch nur so viel als nötig, Raum zu lassen wissen

He returns the crystal to the Pilgrim. Two priests bring a portable altar on which stands a flat golden vessel. The altar must be high enough to prevent anyone from seeing into the receptacle and to oblige those who dip into it to raise their hands above their heads.

Choral Song.

SAR. *(unfolding his scroll).* The lot is mine. I hesitate not an instant to submit to its decree. More, it fulfils a presage. The gods remove me from your midst in order to try both you and me. I am called hence at the portentous moment when inimical powers grow more threatening. The scale of goodness is made lighter by my departure. Be firmly united, endure, do not swerve from the straight path, and we shall meet again joyfully.

> The crown did I without repining
> Surrender to the noble prince.
> Yet held I, brethren, still to serve ye,
> The power given me long since.
> This too I must this day abandon;
> I leave ye, and my duties hand on;
> I leave this holy, cherished place.
>> From ye I part
>> With heavy heart.
>> Brethren, farewell!
> Uphold and guard ye wisdom's well!
>> Away I turn
> And leave this hallowed hall,
> A pilgrim, at a sacred call.

During this aria Sarastro gives away his outer garment and his high-priestly insignia, which are carried away together with the golden receptacle. He receives instead the pilgrim's cloak, the ribbon with the crystal is hung round his neck, and he seizes the staff. The composer will know how to leave room for this between the different parts of the aria, but no more than is necessary.

CHOR.   Wer herrschet nun
                              Am heilig lieben Ort?
                              Er geht von uns als Pilger fort.

Die Priester bleiben zu beiden Seiten stehen, der Altar in der Mitte

SARASTRO.   Mir ward bei euch, ihr Brüder,
                              Das Leben nur ein Tag.
                              Drum singet Freudenlieder,
                              Werft euch in Demut nieder
                              Und gleich erhebt euch wieder,
                              Was auch der Gott gebieten mag.

                              Von euch zu scheiden,
                              Von euch zu lassen,
                              Welch tiefes Leiden!
                              Ich muß mich fassen,
                              O harter Schlag! *Ab.*

CHOR.   Ihr heiligen Hallen,
                              Vernehmet die Klagen!
                              Nicht mehr erschallen
                              An heitern Tagen
                              Sarastros Worte,
                              Am ernsten Orte
                              In edlen Pflichten
                              Zu unterrichten.
                              Es soll die Wahrheit
                              Nicht mehr auf Erden
                              In schöner Klaheit
                              Verbreitet werden.
                              Dein hoher Gang

                              Wird nun vollbracht;
                              Doch uns umgibt
                              Die tiefe Nacht.

CHORUS.   Who is to reign
                         Within this hallowed hall?
                         He leaves us at a sacred call.

The Priests remain standing on both sides, with the
altar in the centre.

SAR.   Once in your midst, my brothers,
                         My life seemed but a day.
                         Rejoice ye in each other's
                         Fraternity and ward ye,
                         Obey the gods who guard ye,
                         Command they what they may.
                                        Alas! to leave ye,
                                        Errant and drifting,
                                        Doth sorely grieve me,
                                        Yet, heart uplifting,
                                        I go this day! *(Exit.)*

CHO.   O sacred dwelling,
                         Our grief upwelling,
                         Here, where no longer
                         Sarastro is stronger
                         In wisdom, so saintly
                         To cheer us, where faintly
                         We followed his leading
                         With praying and pleading.
                         No more the beauty
                         Of noble duty
                         Ever to teach us
                         His voice will reach us
                         His sacred trust
                         He doth assume,
                         But we are thrust
                         In deepest gloom.

Ein feierlicher Zug. Pamina mit ihrem Gefolge. Das Kästchen wird gebracht. Sie will es, einer Vorbedeutung zufolge, der Sonne widmen, und das Kästchen wird auf den Altar gesetzt. Gebet, Erdbeben. Der Altar versinkt, und das Kästchen mit. Verzweiflung der Pamina. Diese Szene ist dergestalt angelegt, daß die Schauspielerin durch Beihilfe der Musik eine bedeutende Folge von Leidenschaften ausdrücken kann.

Wald und Fels. Papagenos Wohnung. Sie haben große schöne Eier in der Hütte gefunden. Sie vermuten, daß besondere Vögel drinnen stecken mögen. Der Dichter muß sorgen, daß die bei dieser Gelegenheit vorfallenden Späße innerhalb der Grenzen der Schicklichkeit bleiben. Sarastro kommt zu ihnen. Nach einigen mystischen Äußerungen über die Naturkräfte steigt ein niedriger Felsen aus der Erde, in dessen Innern sich ein Feuer bewegt. Auf Sarastros Anweisung wird auf demselbigen ein artiges Nest zurechtgemacht, die Eier hineingelegt und mit Blumen bedeckt. Sarastro entfert sich. Die Eier fangen an, zu schwellen, eins nach dem andern bricht auf, und drei Kinder kommen heraus, zwei Jungen und ein Mädchen. Ihr erstes Betragen untereinander, sowie gegen die Alten, gibt zu dichterischen und musikalischen Scherzen Gelegenheit. Sarastro kommt zu ihnen. Einige Worte über Erziehung. Dann erzählt er ihnen den traurigen Zustand, in dem sich Pamina und Tamino befinden. Nach dem Versinken des Kästchens sucht Pamina ihren Gatten auf. Indem sie sich erblicken, fallen sie in einen periodischen Schlaf, wie ihnen angedroht war, aus dem sie nur kurze Zeit erwachen, um sich der Verzweiflung zu überlassen. Sarastro heißt die muntere Familie nach Hofe gehen, um die Betrübnis durch ihre Scherze aufzuheitern. Besonders soll Papageno die Flöte mitnehmen, um deren heilende Kraft zu versuchen. Sarastro bleibt allein zurück und ersteigt unter einer bedeutenden Arie den heiter liegenden Berg.

A Solemn Procession.

Pamina with her retinue. The casket is brought. In response to a premonition she intends to dedicate it to the sun, and it is set upon an altar. Prayer. Earthquake. The altar sinks into the ground, and the casket with it. Pamina despairs. The scene to be laid out in such a way that the actress, with the aid of music, may express a series of significant emotions.

Rocky Woodland: Papageno's dwelling.

They have found large, handsome eggs in their hut, which they suppose to contain birds of a special breed. The poet must see to it that the jests occasioned by this situation remain within the bounds of decency. Sarastro joins them. After a few mystical utterances concerning the forces of nature, a low rock rises from the earth, with a fire burning within. At Sarastro's direction a pretty nest is arranged upon it, into which the eggs are placed, covered with flowers. Exit Sarastro. The eggs begin to swell; they burst one after another, and three children emerge, two boys and a girl. Their first demeanour among themselves and towards their parents gives rise to poetical and musical drolleries. Sarastro rejoins them. A few words on upbringing. He then tells them of the sad situation in which Tamino and Pamina find themselves. After the disappearance of the cask Pamina has sought her husband. At their meeting they have fallen into the periodical sleep with which they had been threatened, from which they awake but for a short time, only to become a prey to despair. Sarastro bids the merry family go to court, to dispel its sorrows by their frolics. Above all, Papageno is to take his flute, in order to try its healing powers. Sarastro remains behind alone and, during a significant aria, climbs the clearly lighted mountain.

*Vorsaal im Palast. Zwei Damen und zwei Herren gehen
auf und ab*

TUTTI.   Stille, daß niemand sich rühre, sich rege,
Daß der Gesang nur sich schläfernd bewege!
Wachend und sorgend bekümmert euch hier:
Kranket der König, so kranken auch wir.

DRITTE DAME *schnell kommend*

Wollet ihr das Neuste hören,
Kann ich euch das Neuste sagen;
Lange werden wir nicht klagen,
Denn die Mutter ist versöhnt.

DRITTER HERR *schnell kommend und einfallend*

Und man saget, Papageno
Hat den größten Schatz gefunden,
Große Gold- und Silberklumpen,
Wie die Straußeneier groß.

ERSTES TUTTI.   Stille, wie mögt ihr das Neue nur bringen
Da wir die Schmerzen der Könige singen? *Pause*
Aber so redet denn, macht es nur kund.

DRITTE DAME.   Wollet ihr das Neuste hören?–

DRITTER HERR.   Und man saget, Papageno–

DRITTE DAME.   Lasset euch das Neuste sagen–

DRITTER HERR.   Hat den größten Schatz gefunden–

VIERTE DAME *schnell kommend und einfallend*

War Sarastro doch verschwunden;
Doch man weiß, wo er gewesen,
Kräuter hat er nur gelesen,
Und er kommt und macht gesund.

VIERTER HERR *geschwind kommend und einfallend*

Ich verkünde frohe Stunden,
Alle Schmerzen sind vorüber;
Denn es ist der Prinz gefunden,
Und man trägt ihn eben her.

TUTTI *der letzten viere, in welchem sie ihre Nachrichten verschränkt wiederholen*

Antechamber in the Palace.

TWO LADIES *and two* GENTLEMEN *walking up and down.*

ALL.	Silence, let no one disturb our devotions,
	Cradle-song follow with somnolent motions!
	Waking and watching our task we must do:
	What the king suffers, that suffer we too.
THIRD LADY *(entering quickly).*	
	Are ye fain to hear the latest?
	Shall I tell the happy tidings?
	Of all pleasures know the greatest:
	For the Queen of Night relents.
THIRD GENTLEMAN *(entering and joining in quickly).*	
	And 'tis said that Papageno
	Now has treasure-trove discovered,
	Richer than the richest ye know,
	Lumps like ostrich-eggs, immense.
ENSEMBLE I.	Silence, what boots us the news ye are bringing,
	While of the grief of our queen we are singing?
	(Pause.)
	Speak then, what is it, what have ye to tell?
LADY III.	Are ye fain to hear the latest?
GENT. III.	And 'tis said that Papageno …
LADY III.	Shall I tell the happy tidings?
GENT. III.	Now has treasure-trove discovered …
FOURTH LADY *(entering and joning in quickly).*	
	True it is, Sarastro vanished;
	Yet we know what was the mission
	That he ventured on, self-banished:
	Herbs he plucked that make all well.
FOURTH GENTLEMAN *(likewise).*	
	Let me prophesy you gladness,
	For the prince has been recovered.
	He is saved, so end your sadness,
	He's restored and all is well.
ENS. II *(of the last four, who continue to repeat their news intertwined).*	

TUTTI *der ersten viere*

> Stille, wie mögt ihr die Märchen uns bringen?
> Helfet die Schmerzen der Herrscher besingen.
> Wär es doch wahr, und sie wären gesund!

Die letzten viere fallen ein, indem sie ihre Nachrichten immer verschränkt wiederholen

Papageno und Papagena, die mit der Wache streitend hereindringen

PAPAGENO. Es soll mich niemand abhalten.

PAPAGENA. Mich auch nicht.

PAPAGENO. Ich habe dem König eher Dienste geleistet, als eure Bärte zu wachsen anfingen, mit denen ihr jetzo grimmig tut.

PAPAGENA. Und ich habe der Königin manchen Gefallen getan, als der böse Mohr sie noch in seinen Klauen hatte. Freilich würde sie mich nicht mehr kennen: denn damals war ich alt und häßlich, jetzo bin ich jung und hübsch.

PAPAGENO. Also will ich nicht wieder hinaus, da ich einmal herein bin.

PAPAGENA. Und ich will bleiben, weil ich hier bin.

HERR. Sieh da das gefiederte Paar! recht wie gerufen. *Zur Wache.* Laßt sie nur! sie werden dem König und der Königin willkommen sein.

PAPAGENO. Tausend Dank, ihr Herren! Wir hören, es sieht hier sehr übel aus.

HERR. Und wir hören, es sieht bei euch sehr gut aus.

PAPAGENO. Bis es besser wird, mag es hingehen.

DAME. Ist's denn wahr, daß ihr die herrlichen Eier gefunden habt?

PAPAGENO. Gewiß.

HERR. Goldne Straußeneier?

PAPAGENO. Nicht anders.

DAME. Kennt ihr denn auch den Vogel, der sie legt?

PAPAGENO. Bis jetzt noch nicht.

DAME. Es müssen herrliche Eier sein.

ENS. I *(of the first four).*

> Silence, incredible tales have ye told us!
> Go, from our loyal lament do not hold us!
> Ah, if we could but believe what ye tell!

The last four join in, again repeating their news intertwined.
Enter Papageno and Papagena, struggling with the guard.

HE. No one shall prevent me!

SHE. Nor me either!

HE. I have served the king before your beards began to grow, wherewith you now make such a grim display.

SHE. And I have often obliged the queen, when she was still in that wicked blackamoor's clutches. It's true, she would no longer recognize me, for I was old and ugly then, and now I am young and pretty.

HE. And so I will not be expelled again, now that I am here.

SHE. And I shall stay too.

A GENTLEMAN. See here, the feathered pair! How welcome! *(To the guard.)* Let them be! The king and queen will be glad to see them.

PAPAGENO. A thousand thanks, gentlemen! We hear that things are in a bad way here.

GENT. And we hear that they are very well with you.

PAPAGENO. Until they improve, they will do.

A LADY. Is it true, then, that you have found such beautiful eggs?

PAPAGENO. True enough.

GENT. Golden ostrich-eggs?

PAPAGENO. Just that.

LADY. And do you know the bird that lays them?

PAPAGENO. Not so far.

LADY. They must be splendid eggs.

PAPAGENO. Ganz unschätzbar.

HERR. Wieviel habt ihr denn bis jetzt gefunden?

PAPAGENO. Ungefähr zwei bis dritthalb Schock.

DAME. Und alle massiv?

PAPAGENO. Bis auf einige, die lauter waren.

HERR. Allerliebster Papageno, Ihr ließt mir wohl eine Mandel zukommen?

PAPAGENO. Von Herzen gern.

DAME. Ich wollte mir nur ein paar in mein Naturalienkabinett ausbitten.

PAPAGENO. Sie stehen zu Diensten.

DAME. Dann habe ich noch ein Dutzend Freunde, alles Naturforscher, die sich besonders auf die edlen Metalle vortrefflich verstehen.

PAPAGENO. Alle sollen befriedigt werden.

HERR. Ihr seid ein vortrefflicher Mensch.

PAPAGENO. Das wird mir leicht. Die Eier sind das wenigste. Ich bin ein Handelsmann, und zwar im großen, wie ich sonst im kleinen war.

DAME. Wo sind denn eure Waren?

PAPAGENO. Draußen vor dem äußersten Schloßhofe. Ich mußte sie stehenlassen.

DAME. Gewiß wegen des Zolls.

PAPAGENO. Sie wußten gar nicht, was sie fordern sollten.

HERR. Sie sind wohl sehr kostbar.

PAPAGENO. Unschätzbar.

DAME. Man kann es nach den Eiern berechnen.

PAPAGENO. Freilich! sie schreiben sich von den Eiern her.

HERR *zur Dame.* Wir müssen ihn zum Freunde haben, wir müssen ihnen durchhelfen.

Mit Papageno und Papagena ab, sodann mit beiden zurück. Sie tragen goldne Käfige mit geflügelten Kindern

PAPAGENO. Inestimable.

GENT. How many have you found, so far?

PAPAGENO. Some three-score and ten.

LADY. And all good?

PAPAGENO. Save a few, which were addled.

GENT. My good Papageno, will you not let me have a bushel or so.

PAPAGENO. With all my heart.

LADY. I should like to ask for a couple for my collection of curiosities.

PAPAGENO. They are at your service.

LADY. And I have a dozen friends or so, all naturalists, who excel especially in their knowledge of precious metals.

PAPAGENO. They shall all be contented.

GENT. You are an excellent fellow.

PAPAGENO. It is easy enough. The eggs are the least. I am a tradesman, and I deal wholesale now, though I was once a retailer.

LADY. But where are your goods?

PAPAGENO. Outside, in the outermost courtyard. I had to leave them there.

LADY. Because of the customs-duty, no doubt?

PAPAGENO. They had not a notion what to charge for them.

GENT. They must be most valuable.

PAPAGENO. Priceless.

LADY. They can be reckoned by the eggs.

PAPAGENO. Doubtless: they are accounted for by the eggs.

GENT. *(to the Lady)*. We must make a friend of him. We must help him through.

Exeunt with Papageno and Papagena. They return with both of them, who carry golden cages with winged children in them.

PAPAGENO und PAPAGENA.

> Von allen schönen Waren,
> Zum Markte hergefahren.
> Wird keine mehr behagen,
> Als die wir euch getragen
> Aus fremden Ländern bringen.
> O höret, was wir singen,
> Und seht die schönen Vögel!
> Sie stehen zum Verkauf.

PAPAGENA *einen herauslassend*

> Zuerst beseht den großen,
> Den lustigen, den losen!
> Er hüpfet leicht und munter
> Von Baum und Busch herunter;
> Gleich ist er wieder droben.
> Wir wollen ihn nicht loben.
> O seht den muntern Vogel!
> Er steht hier zum Verkauf.

PAPAGENO *den andern vorweisend*

> Betrachtet nun den kleinen,
> Er will bedächtig scheinen,
> Und doch ist er der lose,
> So gut als wie der große.
> Er zeiget meist im stillen
> Den allerbesten Willen.
> Der lose kleine Vogel,
> Er steht hier zum Verkauf.

PAPGENA *das dritte zeigend*

> O seht das kleine Täubchen,
> Das liebe Turtelweibchen!
> Die Mädchen sind so zierlich,
> Verständig und manierlich.
> Sie mag sich gerne putzen
> Und eure Liebe nutzen.
> Der kleine zarte Vogel,
> Er steht hier zum Verkauf.

PAPAGENO AND PAPAGENA.

        There is no earthly chattel,
        No market-ware, no cattle,
        You'll find is so attractive,
        So lively and so active,
        As that we have to sell ye.
        From foreign lands, we tell ye,
        Have come our feathered goods:
        Behold our charming broods!

SHE *(releasing one of them).* A fat one here, so wicked,
        As merry as a cricket!
        He hops and skips and pushes
        Through thickets and through bushes;
        And up and down he's flitting,
        As for young birds 'tis fitting.
        Come then, be never shy:
        This merry rascal buy!

HE *(presenting another).* This one's all wistful seeming,
        Reflective, musing, dreaming;
        Yet is the little small one
        As sprightly as the tall one.
        His size is not extensive,
        But he is not expensive;
        And when his song you've heard
        You'll buy the little bird.

SHE *(showing a third).* Oh see this little she-bird,
        More gentle than a he-bird!
        The females are so tender,
        So graceful and so slender,
        Intent on neat perfection,
        Yet full of sweet affection.
        She'd gladden any male:
        The little bird's for sale!

BEIDE.   Wir wollen sie nicht loben,
                          Sie stehn zu allen Proben,
                          Sie lieben sich das Neue.
                          Doch über ihre Treue
                          Verlangt nicht Brief und Siegel:
                          Sie haben alle Flügel.
                          Wie artig sind die Vögel,
                          Wie reizend ist der Kauf!

Es hängt von dem Komponisten ab, die letzten Zeilen eines jeden Verses teils durch die Kinder, teils durch die Alten und zuletzt vielleicht durch das ganze Chor der gegenwärtigen Personen wiederholen zu lassen

DAME. Sie sind wohl artig genug; aber ist das alles?

PAPAGENA. Alles, und ich dächte: genug.

HERR. Habt ihr nicht einige von den Eiern im Korbe? Sie wären mir lieber als die Vögel.

PAPAGENO. Ich glaub's. Sollte man übrigens in dieser wahrheitsliebenden Gesellschaft die Wahrheit sagen dürfen, so würde man bekennen, daß man ein wenig aufgeschnitten hat.

HERR. Nur ohne Umstände.

PAPAGENO. So würde ich sagen, daß dieses unser ganzer Reichtum sei.

DAME. Da wärt ihr weit.

HERR. Und die Eier?

PAPAGENO. Davon sind nur die Schalen noch übrig. Denn eben diese sind herausgekrochen.

HERR. Und die übrigen dritthalb Schock ungefähr?

PAPAGENO. Das war nur eine Redensart.

DAME. Da bleibt euch wenig übrig.

PAPAGENO. Ein hübsches Weibchen, lustige Kinder und guter Humor. Wer hat mehr?

HERR. Du bist also noch immer weiter nichts als ein Lustigmacher.

PAPAGENO. Und deshalb unentbehrlich.

HERR. Vielleicht könnte dieser Spaß den König und die Königin erheitern?

BOTH.
> No need for us to laud them,
> Ye will yourselves applaud them.
> They love what they have newly;
> Yet if they'll serve you truly
> You can but find by trying,
> For wings they have for flying.
> Come then, a songster buy,
> Your luck with it to try!

It is left to the composer to have the last lines of each verse repeated, partly by the children, partly by their parents, and lastly perhaps by all those on the stage in chorus.

LADY. True, they are charming; but is that all?

PAPAGENO. It is, and that's enough, I should think.

GENT. Have you not some of the eggs in the basket? I would rather have them than the children.

PAPAGENO. I'm not surprised. Besides, if it were permitted to tell the truth to this truth-loving company, one would have to confess that one has told a few fibs.

GENT. Don't be backward.

PAPAGENO. Well then, what you see here is our whole fortune.

LADY. Not much to boast about.

GENT. And what about the eggs?

PAPAGENO. Of those only the shells remain, for these have just emerged from them.

GENT. And what of the other three-score and ten or so?

PAPAGENO. That was only a manner of speaking.

LADY. Then there's not much left for you.

PAPAGENO. A pretty little wife, merry children and good humour. Who'd want more?

GENT. So you remain nothing more than a jester?

PAPAGENO. And as such indispensable.

GENT. Perhaps this jest of yours might amuse the king and queen.

DAME. Keineswegs. Es würde vielleicht ihnen nur traurige Erinnerungen geben.

PAPAGENO. Und doch hat mich Sarastro deswegen hergeschickt.

HERR. Sarastro? Wo habt ihr Sarastro gesehn?

PAPAGENO. In unsern Gebirgen.

HERR. Er suchte Kräuter?

PAPAGENO. Nicht daß ich wüßte.

HERR. Ihr saht doch, daß er sich manchmal bückte.

PAPAGENO. Ja, besonders wenn er stolperte.

HERR. So ein heiliger Mann stolpert nicht; er bückte sich vorsätzlich.

PAPAGENO. Ich bin es zufrieden.

HERR. Er suchte Kräuter und vielleicht Steine, und kommt hieher, König und Königin zu heilen.

PAPAGENO. Wenigstens heute nicht; denn er befahl mir ausdrücklich, nach dem Palaste zu gehen, die berühmte Zauberflöte mitzunehmen und beim Erwachen von Ihro Majestäten gleich die sanfteste Melodie anzustimmen, und dadurch ihren Schmerz wenigstens eine Zeitlang auszulöschen.

DAME. Man muß alles versuchen.

HERR. Es ist eben die Stunde des Erwachens. Versucht euer möglichstes. An Dank und Belohnung soll es nicht fehlen.

Pamina und Tamino unter einem Thronhimmel auf zwei Sesseln schlafend. Man wird, um den pathetischen Eindruck nicht zu stören, wohl die Papagena mit den Kindern abtreten lassen, auch Papageno, der die Flöte bläst, kann sich hinter die Kulisse, wenigstens halb, verbergen und nur von Zeit zu Zeit sich sehen lassen

PAMINA *auf den Ton der Flöte erwachend*
> An der Seite des Geliebten
> Süß entschlafen, sanft erwachen,
> Gleich zu sehn den holden Blick –

Papageno hört auf zu blasen und horcht

LADY. Hardly. It would only awaken sorrowful memories in them.

PAPAGENO. And yet Sarastro sent me here for that very purpose.

GENT. He did? And where did you see Sarastro?

PAPAGENO. In our mountains.

GENT. Was he looking for herbs?

PAPAGENO. Not that I know of.

GENT. But you saw him bending down now and then?

PAPAGENO. I did, particularly when he stumbled.

GENT. So holy a man does not stumble; he bent down on purpose.

PAPAGENO. As you will.

GENT. He was looking for herbs, and perhaps for stones, and he comes here to heal the king and queen.

PAPAGENO. Not to-day, though; for he ordered me particularly to go to the palace, to take the famous magic flute with me and, when their majesties awake, to intone at once the gentlest of tunes and with it to still their pain, at least for a time.

LADY. One must try everything.

GENT. This is the very hour of their awakening. Do your utmost. You shall lack neither thanks nor reward.

Pamina and Tamino, asleep on two thrones under a canopy.

In order not to disturb the pathetic impression, it may be preferable to let Papagena and the Children go off-stage. Papageno, as he plays the flute, may be at least half concealed in the wings and become visible only from time to time.

PAM. *(waking at the sound of the flute).*
> At the side of my belovéd,
> Softly sleeping, gently waking,
> Languish I to see his glance ...

PAPAGENO *ceases to play and listens.*

TAMINO *erwachend*   Ach, das könnte den Betrübten
Gleich zum frohen Gatten machen;
Aber ach, was stört mein Glück!

CHOR.   Papageno, blase, blase!
Denn es kehr der Schmerz zurück.

PAMINA *aufstehend und herunterkommend*
Aufgemuntert von dem Gatten
Sich zur Tätigkeit erheben,
Nach der Ruhe sanftem Schatten
Wieder in das rasche Leben
Und zur Pflicht, o welche Lust!

TAMINO *aufstehend und herunterkommend*
Immerfort bei guten Taten
Sich der Gattin Blick erfreuen,
Von der Milden wohlberaten
Sich der heitern Tugend weihen,
O wie hebt es meine Brust!

Sie umarmen sich. Pause, besonders der Flöte

CHOR.   Papageno, laß die Flöte
Nicht von deinem Munde kommen,
Halte nur noch diesmal aus!

PAPAGENO.   Laßt mich nur zu Atem kommen:
Denn er bleibt mir wahrlich aus.

TAMINO *und* PAMINA *sich voneinander entfernend*
Ach was hat man uns genommen!
O wie leer ist dieses Haus!

CHOR.   Blase, Papageno, blase,
Halte nur noch diesmal aus!
Papageno bläst

TAMINO *und* PAMINA *sich einander freundlich nähernd*
Nein, man hat uns nichts genommen,
Groß und reich ist unser Haus.

PAPAGENO.   Ach mir bleibt der Atem aus!

TAM. (waking).

In the sight of my belovéd
Once again my pleasure taking;
Yet alas! who breaks my trance?

CHOR.

Music, Papageno, music!
Play, and do not queer their chance!

PAM. *(rising and advancing)*.

By Tamino's presence heartened,
To the world new ardour giving,
After drowsy sleep's enchantment
Do I now return to living
And to duty; oh, the bliss!

TAM. *(likewise)*.

Given up to deeds of virtue,
In Pamina's love rejoicing,
With my consort, rich in wisdom,
At my side, good counsel voicing,
Naught shall henceforth be amiss.

They embrace. Pause, especially of the flute.

CHOR.

Papageno, music, music!
Never let thy flute be silent,
Lest you interrupt their bliss.

PAPAGENO.

Give me leave to breathe a moment,
For I am not used to this!

PAM. *and* TAM.

Oh, what has been taken from us?
Joyless now our meeting is.

CHOR.

Papageno, do not falter!
Only this time do not miss!

Papageno plays.

TAM. *and* PAM. *(happily approaching each other)*.

No, our gladness is returning,
All again is perfect bliss!

PAPAGENO.

No, I am not used to this.

CHOR.   Halte nur noch diesmal aus!

PAMINA *und* TAMINO.   O wie leer ist dieses Haus!

Es ist wohl überflüssig zu bemerken, daß es ganz von dem Komponisten abhängt,
den Übergang von Zufriedenheit und Freude zu Schmerz und Verzweiflung, nach
Anlaß vorstehender Verse, zu verschränken und zu wiederholen

Es kommen Priester. Es wird von dem Komponisten abhängen, ob derselbe nur
zwei oder das ganze Chor einführen will. Ich nehme das letzte an. Sie geben
Nachricht, wo sich das Kind befinde

PRIESTER.   In den tiefen Erdgewölben
                              Hier das Wasser, hier das Feuer,
                              Unerbittlich dann die Wächter,
                              Dann die wilden Ungeheuer.
                              Zwischen Leben, zwischen Tod,
                              Halb entseelet,
                              Von Durst gequälet,
                              Liegt der Knabe.
                              Hört sein Flehen!
                              Weh! ach er verschmachtet schon.
                              Rettet! rettet euern Sohn!

ALLE.   Welche Stille, welches Grausen
                              Liegt auf einmal um uns her!
                              Welch ein dumpfes fernes Sausen!
                              Welch ein tiefbewegtes Brausen,
                              Wie der Sturm im fernen Meer!
                              Immer lauter aus der Ferne
                              Hör ich alle Wetter drohen.
                              Welche Nacht bedeckt den goldnen
                              Heitern Himmel,
                              Und die Sterne
                              Schwinden schon vor meinem Blick!

CHO.	Once again, oh, do not miss!
PAM. & TAM.	Void again our meeting is.

It may be superfluous to say that it is for the composer to make the most of the verses submitted to him by intertwining and repeating the transitions from contentment and joy to grief and despair.

Enter PRIESTS.

The composer will decide whether he will introduce only two or the whole chorus. I assume the latter. They give news of the child's whereabouts.

PRIESTS.

In a deep and gloomy cavern,
Fire on this, on that side water,
By implacable lions guarded,
By a watch prepared for slaughter,
Half alive, by death endangered,
Starved and wasted,
Thirst-tormented,
Pines the child,
Oh, hear his wailing!
Woe us! Ere the worst be done
Save him, your unhappy son!

ALL.

What a silence, what a terror
Gathers sudden round us! Hear
What a dull and distant roaring,
Like a growing storm, upsoaring,
As from far-off seas comes near.
Loud and louder from the distance
Thund'rous clamour comes approaching,
And the firmament grows darker,
Stars extinguish,
We are blinded,
All in blackness disappear!

Unterirdisches Gewölbe. In der Mitte der Altar mit dem Kästchen, wie er versank. An zwei Pfeilern stehen gewaffnete Männer gelehnt und scheinen zu schlafen. Von ihnen gehen Ketten herab, woran die Löwen gefesselt sind, die am Altare liegen. Alles ist dunkel, das Kästchen ist transparent und beleuchtet die Szene

CHOR *unsichtbar.*   Wir richten und bestrafen:
                                                Der Wächter soll nicht schlafen;
                                                Der Himmel glüht so rot.
                                                Der Löwe soll nicht rasten,
                                                So sei der Knabe tot.

Die Löwen richten sich auf und gehen an der Kette hin und her

ERSTER WÄCHTER *ohne sich zu bewegen.*
                                                Bruder, wachst du?
ZWEITER *ohne sich zu bewegen.*   Ich höre.
ERSTER.   Sind wir allein?
ZWEITER.   Wer weiß!
ERSTER.   Wird es Tag?
ZWEITER.   Vielleicht ja.
ERSTER.   Kommt die Nacht?
ZWEITER.   Sie ist da.
ERSTER.   Die Zeit vergeht.
ZWEITER.   Aber wie?
ERSTER.   Schlägt die Stunde wohl?
ZWEITER.   Uns nie.
ZU ZWEIEN.   Vergebens bemühet
                                    Ihr euch da droben so viel.
                                    Es rennt der Mensch, es fliehet
                                    Vor ihm das bewegliche Ziel.
                                    Er zieht und zerrt vergebens
                                    Am Vorhang, der schwer auf des Lebens
                                    Geheimnis, auf Tagen und Nächten ruht.
                                    Vergebens strebt er in die Luft,
                                    Vergebens dringt er in die tiefe Gruft:
                                    Die Luft bleibt ihm finster,
                                    Die Gruft wird ihm helle.
                                    Doch wechselt das Helle

Subterranean cavern. In the middle the altar with the casket, as it was seen sinking into the ground. Two Armed Men lean against two pillars and seem to be asleep. They hold the ends of chains to which lions, crouching by the altar, are fastened. All is dark; the casket, which is transparent, illuminates the scene.

CHORUS *(invisible).*

Our judgment execute ye,
As guardians do your duty,
For should the cask reveal
The infant that is sleeping
In restless lions' keeping,
His doom its breach would seal.

The lions rise and pace up and down in their chains.

FIRST GUARD *(motionless).*   Brother, wak'st thou?

SECOND GUARD *(likewise).* I hear thee.

GUA. I.   Are we alone?

GUA. II.   Who knows?

GUA. I.   Dawns the day?

GUA. II.   It may.

GUA. I.   Comes the night?

GUA. II.   It's in sight.

GUA. I.   Times passes now.

GUA. II.   But how?

GUA. I.   Strikes the hour thus?

GUA. II.   Not for us!

BOTH.

In vain do ye labour
For ever and aye on high.
Man hastens, yet before him
His goal without ceasing doth fly.
In vain he goes pulling and tearing
The pall that lies heavy and wearing
Upon this life's secret, by day and night.
In vain he struggles for the light,
Descends to earth's deep caverns from the height.
A moment of light in
The dark may he find;
Then radiance, deceptive,

Mit Dunkel so schnelle.
Er steige herunter,
Er dringe hinan;
Er irret und irret
Von Wahne zu Wahn.

Der hintere Vorhang öffnet sich. Dekoration des Wassers und Feuers, wie in der Zauberflöte. Links das Feuer, eine kleine freie Erhöhung, wenn man da durchgegangen ist; alsdann das Wasser, oben drüber ein gangbarer Felsen, aber ohne Tempel. Die ganze Dekoration muß so eingerichtet sein, daß es aussieht, als wenn man von dem Felsen nur durch das Feuer und das Wasser in die Gruft kommen könnte

Tamino und Pamina kommen mit Fackeln den Felsen herunter.
Im Herabsteigen singen sie

TAMINO.

Meine Gattin, meine Teure,
O wie ist der Sohn zu retten!
Zwischen Wasser, zwischen Feuer,
Zwischen Graus und Ungeheuer
Ruhet unser höchster Schatz.

Sie gehen durchs Feuer

PAMINA.

Einer Gattin, einer Mutter,
Die den Sohn zu retten eilet,
Macht das Wasser, macht das Feuer,
In der Gruft das Ungeheuer,
Macht der strenge Wächter Platz.

Indessen hat sich eine Wolke herabgezogen, so daß sie in der Mitte zwischen Wasser und Feuer schwebt. Die Wolke tut sich auf

DIE KÖNIGIN DER NACHT.   Was ist geschehen!
Durch das Wasser, durch das Feuer
Drangen sie glücklich und verwegen.
Auf, ihr Wächter! ihr Ungeheuer!
Stellet mächtig euch entgegen
Und bewahret mir den Schatz.

Leaves darkness behind.
So let him approach us,
He'll meet us in vain:
He'll stray from deception
To error again.

The inner curtain opens. Fire and water scene as in The Magic Flute. *On the left the fire, with a small knoll left free on which to emerge therefrom; next the water with a practicable rock above it, but without a temple. The whole scene must be so arranged that it looks as though the cavern could be reached from the rock only by traversing the fire and water.*

Tamino and Pamina come with torches from the rock. They sing as they descend.

TAM.   My belovéd, my Pamina,
How can we our son deliver?
'Twixt the waters and the fire,
'Twixt wild beasts and horrors dire,
Lies our treasure, all but lost.

(They go through the fire.)

PAM.   From a consort, from a mother
Shrink her infant's grimmest guardians,
Spite the waters, spite the fire,
In this cave of horrors dire
Shall our treasure not be lost.

(They go through the water.)

Meanwhile a cloud has come down and hangs suspended between the fire and water. It opens and reveals the Queen of Night.

QUE.   What is impending?
Through the fire and through the water
Did they penetrate with daring.
Guards, hold my rebellious daughter!
Hold her spouse, no fury sparing!
Keep the child at any cost!

DIE WÄCHTER *richten ihre Speere gegen das Kästchen, doch so, daß sie davon entfernt bleiben. Die Löwen schließen sich aufmerksam an sie an. Die Stellungen sollten auf beiden Seiten symmetrisch sein.*

Wir bewahren, wir bewachen
Mit Speer und Löwenrachen,
O Göttin, deinen Schatz!

TAMINO *und* PAMINA *hervorkommend*

O mein Gatte, mein Geliebter,
Meine Gattin, meine Teure,
Sieh, das Wasser, sieh, das Feuer
Macht der Mutterliebe Platz.
Ihr Wächter, habt Erbarmen!

KÖNIGIN.

Ihr Wächter, kein Erbarmen!
Behauptet euren Platz!

TAMINO *und* PAMINA.

O weh! o weh uns Armen!
Wer rettet unserm Schatz?

KÖNIGIN.

Sie dringen durch die Wachen,
Der grimme Löwenrachen
Verschlinge gleich den Schatz!

Die Wolke zieht weg. Stille.

DAS KIND *im Kästchen*

Die Stimme des Vaters,
Des Mütterchens Ton,
Es hört sie der Knabe
Und wachet auch schon.

PAMINA *und* TAMINO.

O Seligkeit, den ersten Ton,
Das Lallen seines Sohns zu hören!
O laßt nicht Zauber uns betören.
Ihr Götter! welche Seligkeit
Beglückt uns schon!
O laßt uns ihn noch einmal hören,
Den süßen Ton.

GUARDS I & II *(turning their spears towards the casket, but so that they remain at a distance from it. The lions join them attentively. The positions should be symmetrically equal on either side.)*

> We watch it and we ward it,
> The spears and lions guard it:
> The child shall not be lost!

TAM. & PAM. *(coming forward).*

> Oh my consort, my Tamino,
>
> My belovéd, my Pamina,
> Fire and water yield their power
> When a mother supplicates.
> Ye guardians, oh, have pity!

QUE.

> Ye guardians, have no pity!
> Be firm, protect the gates!

TAM. & PAM.

> Alas! Ye gods, have mercy!
> Who'll save our precious child?

QUE.

> Woe! They have won the guardians.
> Then tear the child to pieces:
> The lions still are wild!

The cloud disperses. Silence.

THE CHILD *(in the casket).*

> The voice of his father,
> His mother's dear voice;
> Their child, now to hear them
> Doth, waking, rejoice.

TAM. & PAM.

> Oh, happy we, to hear at last
> The stammer of a cherished infant!
> Ye gods, let not the blessed instant
> Deceive us! What felicity
> We now have found!
> Oh, let us hear it still repeated,
> Th' enchanting sound!

CHOR *unsichtbar*.   Nur ruhig! es schläfet
                               Der Knabe nicht mehr.
                               Er fürchtet die Löwen
                               Und Speere nicht sehr.
                               Ihn halten die Grüfte
                               Nicht lange mehr auf;
                               Er dringt in die Lüfte
                               Mit geistigem Lauf.

Der Deckel des Kastens springt auf. Es steigt ein Genius hervor, der durch die Lichter, welche den Kasten transparent machten, ganz erleuchtet ist, wenn die Lichter so disponiert sind, daß die obere Hälfte der übrigen Figuren gleichfalls mit erleuchtet ist. In dem Augenblick treten die Wächter mit den Löwen dem Kasten näher und entfernen Tamino und Pamina

GENIUS.   Hier bin ich, ihr Lieben!
                               Und bin ich nicht schön?
                               Wer wird sich betrüben,
                               Sein Söhnchen zu sehn?
                               In Nächten geboren,
                               Im herrlichen Haus,
                               Und wieder verloren
                               In Nächten und Graus.
                               Es drohen die Speere,
                               Die grimmigen Rachen–
                               Und drohten mir Heere
                               Und drohten mir Drachen,
                               Sie haben doch alle
                               Dem Knaben nichts an.

In dem Augenblick, als die Wächter nach dem Genius mit den Spießen stoßen, fliegt er davon

CHO. *(invisible)*.

Rest certain, no longer
The child is asleep;
The spears and the lions
At bay will he keep.
The caverns will hold him
No more in their pow'r:
For he is arising
In freedom this hour.

The lid of the casket bursts open. A GENIUS emerges, wholly illuminated by the lights which make the casket transparent. These lights are so arranged that they also illuminate the upper half of the other figures. At this moment the GUARDS approach the casket with the lions and keep TAMINO and PAMINA at a distance.

GENIUS.

Here am I, ye dear ones!
And am I not fair?
Say, will ye regret it
To see me your heir?
By darkness of night born,
In glory and state,
Yet lost by the powers
Of malice and hate;
By spears and by gaolers,
By lions' dread jaws,
By warriors threatened,
And dragons' foul maws;
Yet safe from all ill
The child liveth still!

At the moment when the GUARDS thrust their spears at the GENIUS, he flies away.

Bibliography

Aarne, Antti, ed. *The Types of the Folktale*. Translated by Stith Thompson. Helsinki: Academia Scientiarum Fennica, 1964.

Abert, Hermann. *Goethe und die Musik*. Stuttgart: J. Engelhorns Nachf., 1922.

Adorno, Theodor W. "Huldigung an Zerlina." In *Wolfgang Amadeus Mozart. Don Giovanni*. Edited by Attila Csampai and Dietmar Holland. Hamburg: Rowohlt Taschenbuch Verlag, 1981.

Allanbrook, Wye Jamison. *Rhythmic Gesture in Mozart*. Chicago and London: University of Chicago Press, 1983.

Arnim, Bettina von. "Goethes Briefwechsel mit einem Kind." *Sämtliche Werke*. Edited by Waldemar Oehlke. 8 vols. Berlin: Im Propyläen Verlag, 1920–22.

Asher, Gloria J. *Die Zauberflöte und Die Frau ohne Schatten: Ein Vergleich zwischen zwei Operndichtungen der Humanität*. Bern: A. Francke Verlag, 1972.

Atkins, Stuart. *Goethe's Faust: A Literary Analysis*. Cambridge: Harvard University Press, 1958.

—. "On Goethe's Classicism." In *Goethe Proceedings*. Edited by Clifford A. Bernd *et al.* 1–21. Studies in German Literature, Linguistics, and Culture. Columbia, S.C.: Camden House, 1984.

—. "*Die Wahlverwandtschaften*: Novel of German Classicism." *The German Quarterly*, 53 (1980): 1–45.

Barrington, Daines. "Account of a very remarkable young Musician." In *Philosophical Transactions of the Royal Society of London*, 60 (1770): 54–64.

Barth, Karl. "My Faith in Mozart." In *Religion and Culture: Essays in Honor of Paul Tillich*. Edited by Walter Leibrecht. 61–78. New York: Harper and Bros., 1959.

—. *Wolfgang Amadeus Mozart*. Translated by Clarence K. Pott. Foreword by John Updike. Grand Rapids, Michigan: William B. Eerdmans Publishing Co., 1986.

Barzun, Jacques. *Berlioz and the Romantic Century*. 3rd ed. 2 vols. New York and London: Columbia University Press, 1969.

Batley, E. M. *A Preface to the Magic Flute.* London: Dennis, 1969.

Beaulieu–Marconnay, Carl von. "Goethes cour d'amour." *Goethe–Jahrbuch* 6 (1885): 59–83.

Beer–Hofmann, Richard. *Gedenkrede auf Wolfgang Amadeus Mozart.* Berlin: S. Fischer Verlag, 1921.

Belli, Maria, ed. *Leben in Frankfurt am Main: Auszüge der Frag– und Anzeigungs–Nachrichten.* 10 vols. Frankfurt am Main, 1850–51.

Benn, Gottfried. *Briefe an F. W. Oelze 1932–1945.* 3 vols. Edited by Harald Steinhagen and Jürgen Schröder. Wiesbaden and Munich: Limes Verlag, 1977. Reprint. Frankfurt: Fischer Taschenbuch Verlag, 1979.

Benz, Richard. *Goethe und Beethoven.* Leipzig: Reclam, 1944.

Berlioz, Hector. *New Edition of the Complete Works.* c. 20 vols. Edited by Hugh Macdonald. Kassel, London, New York: Bärenreiter Verlag, 1967– .

Bernstein, Leonard. *The Unanswered Question: Six Talks at Harvard.* Cambridge: Harvard University Press, 1976.

Beutler, Ernst. "Begegnung mit Mozart." In *Essays um Goethe.* 2 vols. Wiesbaden: Dieterich'sche Verlagsbuchhandlung, 1946.

—. "Das Goethesche Familienvermögen von 1687–1885." In *Essays um Goethe.* 2 vols. Wiesbaden: Dieterich'sche Verlagsbuchhandlung, 1946.

Bielschowsky, Albert. *Goethe: Sein Leben und seine Werke.* 2 vols. Munich: C.H. Beck'sche Verlagsbuchhandlung, 1911.

Blackall, Eric A. *The Emergence of German as a Literary Language, 1700–1775.* Cambridge: At the University Press, 1959.

Bloch, Ernst. *Das Prinzip Hoffnung.* 2 vols. Frankfurt am Main: Suhrkamp, 1959.

Blom, Eric, ed. and trans. *The Magic Flute, Part II*, by Johann Wolfgang von Goethe. *Music and Letters*, 23 (1942): 234–254.

—. *Mozart.* London: J.M. Dent & Sons. Paperback edition, 1974.

Blume, Friedrich. *Goethe und die Musik.* Kassel: Bärenreiter Verlag, 1948.

Bode, Wilhelm. *Die Tonkunst in Goethes Leben.* 2 vols. Berlin: E.S. Mittler und Sohn, 1912.

Borchmeyer, Dieter. *Höfische Gesellschaft und Französische Revolution bei Goethe.* Kronberg/Ts.: Athenäum Verlag, 1977.

—. "'Ganz verteufelt human.' Über Mozarts Titus." *Ludwigsburger Schloßfestspiele. Almanach 1983*: 65–69.

Born, Ignaz von. "Über die Mysterien der Ägypter." In *Journal für Freymaurer*. Vienna, bey Christian Friedrich Wappler, 1784.

Bretzner, Christoph Friedrich. *Belmont und Constanze, oder: Die Entführung aus dem Serail. Eine Operette in drey Acten*. Leipzig, bey Carl Friedrich Schneider, 1781.

Brook, Barry S. "Sturm und Drang and the Romantic Period in Music." *Studies in Romanticism*, 9 (1970): 269–284.

Brown, Calvin S. "The Relation Between Music and Literature As a Field of Study." *Comparative Literature*, 22 (1970): 97–107.

Brown, Marshall. "Mozart and After: The Revolution in Musical Consciousness." *Critical Inquiry*, 7 (1981): 689–706.

Burke, John N. *Mozart and his Music*. New York: Random House, 1959.

Butler, E. M. *The Fortunes of Faust*. Cambridge: At the University Press, 1952.

Carlson, Marvin. *Goethe and the Weimar Theater*. Ithaca: Cornell University Press, 1978.

Carr, Francis. *Mozart and Constanze*. London: John Murray Ltd., 1983.

Chailley, Jacques. *The Magic Flute: Masonic Opera*. Translated by Herbert Weinstock. New York: A. Knopf, 1971.

Clive, Geoffrey. *The Romantic Enlightenment*. New York: Meridian Books, 1960.

Cone, Edward T. *The Composer's Voice*. Berkeley: University of California Press, 1974.

Cotti, Jürg. *Die Musik in Goethes "Faust."* Winterthur: Verlag Keller, 1957.

Cottrell, Alan P. *Goethe's Faust: Seven Essays*. Chapel Hill: The University of North Carolina Press, 1976.

Croll, Gerhard, ed. *Wolfgang Amadeus Mozart*. Darmstadt: Wissenschaftliche Buchgesellschaft, 1977.

Davenport, Marcia. *Mozart*. New York: Charles Scribner's Sons, 1960.

Dehmel, Richard. "Der Olympier Goethe." In *Gesammelte Werke*. 3 vols. Berlin: S. Fischer Verlag, 1913.

Dennerlein, Hanns. *Der unbekannte Mozart*. Leipzig: Breitkopf und Härtel, 1951.

Dent, Edward J. *Mozart's Operas: A Critical Study*. 2nd ed. London, Oxford, New York: Oxford University Press Paperback, 1960.

Deutsch, Otto Erich, ed. *Mozart: Die Dokumente seines Lebens*. Kassel: Bärenreiter Verlag, 1961.

—. *Mozart and his World in Contemporary Pictures*. Kassel: Bärenreiter Verlag, 1961.

—. *Franz Schubert: Die Dokumente seines Lebens*. Munich and Leipzig: Georg Müller, 1914.

Dibelius, Ulrich. *Mozart–Aspekte*. Munich: Deutscher Taschenbuch Verlag, 1979.

Dieckmann, Liselotte. "Zum Bild des Menschen im Achtzehnten Jahrhundert: *Nathan der Weise, Iphigenie, Die Zauberflöte*." In *Festschrift für Detlev W. Schumann*. Edited by Albert R. Schmitt, 89–96. Munich: Delp, 1970.

Donnington, Robert. "Don Giovanni goes to Hell." *The Musical Times*, 122 (July, 1981): 446–448.

Dreyer, Ernst–Jürgen. *Versuch, eine Morphologie der Musik zu begründen. Mit einer Einleitung über Goethes Tonlehre*. Bonn: Bouvier Verlag, 1976.

Eckermann, Johann Peter. *Gespräche mit Goethe in den letzten Jahren seines Lebens*. Munich: Deutscher Taschenbuch Verlag, 1976.

Eibl, Joseph Heinz, ed. *Wolfgang Amadeus Mozart: Chronik seines Lebens*. Kassel: Bärenreiter Verlag, 1977.

Eichner, Hans. "The Eternal Feminine: An Aspect of Goethe's Ethics." In *Faust*. Edited by Cyrus Hamlin. Translated by Walter Arndt, 615–624. New York: W. W. Norton, 1976.

Einstein, Alfred. *Greatness in Music*. Translated by César Saerchinger. New York: Oxford University Press, 1941.

—. *Mozart. His Character, His Work*. Translated by Arthur Mendel and Nathan Broder. New York: Oxford University Press Paperback, 1962.

Eissler, Kurt Robert. *Goethe: A Psychoanalytic Study 1775–1786*. 2 vols. Detroit: Wayne State University Press, 1963.

Enzinger, Moriz. "Randbemerkungen zum Textbuch der 'Zauberflöte'." In *Sprachkunst als Weltgestaltung. Festschrift für Herbert Seidler*. Edited by Adolf Haslinger, 49–74. Salzburg and Munich: Anton Pustet, 1966.

Fähnrich, Hermann. "Goethes Musikanschauung in seiner Fausttragödie – die Erfüllung und Vollendung seiner Opernreform." *Goethe*, N. F. 25 (1963): 250–263.

Fairley, Barker. *Goethe as Revealed in His Poetry*. New York: Frederic Ungar, 1963.

Finney, Gail. "Type and Countertype: The Dialectics of Space in *Die Wahlverwandtschaften*." *The Germanic Review*, 58 (1983): 67–74.

Flaherty, Gloria. *Opera in the Development of German Critical Thought*. Princeton: Princeton University Press, 1978.

Flemming, Willi. *Goethe und das Theater seiner Zeit*. Stuttgart: W. Kohlhammer Verlag, 1968.

Flower, Newman. *Franz Schubert: The Man and His Circle*. New York: Frederick A. Stokes, 1928.

Friedell, Egon. *Cultural History of the Modern Age*. 2 vols. New York: A. Knopf, 1931.

Friedlaender, Max, ed. *Gedichte von Goethe in Compositionen seiner Zeitgenossen*. 2 vols. Weimar: Verlag der Goethegesellschaft, 1896 and 1916.

Gerhard, Melitta. "Faust: die Tragödie des 'neueren Menschen'." *Jahrbuch des Freien Deutschen Hochstifts 1978*: 160–164.

—. "Götter–Kosmos und Gesetzessuche: Zu Goethes Versuch seines Achilleis–Epos." *Monatshefte*, 66 (1964): 145–159.

—. "Rom in seiner Bedeutung für Goethe – Eine 'Neue Welt'." *Jahrbuch des Freien Deutschen Hochstifts 1977*: 83–91.

Gide, André. "Leben mit Goethe." *Die neue Rundschau*, 43(1932): 514–522.

Gilman, Sander L. "'Das–ist–der–Teu–fel–si–ch–er–lich:' The Image of the Black on the Viennese Stage from Schikaneder to Grillparzer." In *Austriaca: Beiträge zur österreichischen Literatur. Festschrift für Heinz Politzer*. Edited by Winfried Kudszus and Hinrich C. Seeba, 78–101. Tübingen: Max Niemeyer Verlag, 1975.

Girdlestone, Cuthbert. *Mozart and his Piano Concertos*. New York: Dover Publications, 1964.

Göres, Jörn, ed. *Gesang und Rede, sinniges Bewegen. Goethe als Theaterleiter*. Düsseldorf: Goethe–Museum, 1973.

Görner, Rüdiger. "Die Sprache in der Musiktheorie Jerome–Joseph de Momignys." In *Logos Musicae. Festschrift für Albert Palm*. Edited by Rüdiger Görner, 100–109. Wiesbaden: Franz Steiner Verlag, 1982.

—. "'Die Zauberflöte' in Kierkegaards 'Entweder–Oder'." *Mozart–Jahrbuch 1980–83*: 247–257.

Goethe, Johann Wolfgang. *Conversations with Eckermann*. Translated by John Oxenford. London: G. Bell and Sons, 1875. Reprint. San Francisco: North Point Press, 1984.

—. *Der junge Goethe*. 6 vols. Edited by Max Morris. Leipzig: Insel Verlag, 1909–12.

—. *Hermann and Dorothea*. Translated by Daniel Coogan. New York: Frederick Ungar, 1966.

—. *Italian Journey 1786–1788*. Translated by W. H. Auden and Elizabeth Mayer. New York: Pantheon Books, 1962. Reprint. San Francisco: North Point Press, 1982.

—. *Goethes Leben und Werk in Daten und Bildern*. Edited by Franz Götting. Frankfurt: Insel Verlag, 1966.

—. *Goethe's Schriften*. 8 vols. Leipzig: Joachim Göschen, 1787–91.

—. *Goethe: Selected Poems*. Edited by Christopher Middleton. Boston: Suhrkamp/Insel, 1983.

—. *Goethe: Selected Verse with an Introduction and Prose Translations*. Edited and translated by David Luke. Baltimore: Penguin Books, 1964.

—. *Theory of Colours*. Translated by Charles Lock Eastlake. London: T. Murray, 1840. Reprint. Cambridge, Mass.: MIT Press, 1970.

—. *Zeittafel zu Goethes Leben und Werk*. Edited by Heinz Nicolai. Munich: C. H. Beck, 1977.

Gounod, Charles. *Mozart's Don Giovanni*. Translated by Windeyer Clark and J. T. Hutchinson. 3rd ed. New York: Da Capo Press, 1970.

Grabbe, Christian Dietrich. *Don Juan und Faust*. Edited by Alfred Bergmann. Stuttgart: Reclam, 1963.

Greither, Alois. *Mozart*. Hamburg: Rowohlt Taschenbuch Verlag, 1962.

Grillparzer, Franz. *Sämtliche Werke*. 4 vols. Edited by Peter Frank and Karl Pörnbacher. Munich: Carl Hanser, 1960–65.

Grout, Donald Jay. *A Short History of Opera*. 2nd ed. London and New York: Columbia University Press, 1947.

Gruenter, Rainer, ed. *Das deutsche Singspiel im 18. Jahrhundert*. Heidelberg: Carl Winter, 1981.

Guttmann, Alfred. *Musik in Goethes Wirken und Werken*. Berlin–Halensee, Wunsiedel: Deutscher Musikliteratur Verlag, 1949.

Hadow, William H. "A Comparison of Poetry and Music." In *Collected Essays*. London: Oxford University Press, 1928.

Harvard Dictionary of Music. Edited by Willi Apel. 2nd ed. Cambridge: Harvard University Press, 1972.

Hatfield, Henry. *Goethe. A Critical Introduction*. New York: New Directions Paperback, 1963.

—. "The Walpurgis Night: Theme and Variations." *Journal of European Studies*, 13 (1983): 56–74.

Heidegger, Martin. "Neunte Stunde." In *Der Satz vom Grund*. Pfullingen: Günther Neske, 1957.

Heine, Heinrich. *Werke und Briefe*. 10 vols. Edited by Hans Kaufmann. Berlin: Aufbau Verlag, 1961–64.

Heller, Erich. "The Ambiguity of Goethe's 'Faust'." *The Cambridge Journal*, 2 (1949): 579–597.

—. "Goethe and the Scientific Truth." In *The Disinherited Mind*. New York: Farrar, Straus and Cudahy, 1957.

Helm, Eugene. "Carl Philipp Emanuel Bach." In *The New Grove: Bach Family*. Edited by Christoph Wolff *et al*. New York: W.W. Norton, 1983.

Helmholtz, Hermann von. "Über Goethe's naturwissenschaftliche Arbeiten." In *Vorträge und Reden*. Braunschweig: Friedrich Vieweg und Sohn, 1884.

Henel, Heinrich. "Der junge Goethe." *Monatshefte*, 41 (1949): 129–169.

Henkel, Arthur. "Goethes 'Hommage à Mozart' – Bemerkungen zu 'Der Zauberflöte zweiter Theil'." In *Philomathes. Studies and Essays in the Humanities in Memory of Philip Merlan*. Edited by Robert B. Palmer and Robert Hamerton–Kelly, 485–502. The Hague: Martinus Nijhoff, 1971.

Herder, Johann Gottfried. "Wirkt die Musik auf Denkart und Sitten?" *Sämmtliche Werke*. 33 vols. Edited by Bernhard Suphan. Berlin: Weidmannsche Buchhandlung, 1877–1913.

Hertling, Gunther H. *Theodor Fontanes Stine: Eine entzauberte Zauberflöte?* Bern and Frankfurt: Peter Lang, 1982.

Hesse, Hermann. *Dank an Goethe*. Edited by Volker Michels. Frankfurt: Insel Taschenbuch, 1975.

—. *Piktors Verwandlungen*. Edited by Volker Michels. Frankfurt: Insel Verlag, 1975.

—. *Steppenwolf*. Translated by Basil Creighton. New York: Holt, Rinehart & Winston, 1963.

Hicks, W.C.R. "Was Goethe Musical?" *Publications of the English Goethe Society*, N. S., 27 (1958): 73–139.

Hildesheimer, Wolfgang. *Betrachtungen über Mozart*. Pfullingen: Günter Neske, 1963.

—. *Mozart*. Translated by Marion Faber. New York: Farrar Straus Giroux, 1982.

—. *Wer war Mozart?* Frankfurt: edition suhrkamp, 1966.

Hiller, Ferdinand. *Goethes musikalisches Leben.* Cologne: Du Mont–Schauberg, 1883.

Höffner, Johannes. *Goethe und das Weimarer Hoftheater.* Weimar: Gustav Kiepenheuer, 1913.

Hoelzel, Alfred. "The Conclusion of Goethe's *Faust*: Ambivalence and Ambiguity." *The German Quarterly*, 55 (1982): 1–12.

—. "*Faust*, the Plague, and Theodicy." *The German Quarterly*, 52 (1979): 1–17.

Hofmannsthal, Hugo von. "Ein Brief." *Ausgewählte Werke.* 2 vols. Edited by Rudolf Hirsch. Frankfurt: S. Fischer, 1957.

—. *Gesammelte Werke in Einzelausgaben.* Edited by Herbert Steiner. Frankfurt: S. Fischer Verlag, 1952–66.

Hollander, John. *The Untuning of the Sky: Ideas of Music in English Poetry, 1500–1700.* Princeton: Princeton University Press, 1961.

Hughes, Spike. *Famous Mozart Operas.* New York: Dover Publications, 1972.

—. "Notes on the Flute." *Opera News* (January, 1977): 12–14.

Humboldt, Wilhelm von. *Wilhelm und Caroline Humboldt in ihren Briefen.* 7 vols. Edited by Anna von Sydow. Berlin: E. S. Mittler, 1906–1916.

Istel, Edgar. "Goethe and Music." *The Musical Quarterly*, 14 (1928): 216–254.

Ives, Charles E. *Ilmenau.* New York: Peer International Corp., 1952.

Jahn, Otto. *The Life of Mozart.* 3 vols. Translated by Pauline D. Townsend. London: Novello, Ewer and Co., 1882.

—. *W. A. Mozart.* 2 vols. Fifth rev. ed. Edited by Hermann Abert. Leipzig: Breitkopf und Härtel, 1919–21.

Jantz, Harold. *The Form of Faust.* Baltimore: The Johns Hopkins University Press, 1978.

Jaspers, Karl. "Goethes Menschlichkeit." In *Basler Universitätsreden.* Basel: Helbing und Lichtenhahn, 1949.

—. *Unsere Zukunft und Goethe.* Zurich: Artemis Verlag, 1948.

John, Hans. *Goethe und die Musik.* Langensalza: H. Beyer und Söhne, 1927.

Jouve, Pierre Jean. "The Present Greatness of Mozart." *Horizon*, 1 (1940): 84–94.

Kaiser, Hartmut. "Betrachtungen zu den neapolitanischen Wasserspielen von Mörikes Mozartnovelle." In *Jahrbuch des Freien Deutschen Hochstifts 1977*: 364–400.

—. "Mozarts Don Giovanni und E. T. A. Hoffmanns Don Juan." In *Mitteilungen der E. T. A. Hoffmann–Gesellschaft*, 21 (1975): 6–26.

—. "Mozarts 'Zauberflöte' und 'Klingsohrs Märchen'." In *Jahrbuch des Freien Deutschen Hochstifts 1980*: 238–258.

Kaiser, Joachim. *Mein Name ist Sarastro*. Munich: Piper Verlag, 1984.

Kalbeck, Max. *Johannes Brahms*. 4 vols. Berlin: Verlag der Deutschen Brahms–Gesellschaft, 1904–14.

Kerman, Joseph. *Opera as Drama*. New York: Vintage Books, 1959.

Kierkegaard, Søren. *Either/Or*. 2 vols. Edited by Howard A. Johnson. Translated by David F. Swenson and Lillian Marvin Swenson. Princeton: Princeton University Press Paperback, 1971.

Koch, Hans–Albrecht. *Das deutsche Singspiel*. Stuttgart: Sammlung Metzler, 1974.

—. "Das Textbuch der 'Zauberflöte'." In *Jahrbuch des Freien Deutschen Hochstifts 1969*: 76–120.

—. "Goethes Fortsetzung der Schikanederschen 'Zauberflöte'," in *Jahrbuch des Freien Deutschen Hochstifts 1969*: 121–163.

Köster, Albert, ed. *Die Briefe der Frau Rath Goethe*. 2 vols. Leipzig: Carl Ernst Poeschel, 1904.

Kraemer, Uwe. "Wer hat Mozart verhungern lassen?" *Musica*, 30 (1976): 203–211.

Kramer, Lawrence. *Music and Poetry: The Nineteenth Century and After*. Berkeley, Los Angeles, London: University of California Press, 1984.

Kreutzer, Hans Joachim. "Der Mozart der Dichter. Über Wechselwirkungen von Literatur und Musik im 19. Jahrhundert." *Mozart–Jahrbuch 1980–83*: 208–227.

—. "Proteus Mozart: Die Opern Mozarts in der Auffassung des 19. Jahrhunderts." *Deutsche Vierteljahrsschrift für Literaturwissenschaft und Geistesgeschichte*, 60 (1986): 1–23.

Kusche, Ludwig, ed. *Zweihundert Jahre Liebe zu Mozart*. Munich: Süddeutscher Verlag, 1956.

Landon, Robbins H. C. "Mozart on the Eighteenth–Century Stage." *High Fidelity*, 15 (November, 1965): 62–64, 183.

Landon, Robbins H. C. and Donald Mitchell, eds. *The Mozart Companion.* New York: W. W. Norton, 1956.

Lange, Victor. "Art and Literature." In *Goethezeit: Studien zur Erkenntnis und Rezeption Goethes und seiner Zeitgenossen. Festschrift für Stuart Atkins.* Edited by Gerhart Hoffmeister, 157–178. Bern: Francke Verlag, 1981.

Leichtentritt, Hugo. *Music, History, and Ideas.* Cambridge: Harvard University Press, 1958.

Leppmann, Wolfgang. *The German Image of Goethe.* Oxford: At the Clarendon Press, 1961.

Liebner, Janos. *Mozart on the Stage.* New York: Praeger Publishers, 1972.

Lützeler, Paul Michael. "Hermann und Dorothea." In *Goethes Erzählwerk: Interpretationen.* Edited by P. M. Lützeler and James E. McLeod, 216–265. Stuttgart: Reclam, 1985.

Malloy, Joseph T. "Genius is Served: Ingmar Bergman Redefines Mozart's *Zauberflöte.*" In *Film Studies: Proceedings of the Purdue University Sixth Annual Conference on Film,* April 1–4, 1982: 188–193.

Mann, Thomas, ed. *The Permanent Goethe.* New York: The Dial Press, 1948.

Mann, William. "Mozart alla Turca." *Opera News,* 44 (April 1980): 14–16.

Marks, Emerson R. *Coleridge on the Language of Verse.* Princeton: Princeton University Press, 1981.

Marlowe, Christopher. *The Tragical History of Dr. Faust.* Edited by Paul H. Kocher. New York: Meredith Corporation, 1950.

Mason, Eudo C. "Goethe's Sense of Evil." *Publications of the English Goethe Society,* N.S. 34 (1964): 1–53.

May, Kurt. "Entwürfe zu Operntexten." In *Goethes Gedenkausgabe* VI, 1252–1256.

Mayer, Hans. *Doktor Faustus und Don Juan.* Frankfurt a. M.: Suhrkamp Verlag, 1979.

Mendelssohn, Felix. *Mendelssohn: Letters.* Edited by G. Selden–Goth. New York: Random House, 1972. Reprint. Vienna House, 1973.

Metzger, Heinz–Klaus and Rainer Riehm, eds. *Mozart: Ist die Zauberflöte ein Machwerk? Musik–Konzepte,* 3 (1978): 3–76.

Middleton, Christopher, ed. *Goethe: Selected Poems.* See Goethe, Johann Wolfgang.

Mitchells, K. "'Nur nicht lesen! Immer singen!': Goethe's 'Lieder' into Schubert Lieder." *Publications of the English Goethe Society,* N. S., 44 (1974): 63–82.

Mittenzwei, Johannes. *Das Musikalische in der Literatur. Ein Überblick von Gottfried von Straßburg bis Brecht.* Halle: VEB Verlag Sprache und Literatur, 1962.

Mommsen, Katharina, ed. *Goethe Novellen.* Frankfurt a. M.: Insel Taschenbuch, 1979.

Morris, Max. *Der junge Goethe.* See Goethe, Johann Wolfgang.

Mozart, Wolfgang Amadeus. *Don Giovanni.* Edited by Attila Csampai and Dietmar Holland. Hamburg: Rowohlt Taschenbuch Verlag, 1981.

—. *Mozart and his World in Contemporary Pictures.* Edited by Otto Erich Deutsch. Kassel: Bärenreiter Verlag, 1961.

—. *Mozart Briefe.* Edited by Wolfgang Hildesheimer. Frankfurt a. M.: Insel Taschenbuch, 1975.

—. *Mozart. Briefe und Aufzeichnungen. Gesamtausgabe.* 7 vols. Edited by W. A. Bauer and O. E. Deutsch. Kassel: Bärenreiter Verlag, 1962–75.

—. *Mozart. Die Dokumente seines Lebens.* Edited by Otto Erich Deutsch. Kassel, London, New York: Bärenreiter Verlag, 1961.

—. *Mozart. Die Dokumente seines Lebens. Addenda und Corrigenda.* Edited by Joseph H. Eibl. Kassel: Bärenreiter Verlag, 1978.

—. *Mozart's Letters.* Edited by Eric Blom. Baltimore: Penguin Books, 1956.

—. *The Letters of Mozart and His Family.* 3rd ed. Edited by Emily Anderson. New York: W. W. Norton, 1985.

—. *The Great Operas of Mozart.* Edited by Nathan Broder. New York: G. Schirmer, 1962.

—. *W. A. Mozart: Klavierstücke. Urtext.* Edited by B. A. Wallner. Munich: G. Henle Verlag, 1974.

—. *Die Zauberflöte.* Edited by Attila Csampai and Dietmar Holland. Hamburg: Rowohlt, 1982.

—. *Die Zauberflöte.* Text by Emanuel Schikaneder. Edited by Wilhelm Zentner. Stuttgart: Reclam, 1969.

Müller, Kanzler von. *Unterhaltungen mit Goethe.* 2nd ed. Edited by Renate Grumach. Munich: Verlag C.H. Beck, 1982.

Müller–Blattau, Joseph. *Goethe und die Meister der Musik.* Stuttgart: Klett Verlag, 1969.

Muschg, Walter. *Studien zur tragischen Literaturgeschichte.* Bern and Munich: Francke Verlag, 1965.

Nettl, Paul. *Goethe und Mozart*. Esslingen: Bechtle Verlag, 1949.

—. "Goethe and Mozart." In *Goethe Bicentennial Studies*. Edited by H. J. Meessen. Bloomington: Indiana University Press, 1950.

—. *W. A. Mozart*. Frankfurt a. M.: Fischer Bücherei, 1955.

Neubauer, John. "Absolute and Affective Music: Rameau, Diderot, and Goethe." In *Johann Wolfgang von Goethe: One Hundred and Fifty Years of Continuing Vitality*. Edited by Ulrich Goebel and Wolodymyr T. Zyla, 115–131. Lubbock, Texas: Texas Tech Press, 1984.

Niemetschek, Franz Xaver. *Ich kannte Mozart*. Munich: Bibliothek der zeitgenössischen Literatur, 1798. Photomechanical reprint, 1984.

Nissen, Georg Nikolaus von. *Biographie W. A. Mozarts*. Leipzig: Breitkopf und Härtel, 1828. Photomechanical reprint. Hildesheim, New York: Georg Olms Verlag, 1972.

Nietzsche, Friedrich. "Nietzsche contra Wagner." *Gesammelte Werke*, 23 vols. Edited by Max Oehler, Richard Oehler, and Friedrich Würzbach. Munich: Musarion Verlag, 1920–29.

Novello, Vincent and Mary Novello. *Eine Wallfahrt zu Mozart*. Edited by Nerina Medici di Marignano and Rosemary Hughes. Translated by Ernst Roth. Bonn: Boosey und Hawkes, 1955.

Orel, Alfred. *Goethe als Operndirektor*. Bregenz: Eugen Russ Verlag, 1949.

Ortheil, Hanns–Josef. *Mozart im Innern seiner Sprache*. Frankfurt a. M.: S. Fischer Verlag, 1982.

Osborne, Conrad L. "The Operas of Mozart on Microgroove." *High Fidelity*, 15 (November, 1965): 65–72, 128–140.

Perinet, Joachim. *Der Fagottist, oder die Zauberzither. Ein Singspiel in drey Aufzügen*. Vienna: Mathias Andreas Schmidt, 1791.

Pestelli, Giorgio. *The Age of Mozart and Beethoven*. Translated by Eric Cross. Cambridge: Cambridge University Press, 1984.

Petersen, Julius. *Die Entstehung der Eckermannschen Gespräche und ihre Glaubwürdigkeit*. 2nd edition. Frankfurt a. M.: Verlag Moritz Diesterweg, 1925.

Pietsch, J. *Johann Wolfgang v. Goethe als Freimaurer*. Leipzig: Bruno Zechel, 1880.

Prawer, Siegbert Salomon, ed. and trans. *The Penguin Book of Lieder*. Harmondsworth, England: Penguin Books, 1964.

Rech, Géza. *Das Salzburger Mozart–Buch*. Hamburg: Rowohlt Taschenbuch Verlag, 1964.

Reich, Willi. *Goethe und die Musik*. Zurich: Ex Libris–Verlag, 1949.

Rolland, Romain. "Mozart: According to his Letters." In *Essays on Music*. Edited by David Ewen, 245–261. New York: Dover Publications, 1959.

Rommel, Otto. *Die Alt–Wiener Volkskomödie*. Vienna: Anton Schroll, 1952.

—, ed. *Die Maschinenkomödie*. Leipzig: P. Reclam jun., 1935.

Rosen, Charles. *The Classical Style. Haydn, Mozart, Beethoven*. New York: W. W. Norton, 1972.

Rosenberg, Alfons. *Don Giovanni*. Munich: Prestel Verlag, 1968.

Rushton, Julian. *W. A. Mozart: Don Giovanni*. Cambridge: Cambridge University Press, 1981.

Sadie, Stanley. *The New Grove Mozart*. New York: W. W. Norton, 1983.

Salmen, Walter. *Johann Friedrich Reichardt*. Freiburg and Zurich: Atlantis Verlag, 1963.

Sargeant, Winthrop. "Force of Nature: Don Giovanni as an Arche–Type." *Opera News,* 42 (1978): 19–21.

Schenk, Erich. *Mozart, sein Leben – seine Welt*. 2nd edition. Vienna, Munich: Amalthea Verlag, 1975.

Scher, Steven Paul. "Literature and Music." In *Interrelations of Literature*. Edited by Jean–Pierre Barricelli and Joseph Gibaldi, 225–250. New York: MLA, 1982.

—, ed. *Literatur und Musik: Ein Handbuch zur Theorie und Praxis eines komparatistischen Grenzgebietes*. Berlin: Erich Schmidt Verlag, 1984.

—. "Theory in Literature, Analysis in Music: What's Next?" *Yearbook of Comparative and General Literature,* 32 (1983): 50–60.

—. *Verbal Music in German Literature*. New Haven: Yale University Press, 1968.

Scherman, Thomas and Louis Biancolli, eds. *The Beethoven Companion*. New York: Doubleday, 1972.

Schiebeler, Daniel. *Lisuart und Dariolette, oder die Frage und Antwort. Eine Operette in zwey Aufzügen*. 1766.

Schikaneder, Emanuel. *Die Zauberflöte*. See Mozart, W. A.

—. *Die Zauberflöte*. Newly arranged by C. A. Vulpius. Leipzig: Johann Samuel Heinsius, 1794.

Schiller, Friedrich. "Über Egmont, Trauerspiel." In *Schillers Sämtliche Werke,* 22 vols. Edited by Conrad Höfer. Munich and Leipzig: Georg Müller Verlag; and Berlin: Propyläen Verlag, 1910–26.

Schindler, Anton. *Biographie von Ludwig van Beethoven.* Bonn: Karl Glöckner, 1949.

Schlegel, Friedrich. *Kritische Schriften.* Edited by Wolfdietrich Rasch. Munich: Carl Hanser, 1964.

Schlichtegroll, Friedrich. *Mozarts Leben.* Grätz, bey Joseph Georg Hubeck. Reprint. Kassel: Bärenreiter Verlag, 1974.

Schonberg, Harold C. *The Lives of the Great Composers.* New York: W.W. Norton, 1970.

Schopenhauer, Arthur. *Gespräche.* Edited by Arthur Hübscher. Stuttgart–Bad Canstadt: Friedrich Frommann, 1971.

Schrade, Leo. *W. A. Mozart.* Bern: A. Francke Verlag, 1964.

Schuh, Willi, ed. *Goethe–Vertonungen. Ein Verzeichnis.* Zurich: Artemis Verlag, 1952.

Schumann, Robert. *Gesammelte Schriften über Musik und Musiker.* 2 vols. 5th ed. Edited by M. Kreisig. Leipzig: Breitkopf und Härtel, 1914.

Seidlin, Oskar. "Goethe's Magic Flute." In *Essays in German and Comparative Literature,* 45–59. Chapel Hill: University of North Carolina Press, 1961.

—. "Is the 'Prelude in the Theatre' a Prelude to *Faust?*" In *Essays in German and Comparative Literature,* 60–69. Chapel Hill: University of North Carolina Press, 1961.

Sessions, Roger. *Roger Sessions on Music. Collected Essays.* Edited by Edward Cone. Princeton: Princeton University Press, 1979.

Shaw, George Bernard. *Music in London 1890–1894.* 3 vols. New York: Wm. H. Wise and Co., 1931.

Singer, Irving. *Mozart and Beethoven. The Concept of Love in Their Operas.* Baltimore and London: The Johns Hopkins University Press, 1977.

Smeed, J. W. *Faust in Literature.* London: Oxford University Press, 1975.

Smend, Friedrich. *Goethes Verhältnis zu Bach.* Berlin: Verlag Carl Merseburger, 1954.

Spaethling, Robert. "Folklore and Enlightenment in the Libretto of Mozart's *Magic Flute.*" *Eighteenth–Century Studies,* 9 (1975): 45–68.

—. "The Unwritten Masterpiece of German Classicism: Mozart's Music for Goethe's *Faust.*" *Forum,* 14 (1976): 24–31.

Staiger, Emil, ed. *Der Briefwechsel zwischen Schiller und Goethe*. Frankfurt a. M.: Insel Verlag, 1966.

—. "Goethe und Mozart." In *Musik und Dichtung*, 41–60. Zurich: Atlantis Verlag, 1959.

Starobinski, Jean. *1789: The Emblems of Reason*. Translated by Barbara Bray. Charlottesville: University Press of Virginia, 1982.

Steffan, Joseph Anton, ed. *Sammlung deutscher Lieder für das Klavier*. 4 vols. Vienna, bey Joseph Edlen von Kurzböck, 1778–1782.

Stein, Jack M. "Musical Settings of the Songs from *Wilhelm Meister*." *Comparative Literature*, 22 (1970), 125–146.

—. *Poem and Music in the German Lied from Gluck to Hugo Wolf*. Cambridge: Harvard University Press, 1971.

—. "Was Goethe Wrong About the Nineteenth–Century Lied? An Examination of the Relation of Poem and Music." *Publications of the Modern Language Association of America*, 77 (1962): 232–239.

Steinhauer, Harry, ed. and trans. *German Stories*. New York: Bantam Books, 1964.

Stendhal [Henri Beyle, pseud.] *Life of Rossini*. Edited and translated by Richard N. Coe. New York: The Orion Press, 1970.

Sternfeld, Frederick W. *Goethe and Music. A List of Parodies and Goethe's Relationship to Music*. New York: The New York Public Library, 1954.

Stravinsky, Igor. *Themes and Conclusions*. Berkeley and Los Angeles: University of California Press Paperback, 1982.

Szabolcsi, Bence. "Mozarts faustische Dramaturgie." In *Festschrift zum achtzigsten Geburtstag von Georg Lukàcs*. Edited by Frank Benseler, 535–539. Neuwied und Berlin: Luchterhand, 1965.

Szövérffy, Joseph. "Zauberflöte und Welttheater." In *Archiv für Kulturgeschichte*, 48 (1966): 262–277.

Tappolet, Willy. *Begegnungen mit der Musik in Goethes Leben und Werk*. Bern: Bentelli Verlag, 1975.

Terrasson, Jean. *Geschichte des egyptischen Königs Sethos*. 2 vols. Translated by Matthias Claudius. Breslau, bei Gottlieb Löwe, 1777–78.

—. *Sethos, histoire ou vie tirée des monuments, anecdotes de l'ancienne Egypte; traduite d'un manuscript Grec*. Paris, 1731.

Tovey, Donald Francis. *Essays in Musical Analysis*. 6 vols. London: Oxford University Press, 1972.

Tschitscherin, Georgi W. *Mozart: Eine Studie.* Leipzig: Deutscher Verlag für Musik, 1975.

Viëtor, Karl. *Goethe. The Poet.* Translated by Moses Hadas. Cambridge: Harvard University Press, 1949.

Vulpius, Christian A., ed. *Die Zauberflöte.* Leipzig: Johann Samuel Heinsius, 1794.

Wade, Gerald. E. *El Burlador de Sevilla y convidado de piedra.* New York: Charles Scribner's Sons, 1969.

Wahle, Julius. *Das Weimarer Hoftheater unter Goethes Leitung.* Weimar: Verlag der Goethe–Gesellschaft, 1892.

Wallace, Robert K. *Jane Austen and Mozart. Classical Equilibrium in Fiction and Music.* Athens, Ga.: The University of Georgia Press, 1983.

Walter, Bruno. *Vom Mozart der Zauberflöte.* Frankfurt a. M.: S. Fischer Verlag, 1956.

Waltershausen, Hermann W. von. *Die Zauberflöte.* Munich: Bruckmann Verlag, 1920.

Walwei–Wiegelmann, Hedwig, ed. *Goethes Gedanken über Musik.* Frankfurt a. M.: Insel Taschenbuch, 1985.

Wapnewski, Peter. "Goethe: Todesgedenken," *Die Zeit,* Nr. 12, March 1982, "Feuilleton," p. 7.

Weigel, Hans. *Apropos Musik.* Zurich and Stuttgart: Artemis Verlag, 1965.

Weinstein, Leo. *The Metamorphoses of Don Juan.* New York: AMS Press, 1967.

Weiss, Walter. "Das Weiterleben der 'Zauberflöte' bei Goethe." In *Studien zur Literatur des 19. und 20. Jahrhunderts in Österreich: Festschrift für Alfred Doppler.* Edited by Johannes Holzner *et al.,* 15–24. Innsbruck: Kowatsch, 1981.

Weisstein, Ulrich, ed. *The Essence of Opera.* New York: W. W. Norton, 1964.

—. "Reflections on a Golden Style: W. H. Auden's Theory of Opera." *Comparative Literature,* 22 (1970): 108–124.

Weizsäcker, Carl Friedrich von. "Nachwort zu Goethe's *Farbenlehre.*" *Goethes Werke. Hamburger Ausgabe,* XIII.

Wieland, Christoph Martin. *Dschinnistan oder auserlesene Feen– und Geister–Mährchen, theils neu erfunden, theils übersetzt und umgearbeitet.* 3 vols. Winterthur, bey Heinrich Steiner, 1786.

—. "Versuch über das deutsche Singspiel." *Wielands Gesammelte Schriften. Werkausgabe.* 23 vols. Edited by the Preußische Akademie der Wissenschaften. Berlin: Weidmann'sche Buchhandlung, 1909–69.

Wilkinson, Elizabeth M. "Goethe's Poetry." In *German Life and Letters*, N. S., 2, (1949): 316–329.

Williams, Bernard. "Don Giovanni as an Idea." In *W. A. Mozart: Don Giovanni*. Edited by Julian Rushton, 81–91. Cambridge: Cambridge University Press, 1981.

Winn, James Anderson. *Unsuspected Eloquence: A History of the Relations Between Poetry and Music*. New Haven and London: Yale University Press, 1981.

Winternitz, Emanuel. *Musical Instruments and their Symbolism in Western Art*. London: Faber and Faber, 1967.

Wolf, Christa. *Büchner–Preis–Rede 1980*. Sonderdruck für die Freunde des Luchterhand Verlages, 1980.

Zeydel, Edwin H. *Goethe, the Lyrist*. Chapel Hill: The University of North Carolina Press, 1955.

Index